My Life of Adventure

My Life of Adventure

Norman D. Vaughan
with Cecil B. Murphey

STACKPOLE
BOOKS

Published by
STACKPOLE BOOKS
5067 Ritter Road
Mechanicsburg, PA 17055

Published in association with the literary agency of Alive Communications, P.O. Box 49068, Colorado Springs, CO 80949.

Printed in the United States of America

10 9 8 7 6 5 4 3 2 1

First edition

Library of Congress Cataloging-in-Publication Data

Vaughan, Norman D.
    My life of adventure / Norman D. Vaughan, with Cecil B. Murphey.
        p. cm.
    ISBN 0-8117-0892-6
    1. Vaughan, Norman D. 2. Adventure and adventurers—United States—
Biography. I. Murphey, Cecil B. II. Title.
G530.V38V38 1995
919.804—dc20
    [B]   95-2271
                                                                                              CIP

*Far better it is to dare mighty things, to win glorious triumphs,
even though checkered by failure, than to take rank with those poor
spirits who neither enjoy much nor suffer much, because they live in the
gray twilight that knows not victory nor defeat.*

—Theodore Roosevelt, 1899

Foreword

Since the beginning of time, the world has been fascinated by explorers and adventurers who dared to go where no man has ventured before. Their daring feats and journeys have been a source of inspiration for countless generations.

What child has not yearned to be a sailor on Columbus's ship? Or dreamed of being an Army scout in the winning of the West? Or perhaps envisioned being an astronaut risking the vast wilderness of space?

Such a man is Colonel Norman Vaughan . . . from his burning desire, as a young man attending Harvard University, to be a member of Admiral Byrd's expedition, to the realization of his lifelong quest to become the first person to climb the mountain named after him on the continent of Antarctica.

In my twenty-five years of telecasting the *Hour of Power*, I have had the privilege of meeting the greatest personalities of our time—and no one ranks higher in my mind than Norman Vaughan. He's the single most authentic and inspiring "Possibility Thinker" I've ever met in my life.

The story of Colonel Vaughan in World War II is that of a true hero in every sense of the word—from his daring plan to transport wounded soldiers during the Battle of the Bulge with his dog sled teams to his rescue of members of the Army Air Corps whose planes had crashed. He had two hundred dogs and seventeen men under his command in search-and-rescue missions and was called upon many times to deliver men and equipment.

Although his life has been filled with excitement and great adventure, he has also known disappointment, bankruptcy, and divorce. At the age of sixty-eight he went alone to Alaska without money, food, or shelter. But his strong will to survive never left him, and he soon found himself entering the longest dog sled race in the world, the famous Iditarod, 1,151 miles.

His dreams have been majestically fulfilled and he continues to be a source of inspiration to all who know him.

Our God gives us the tools with which to make a difference in today's world; whether or not we use those tools and answer His call depends on our faith that God will guide us.

Colonel Vaughan is a man who answered that call, loud and clear. He has stirred up the adventurer in all of us. His story makes our pulse quicken; he has inspired us to wish that we could have been with him in all of his many fantastic adventures. We are indebted to him for forging beyond the borders of safety to know the thrill of doing what no one before has done— and very few, if any, will ever do.

After reading this book, anyone who knows about Colonel Vaughan will want to stand and shout out with me, "God loves you, Norman Vaughan, and so do I."

Dr. Robert H. Schuller

Introduction

"Write something that's just for me. Anything," said the boy, thrusting the book at me. As I stared at the dimpled smile, I estimated that he was twelve or fourteen years old. He leaned forward and whispered, "I've already read the first two chapters while I was standing in line. It's pretty good." He was the last person in line on a day when I autographed and sold copies of my book *With Byrd at the Bottom of the World*. "Just anything you want to write is all right," he said. "My name is Ken."

"Dream big, Ken," I said as I took the book from him. Despite the long line and the numbness my fingers were beginning to feel from autographing, I liked to personalize each book. Quickly I wrote this brief message addressed to Ken:

"Live out your dreams. Take every opportunity to face your challenges with enthusiasm and then live adventurously." I finished with my signature.

"Hey, thanks. I'm going to finish the book this week!" he said as he left.

I smiled at Ken and thought about what I had inscribed in his book. In each book, no matter what the message, I ended, "Live adventurously," before my signature. I hadn't consciously decided to write those two words; they just felt right when I did.

$$\succ$$

The more I thought about that message, the more I realized that they summed up my philosophy of life. I began my real adventures, as best I can remember, at age twelve with my first sled dog. Since then, I have looked for adventure wherever I thought I could find it. On December 16, 1994, three days before my eighty-ninth birthday, I celebrated at the summit of

Mount Vaughan, a previously unscaled mountain named in my honor by Admiral Richard E. Byrd. As I surveyed the glorious beauty of nature, stared at the glacier-filled valleys, and pondered the treacherous crevasses that lurked beneath the snow, I realized that I hadn't done anything anyone else couldn't do. The only difference is that I actually did it.

One

ALL MY LIFE I'VE SOUGHT ADVENTURE. IT'S EXCITING TO DREAM BIG AND DARE to fail and be bold enough to try. When I succeed, well, that's just icing on the cake. It's the *adventure* that drives me—and sometimes gets me into trouble.

When I was twelve, my family moved from Salem, Massachusetts, to a rural area outside Hamilton, also in Massachusetts. My father, a prosperous leather tanner and shoe manufacturer, had made a fortune when he invented a process for dyeing leather white for nurses' shoes, calling it Vaughan's Ivory Sole Leather. He believed that my younger brother and sister and I would benefit more from country living. Our physical health was quite important to him because my two half-brothers had both died of tuberculosis. In those days, the treatment was to have the patients spend a lot of time outdoors.

My special companion in the country was Rex, a mixed German shepherd. Rex was my pal at every possible opportunity. My best friend, Edward Goodale, who lived five miles away in Ipswich, also had a dog of uncertain pedigree called Fido. I tell my friends that's when I went astray, either leading or following Eddie down the path of adventure.

Both Eddie and I enjoyed reading real-life stories. My personal heroes were the explorers Robert Peary, Roald Amundsen, Sir Robert Falcon Scott (who died returning from the South Pole), Sir Douglas Mawson, and Sir Ernest Shackleton. Later I added then-Commander Richard E. Byrd, who became the first man to fly over the North and South Poles.

As I recall, our search for adventure began when we read in a school textbook that Eskimos used sealskin to make harnesses for their teams of sled dogs.

"Let's make our own harnesses," I said to Eddie.

"What'll we use for sealskin?" he asked.

I pointed to a long coil of old rope that I had found in the barn. I had a good imagination. "It's not stiff and it won't kink," I said.

"Yeah, and we can go everywhere by sled, just like the Eskimos," he said.

We set to work with the rope, figuring, measuring, and splicing. We had learned how to splice by being sailors on any kind of boat we could get on, including fishing schooners that tied up at the wharves. After we finally had the harnesses made, we waited for the first snowfall. The days seemed to pass slowly, but it was probably less than a week before we had a nice four-inch snowfall. On the next morning after the snow, we hitched Rex and Fido to Eddie's Flexible Flyer sled.

"Ready?" I asked Eddie as he lay flat on the sled, ready for the dogs to race across the countryside.

"I'm ready."

We had put the dogs on a line ten feet in front of the sled. "Mush!" I yelled because that was the only command I knew.

The dogs didn't move.

"Mush, Rex! Mush, Fido!" The dogs, knowing nothing of our ambitious plans, thought we were calling them. Both animals turned and came back to the sled, wagging their tails. Fido put his feet on the sled and bent forward to lick Eddie's face.

"No! Pull! Mush! Fido, mush!" Eddie yelled and tried to push his dog away.

"It's not going to work this way," I said.

Eddie got up and told me to get on the sled; he went around to the front and called the dogs to follow him. As soon as their rope was taut, Eddie smiled. "Ready?" he asked. I held on and Eddie walked ahead, calling the dogs' names. They followed at a lope, tails wagging. Say, this is wonderful, I thought. In my mind, I was an Eskimo being pulled by a team of huskies across the frozen tundra of Alaska. We had our first sled-dog team. That was the beginning.

We had lessons to learn about dogs and sleds, the first of which was that dogs got tired of pulling loads. Eddie quickly solved that problem. As soon as our fathers left for work in the morning, we would tie up our dogs. I tied up Rex far away from the house so that Mother wouldn't hear him bark. I explained to Rex that he had to rest all day. As soon as we got home from school, we were ready for our dogs to pull the sled. Since they had been tied up all day, they were anxious for exercise. They cooperated beautifully. When we harnessed the dogs, they would feel the slack rope and think they were free. They were so glad to get moving after being tied up, they would pull like crazy.

At first we tried to ride across the fields. But that didn't work because the dogs had no sense of direction. Sometimes Rex tried to pull in one direction and Fido in another, and we didn't know how to take charge. We soon learned that we had to be on trails with our untrained dogs. In 1917, there were plenty of horse trails through the woods that were easy to follow. We went over the same track every day with the dogs. It took about a week of leading the dogs before they could do it on their own. When the trail was icy, we could both ride on Eddie's sled. Other times one rode and the other ran beside the sled yelling, "Mush!"

In our young minds, we had learned to drive dogs. For the next two winters, Eddie and I got our dogs out on the trail right after the first snow and mushed across the countryside. Spring thaws ruined our winter adventures, and our dogs went back to being family animals, until winter came again.

➤

"What if we had more dogs?" I asked, already beginning to think of a team. I had read of the larger teams used by explorers. Driving three or four dogs would be more of a challenge than two. And if we could train two dogs, why not three or four—maybe even six?

Eddie's eyes lit up. "We could buy another one!"

"At the dog pound," I said.

Eddie agreed. We withdrew our savings and went to the dog pound in Hamilton. When we got there, I walked up to the man in charge and asked, "Do you have any big dogs for sale cheap?"

"Look around," he said indifferently. "See if you like what you see." He took us into the shed out back where dogs were barking and trying to get out of their cages.

Immediately I saw the dog I wanted. He was a powerfully built Saint Bernard cross and weighed well over one hundred pounds. That meant he would be good at pulling. His single defect was that he had only one eye. That factor and his red-and-white coloring made him look lovable as well as strong. "That one." I pointed.

Eddie nodded in agreement.

"The Saint Bernard," I said to the man. "How much is he?"

"Ten dollars," he said.

Ten dollars in those days at a dog pound was high, and who would buy a dog with one eye? Had we thought it through, we could have bargained for him. The asking price was more than we had wanted to spend, but not knowing how to bargain, we paid the full amount. Eddie and I counted out $5 each. We named him Storm and he was *our* dog.

Immediately, we faced a new obstacle. Feeding an animal of that size was going to be a problem. We decided that we would stop at the butcher shop and ask for unsold meat and bones. The butcher handed us a bag of meat and bones in a paper bag. Later, we realized the meat was spoiled, but Storm didn't care. I was getting ready to feed him when he smelled the meat. Storm snatched the bag out of my hands. Protecting his meal with his large body, he sat down and began to eat. I reached toward him to remove the bag, and he growled ferociously. I pulled my hand back and didn't try to touch him until after he had eaten the meat and was gnawing contentedly on the bones. Once he had finished, he acted docile enough, but Eddie and I were still a little afraid of him. When we got ready to move out, Storm growled and tried to guard the bones. Using the rope around his neck, we pulled him away so that we could pick them up and feed him the rest later.

We had decided to share the dog, but that never created any problems for us. For a few days we kept him chained at my house, and then Eddie took him for a while.

By then we allowed the other two dogs to roam around freely, because they came when we called. But we didn't dare let Storm loose because we were afraid we'd lose him. So we kept him tied up all the time.

We were making progress. We had a sled pulled by three dogs. By using the same method as before, we taught Storm to lead by extending his trace line a little each day with Rex and Fido pulling behind him.

We began to winter camp. We persuaded our fathers to let us wear their coonskin coats. We kept warm except for our feet. From that we learned that we had to put on dry socks. We also filled small bags with hay that we wore on our feet in order to get an intermittent sleep.

➤

My love for the outdoors didn't end with winter. I must have been fifteen when I told my father, "I love to go beachcombing on Crane's Beach. I want to see if I can live like an Indian down there for a week. I'd like to do it by myself. Would that be all right?" Crane's Beach, a lovely, sandy stretch five hundred feet wide with sand dunes seventy feet high, was sculpted into steep, curving sides on the windward north. Although dunes change their shape with every high wind, they gradually sloped to the south. The north side was too steep to climb because our feet wouldn't hold, and if we tried, the sand flowed downward in a miniature avalanche.

By then my father had gotten used to my strange ideas of adventure. He didn't oppose the idea, but he didn't like my going there alone. "Can't you get somebody to go with you? Can't you get Eddie to go along?"

"I asked, but he's going away on a trip to Maine with his parents. And anyway, I can take care of myself." In those days, no one worried about strangers or abductors. I knew my father was concerned about my being alone in case I got hurt. "I'll be fine, Father," I assured him. I was tall for my age, already nearly six feet, and broad shouldered. I looked sixteen or seventeen.

"Norman, I'm not sure that's a good idea."

"Why not? I'll be perfectly safe. It's summer and there's no danger down there. I've been on many daytime picnics at Crane's Beach. Father, this is important to me. I've read about how the Indians used to live. I want to go and not take anything with me. I want to see if I can live off the beach."

"What will you eat?"

"I'll live like the Indians did. I won't get cold, you know. I'll have plenty of good wood for a fire. And I know how to start a fire by rubbing two sticks together. Mainly, I'll eat clams. The Indians did it for centuries. Certainly I can do it for a week."

"What about water?"

"I can get my water where the deer do." I had learned that I could find water by tracking deer, which was fun. I had watched them scrape a hole with their hooves where the sand was shallow in depressions. At high tide, the water table rises among the dunes and fills the hole. It is brackish but drinkable. "Please, Father, I want to see what it's like to be absolutely alone."

Father thought I was crazy. He stared at me as if he could not understand why anyone would have such a desire. "What are you going to do if it rains?"

"I'll get wet," I said. "But it's summer, and I'll dry off, won't I?"

"I shall have to think about it," he answered.

I persisted. Each day I asked, assuring him that I would be safe, that I wouldn't take chances, and that I would walk home if it didn't work for me. It was only five miles.

"All right, Norman," he said. "You have proven you're trustworthy. You may go for one week."

"Thank you, Father," I said. He gave me permission on a Monday. The following morning, after he left for work, I rode in his chauffeur-driven car to Crane's Beach. Before the car left me, I had to promise Arthur, the driver, I wouldn't do anything dangerous. A keen hunter, Arthur had taught me how to handle a gun and how to shoot.

I wore what today would be called sneakers, jeans, and a cotton shirt. I carried no other clothes, no food, no knife, and no matches. After waving good-bye, I began to orient myself. As I walked, I took note of which way it was back to the road. I followed the swampy areas in the sand dunes, where I came upon two deer. They had been drinking at one of their oases. I dug in the same place, made the hole deeper, and soon had good, clear water. I found a sea clam shell on the beach and used it as a dipper, being sure the sand that flowed over the edge of the shell wouldn't get into my mouth. I used the same hole for the whole week and had all the water I wanted.

On the second day, I discovered the iron top of a galley stove in the wreck of a long-ago-grounded ship. Around the stove top were an inordinate number of broken clam shells. One or two of them were fresh, but most had been parched by the sun. I also recognized guano deposits from sea gulls. It puzzled me why sea gulls would rest on a stove top, because they usually chose an elevated place such as a buoy or a moored boat.

Later, when I was walking along the dunes, a sea gull dove over the top of that same dune. I ran over and saw a new splash of guano as well as a freshly cracked clam shell without any insides. Then I understood. The gulls flew over the stove, judged the wind, and dropped the mollusk to break on the heavy iron. (A live clam is hard to open.) I wondered how the birds learned the bombing techniques of figuring wind and height above the stove top.

Their actions made me think about trying the same method, but I could not get up high enough to drop the clams. I decided I would hide and wait until a gull bombed the stove top, and then I would dash over and steal the smashed clam before the bird swooped in. It seemed like a good idea.

I waited at least two hours in a hastily built blind and not one sea gull came by. "A good idea that just didn't work," I said aloud.

I never forgot that incident. Over the years, other good ideas sometimes just didn't work. But just because they didn't work was no reason to stop trying new approaches.

Continuing my explorations, I picked up an old discarded raincoat that protected me from the rainstorm that struck on the third day. Using a broken clam hoe with four tines and no handle, I was able to dig all the clams I wanted at low tide. Because I had nothing to tie the hoe to, I had to hold it with both hands to dig. But that didn't matter. I went clamming every low tide. I didn't build a fire the whole week. I consumed only water and raw clams. I thought it was adventuresome and exciting.

People ambled along the shore and up and down the river in back of this mile-long sandy beach. We exchanged friendly waves, but I'm sure they didn't know I was roughing it, or they might have stopped to talk or to offer me food.

The first afternoon, I saw a stranger walking in the dunes. I would have paid little attention to this man except that he wore a tie. He was quite a distance away, so I couldn't recognize him, but I felt certain he saw me. Then he turned and left the beach by walking back into the dunes. Curious, I ran the quarter mile or so to where I'd seen him, but he was gone. I stared at his footprints. He wore a pair of shoes with a distinctively large heel. I laughed. The man was Father's chauffeur, Arthur. "He's come down to check on me," I said to myself.

Every afternoon of that week at Crane's Beach, I spotted Arthur in the distance. He never waved, but as soon as he saw me, he turned around and went back the way he had come.

I stayed six nights. My father and Arthur picked me up just before dark on the seventh day. I loved it on the beach. I had plenty to eat and drink, and did not feel lonely. I felt like an explorer entering virgin territory. I had done it alone. I felt I could conquer the world.

My father asked, "Norman, did you enjoy yourself?"

"Oh, enormously," I said as I got into the car. "And, Dad, a skunk came up to me while I was asleep and smelled my head. I saw its prints."

I don't recall anything he said, but I could tell that he was both pleased and surprised that I had spent the whole week alone.

My Crane's Beach adventure was typical of the spirit I've had my whole life. Even as a boy, I was already beginning to live a life of adventure.

TWO

MY PARENTS ASSUMED I WOULD OUTGROW MY DAREDEVIL IDEAS. OF COURSE, I never did. Father said little to me of my antics, but Mother often did. "Oh, Norman, I do worry so about you."

Actually that was the wrong thing to say to me. Her concern made me even more determined to show my courage and to try new things. Nevertheless, I would answer, "Mother, I assure you that I won't take foolish chances. I enjoy these things so much, that's all."

She didn't demand that I stop—that wasn't her way. But she made it clear that she didn't like my way of life, even when I was still a boy at home.

One of the people who shaped my life of adventure was Coach Nash. He was the coach for most of the sports at Milton Academy, a private boarding school. I was twelve years old when I entered in the fall of 1918.

I loved Milton Academy, and it remains the highlight of my childhood. Father had always encouraged me to go out for sports, and I did. I was large, muscular, and quite good at most sports I tried. Besides the usual sports at Milton, I learned to play polo. Years later, my knowledge of polo would become an important part of my life and would even take me to Iran. But back then, I preferred the contact sports. I won four letters during my years at Milton—in football, basketball, track, and wrestling. By my senior year, I had become captain of the football team.

The lesson I remember most vividly from Coach Nash happened in the middle of a football scrimmage. Everyone on our team was playing poorly that afternoon. Our first team should have walked all over the second team, but instead they were slaughtering us. The small crowd started cheering for the other team as they pushed us around. Nash was upset because we had a big game on Friday. It was then Wednesday, the last day of scrimmage.

I suddenly became aware of a sharp, painful sting in my heel. In those days, we had spikes nailed to the soles of our shoes. One of the nails had poked through into my heel. It hurt. I ignored the pain for a few minutes, but it got worse.

"Coach Nash," I called out, "may I go up to the locker room and hammer a nail out of my shoe? It's coming through."

For a few seconds he just stared at me, hands on his hips. In a low, deep voice he growled, "If you're tough enough to make this team, you're tough enough to drive that nail back with your foot."

I prided myself on being a tough guy, so I didn't leave the field. That didn't take away the pain. We played for another forty-five minutes. When I finally pulled off my shoe, the bottom of my sock was blood stained. I winced as I hobbled to the showers.

"Your foot really looks chewed up," one of my teammates commented.

"Ah, it's nothing," I said. But it was something. And it hurt. Naturally, I acted as if it didn't.

It was silly of me, of course, but I learned something. I had stayed in the game and had been able to push the pain aside and concentrate. To my surprise, I had played better after that than before. Maybe part of the reason is that I felt I had to prove to the coach that I really was tough. That attitude has stayed with me all my life.

➤

I loved life at Milton Academy so much that I didn't want to leave. I had lost something by graduating. I felt I was being severed from something I owned. I loved being there, loved being captain of the football team. Milton had three houses, and I was the elected head of one of them. Especially during my senior year, I had a feeling of ownership so strong that I wished I could find a way to stay. The challenge of college never entered my mind.

Once I left Milton, I couldn't go back. Nostalgia wouldn't let me. I have driven past the campus many times, but I've never been able to stop. Even now, some seventy years later, I still feel a sense of loss and a kind of homesickness for the school and Coach Nash. Milton was where I found unqualified acceptance by my peers and by my teachers. It was a time of innocence, and it was the happiest period of my childhood.

➤

In the spring I loved to canoe white water. I took three friends with me on weekend canoe trips in Maine and New Hampshire. We would strap two canoes on top of my first automobile, a Model T Ford station wagon with three pedals.

We enjoyed white water and thought we were pretty good at it. In fact, we became so cocky, we decided that we were the best at the sport in all of New England. Even after we entered Harvard, we carried on with this springtime sport of running white water.

One particular weekend stands out in my memory. I had boasted that we could beat anyone. To back up my boast, I sent a message to the fish and game wardens of Maine asking them if they would send a team down to the Rapid River to compete against us. We also challenged two Maine guides. I went to the Old Town Canoe Company and talked them into donating four new canoes for this event. "We are going to outmaneuver the guides and the wardens," I said. They thought it sounded like a good idea that would give them advertising for their product, so they agreed.

Thanks to some newspaper coverage, this challenge became a big event in that part of the country. More than twenty-five people showed up to watch the race. Four new seventeen-foot canoes, all wrapped in burlap to keep them from getting scratched, were shipped to the starting spot.

What I hadn't told the people at Old Town Canoe was that we were going to run on a river that we had never been on. But we had no doubts of our invulnerability. Laughingly calling ourselves the Vassar Girls, we were sure we could outmaneuver the professional canoeists.

We exchanged a lot of friendly put-downs and challenges with the game wardens and guides who had accepted our challenge. Then we climbed into two canoes, and they got into the other two. We weren't smart enough to wear life preservers. In our brashness, we figured that if we went over, we'd simply swim ashore. Our wiser competitors did use life preservers. Soon after starting, I realized the Vassar Girls had made a terrible mistake by refusing to wear life preservers.

We started to paddle down the fast-rushing river. The fish and game wardens had the first accident. Paddling around a bend in the river, they confronted a large, smooth rock on the outside of the flow. Water rolled over the upstream edge of the rock and beside it. They could see where they wanted to go, but they were going so fast they couldn't paddle their way out, and the current lifted them up onto the rock. They were high, but certainly not dry. The smash caused a sixteen-inch rip on the bottom of the boat. That accident eliminated them. The crowd on the shore cheered us on, for we stopped at every slack water cove to position ourselves for the next rapids. The crowd kept moving down a path along the riverbank, gathering at the next difficult spot.

A short time later, the guides' canoe pulled out. "Too swift for us," they said. "We never do water like this."

"Go ahead and pull out," we yelled. We thought of them as old men, but they were probably in their thirties. Not only were we young and fresh, but we were crazy. The Vassar Girls headed on.

The other canoe was just ahead of mine, when it was suddenly thrown ashore. The crash was so bad it tore a hole in the side of the canoe, which meant it couldn't be safely relaunched. Fortunately, the two paddlers, Alexander Bright and Skippy Clark, were all right.

Only our canoe was left. The crowd yelled encouragement to us, and we waved, momentarily losing our concentration. My companion, Bob Livermore, and I went over a small waterfall. The nose of the canoe went down. In the bow, I went underwater, but soon came up. Even though the canoe was filled, we weren't ready to give up.

"Paddle, Bob. Paddle!"

That's what he was doing, of course. Both of us paddled as rapidly as possible, unable to take time to bail out the water. It was hopeless. We were trying to paddle a canoe full of water. Just then we hit something—a large rock, undoubtedly, although I never saw it—and turned sideways and rolled upside down. Livermore and I were thrown out of the boat into the water. As I came to the surface, I saw our brand-new canoe being carried downstream.

Once ashore, I considered the damage. Two of the four new canoes were wrecked and a third one lost. It had been a crazy, dangerous, stupid thing to do that proved nothing. But we weren't wise enough to see it then. We had been the last to give up. To us, it was a victory and therefore worth it all.

I loved those minutes facing the white water, feeling the adrenaline rushing through me. I still remember it as one of the great times of my life. It was years later before I realized I could have been seriously injured or killed on that river, although after that trip, we did begin wearing preservers.

➤

During my senior year at Milton Academy in 1925, I faced the Harvard entrance examination. Two of us seniors at Milton were weak in history, and we engaged Stanley Osborne as our tutor. Stanley, an undergraduate tutor at Harvard, was superb in history. He could recall the date of any historical event and expected me to do likewise. He knew how much I had concentrated on sports at Milton and that I had neglected my other work. He was kind but tough,

"It is like this, Vaughan," he said. "I don't think you will pass your exams for Harvard without more study." Then he added, "And I mean a great deal of study."

I knew he was correct. He began to work with me, and then school ended for the year. Both of us knew I still hadn't caught up.

"I have a suggestion that may help you," he said. "If you would like to come home with me for the summer, I shall work with you every morning."

"I'd love to," I said. His home was then in Guatemala, where his father worked for the American government.

Harvard accepted a postponement of the entrance examination until fall but stipulated that I must pass all subjects before entering the class of 1929. If I gambled and failed the examinations in the spring, I could not take them in the fall. I thought I could pass if I waited until fall. So I went with Stanley Osborne to his home in Guatemala for the summer.

I studied hard for those two months. There were four subjects I had to pass: American history, French, mathematics, and English. I was lucky and passed the exams in the fall and entered in regular full standing with the Harvard class of 1929. Stanley couldn't believe it.

I had fallen in love with Jessie Bancroft while I was still enrolled at Milton Academy. We met at a dance social shortly before my fifteenth birthday. She was my first love, and I was positive I would marry her and never love another. Jessie was an attractive brunette, who was nearly two years younger than I. She attended Miss Windsor's, a girls' day school in Boston, and her primary interest was horses. She particularly liked to drive hackneys, and I was interested in riding horses because I had played polo during my summer vacations. She was an expert with high-stepping gaited breeds. Her grandfather owned *Barron's Weekly*, and he encouraged Jessie's fascination with hackneys. Jessie drove in all the fashionable horse shows, including the big one at Madison Square Garden. She looked gorgeous sitting in the middle of the four-wheel, rubber-tired light carriage, gripping a whip and reins in her gloved hands, a plaid checkered robe over her legs.

I was so in love with her that I went to Boston to see her just about every weekend. Jessie came to all of my football games and other athletic events. In turn, I took her duck hunting and to other sporting events, especially those that involved horses. We spent weekends at each other's homes in Hamilton, Cohassel, and Boston. Several times Jessie and I went to her grandfather's house. I always looked at him in awe as he used a phone at the dining table to conduct business all over the world.

I thought we were engaged, even though I had not given her a ring, and I'm sure she thought so, too. I hoped to marry her as soon as I finished Harvard, but going to Guatemala changed everything. While I was gone, the Bancroft family hired a Milton Academy classmate, Bill Cox, as a tutor to work with their younger son, Hugh. That meant Bill was constantly at their home. When I came back, I learned that Jessie had fallen in love with Bill. I was shattered. I told her she had to choose between him and me. She couldn't make a choice, so we parted. That was the end of my first love affair, in 1925.

Heartbroken, I felt the world was at an end. The pain had cut so deeply, I didn't want to think about romance, and I didn't want to go steady or even date anyone. In fact, I didn't date anyone until I got back from the Antarctic in 1930—five years after losing Jessie.

Three

THE NAME OF SIR WILFRED GRENFELL MAY NO LONGER STIR HEARTS, BUT HE was one of the international heroes of my youth. In 1892, this dedicated doctor left England and went to Labrador, part of the most easterly Canadian province of Newfoundland. He spent the next forty years of his life ministering to the health and educational needs of Newfoundlanders and Labradoreans. Fishing was their primary occupation, and they were constantly cutting their fingers or hands on the lines. They had no knowledge of sanitation, and their wounds often became seriously infected. Because of his utter devotion to them, Grenfell won their respect. He traveled the coastal waters in a specially equipped hospital ship each summer. In the winter, he went overland by dog sled. With a hospital at St. Anthony, Newfoundland, and nursing stations, he gave the people their first medical education and lessons in personal sanitation.

Dr. Grenfell is important to me because I had the opportunity to spend a good part of a school year working for him. I observed firsthand the good he did. It gave me great satisfaction to do good for others.

This opportunity came about after I had entered Harvard in 1925 as a freshman. I didn't do well because I paid too much attention to football and coming-out parties. In December, the school held an examination called November Hours. I did so poorly on that test that my name appeared on the dean's list. In those days, the dean's list was not an honor roll. Being on the list meant I had to give up all athletics and concentrate on my studies.

"Norman," my father said to me when I went home for the weekend, "you have not been doing your best."

"No, sir," I said. "But I promise to do better." I really had no choice if I wanted to stay at Harvard, which I did. I resigned myself to playing no sports for the rest of the year.

My life would have gone on like that except for an American surgeon named Charles Curtis. On behalf of Dr. Grenfell's mission, he traveled throughout New England, giving talks to raise the money needed at the mission. He met my father, they liked each other, and they spent time talking together. During their conversation, the matter of my being on the dean's list came up.

"Why don't you send Norman to Newfoundland with me?" suggested Dr. Curtis. "I'll give him a winter of hard work. He'll have no football or social activities to distract him. Just hard work."

"That's an excellent idea," said my father.

"When he comes back, he'll also be in better shape because life there is physically demanding. And maybe he can work it out to get himself off the dean's list."

My father mentioned to Dr. Curtis my interest in sled dogs.

"That would make him even more valuable to our mission."

When Father told me of his conversation, I could hardly contain my excitement. I envisioned what it must be like traveling to desolate fishing villages and mushing sled dogs through the woods, across the swamps, and over the ice. I discussed this trip with the dean, who thought it was a good idea. Not only that, but he said that if I spent the remaining academic year with the Grenfell mission and earned a good report, they would let me back into college. In the meantime, they would list me as a dropped freshman.

"Yes, that will be satisfactory," I replied, hardly able to believe my good fortune. I had a week to get ready before I left by train with Dr. Curtis.

I liked Dr. Curtis from the time we met. He was short, stout, and of medium complexion. He was in charge of Dr. Grenfell's mission hospital at St. Anthony. "You can live at my house when we reach St. Anthony," he told me. A brilliant, serious man, he was a first-rate leader whom people naturally followed. As I learned once I arrived, the hospital staff loved him.

"Just one thing," I said to Dr. Curtis. "I have a sled dog leader. His name is Storm. I'd like to take him."

"Oh, really?" he asked. "What kind of dog is he?"

"A Saint Bernard cross." I explained that he was twenty-eight inches tall and in good shape except for the one eye.

"Why not take him?" he said with a smile. "Our sled dogs are rather small in stature. By taking Storm, we might put some big-boned blood into the mission team."

He meant we could breed Storm, so I felt even better for having offered his services. The fact that Storm had never been the leader of a real team of huskies didn't bother me. Although he was getting old, he still pulled a sled with energy. In my mind, that made him good enough to go.

With rising expectations, I boarded a train at Boston and traveled to North Sydney, Nova Scotia. From there we took a boat to Stephensville, Newfoundland, then an all-day train ride through desolate, snow-covered countryside. At one o'clock in the morning, our train pulled into Deer Lake. I knew we still had three hundred miles to go to reach the hospital. It would be a long trip by dog sled and I was excited. Dr. Curtis had sent a wire from Boston to have two dog teams waiting for us at Deer Lake, and we were to leave at dawn.

Storm was used to being outdoors, so when we reached the Newfoundland inn, I tied him to a post near the front door. He had been fed that evening, and he wouldn't need water before morning. So I patted him, talked to him a minute, and then left him. Storm curled up into a ball, ignoring the light spray of snow that gingerly struck his heavy coat. I estimated that the temperature was about fifteen degrees above zero.

The front door of the inn was unlocked, and we walked inside. The wind slammed the door shut behind us. To my amazement, no one sat at the desk. No lights shone anywhere. I knew they didn't have electricity, but I didn't see lamps burning. Darkness enclosed everything.

"What do we do now? Wake up somebody?" I asked.

"Oh, no," Dr. Curtis laughed. "We'll tramp upstairs and find ourselves a bed." He was so casual about it, I assumed he meant that they expected us and had saved a room.

We went up the steps. There were eight or ten rooms. One by one, he opened each door. We stepped inside and looked around. Each room held bunk beds, sometimes four, but often as many as eight.

After we had tried the last room, with men sleeping in all of the beds, I said, "Everything looks full, so what do we do now?"

"Let's go back to the first room."

"I saw a man in every bed."

"Yes, I know," he said. He opened the door. "Norman, just hop in with anybody who has any space left."

"Just like that?"

"Of course," he said. He walked across the room and dropped his coat and bag on the floor. Then he pulled himself up onto an upper bunk and bedded down. "Try that one on the far side of the room," he said and rolled over on his side.

"All right," I said. Very carefully I inched into a bed. I was scared. I didn't know who the man was, didn't know what to expect, wondered if he would wake up and kick me out or start punching and ask questions later. I squeezed myself as close to the edge as I could, lying on my left side. Every time my bed companion made the slightest movement, I snapped wide awake.

The four days of travel had tired me. I had looked forward to a warm, comfortable bed, and now I couldn't sleep. I have no idea how long I lay tensed on the edge of the bed, but eventually I did fall asleep out of pure physical exhaustion.

Dr. Curtis awakened me just as the first morning light filtered into the room. I never did learn who I had crawled into bed with. He had already gotten up and was gone. I was so tired, I hadn't felt him climb over me.

"Sleep well, Norman?" Dr. Curtis asked.

"I was too scared to sleep much," I said. "I didn't know who that was in bed next to me. I've never done anything like this before."

"We do it this way all the time," he said. "Get up now, and we'll have breakfast in a few minutes."

Downstairs, we met the husband and wife who ran the inn, but I was too tired to pay them much attention. Breakfast consisted of oatmeal, bread, and hot tea. As I would learn during the next ten months, Newfoundlanders needed three staples for their diet: flour, sugar, and tea. Aside from occasional potatoes, or fish that came from the coast, they had little variety.

By the time we had finished breakfast, I felt invigorated and was eager to get on the trail for St. Anthony. Two hours after daybreak, we left the table. My first task was to put a harness on Storm and let him become the leader of my dog team. At home he had been trained to lead, so he knew his job.

Both sleds waited in front, and our luggage was already lashed on. They were the old-fashioned Newfoundland komatic sleds, about twelve feet long, made of wood with steel runners. In front of the sled, I saw twelve huskies harnessed in a fan hitch. With a fan hitch, each dog had its own trace back to the sled, unlike the gang hitch we use today with one single line and dogs paired along that line. This fan hitch held a team of dogs pulling on individual traces that led back to the sled, much the way Eskimos harnessed their dogs. Eskimos wanted each dog able to get free because they never knew when a polar bear would appear.

As I was to learn, all dogs had the same length trace except when they went through woods. Then they were staggered. In reality, on narrow trails they followed one right behind the other. If it wasn't possible for two dogs to run side by side, the Newfoundlanders would shorten the traces and the dogs would automatically fall in line.

The two teams were waiting for us in front of the inn. The drivers had anchored their sleds by dropping a chain in front and under the runners and hooking it around a tree trunk. The dogs didn't move. They stood only a dozen feet or so away from Storm and stared at the large, one-eyed dog. Suddenly, they started to bark at the strange sight.

The driver cracked his long whip above their heads, making a horrible, popping sound. "Shut up!" he yelled. That was another thing I was to learn: "Shut up!" was the favorite command to get the dogs to quiet down—that along with the crack of a whip. (In Newfoundland, I never saw a man drive a team without a whip. When not on the trail, drivers wore the whips around their necks as emblems identifying them as dog drivers.)

The dogs stopped yelping, but they didn't stop staring at Storm.

When I came outside, the driver of the sled with whom we would travel was checking the lashing of the load. I introduced myself.

"Hello and welcome," he said, extending his hand. "My name is Walter Patti. You and I are taking this sled." Meanwhile, Dr. Curtis got onto his sled, waved, and took off.

Our twelve dogs started to bark when they saw the other team start out. They strained forward in anticipation of following. Walter poised, waiting to pull the hook (that is, undo the anchor and release the chain from the front of the sled, which meant that nothing was under the runners and we should slide along nicely).

I hitched Storm about fifteen feet in front of the other dogs. He turned his head and stared at the yipping dogs. By now they were barking loudly at Patti to pull the hook. It's the trait of a waiting team to push hard to catch up with whoever is in front of them.

"Get ready, Storm!" I yelled.

Storm stared up at me with his one good eye, and then he surveyed the area around him. I don't think he even realized that the other team had started on the trail. He had no idea which way to go. Trails were everywhere, and there was no distinctive one to follow. The twelve other dogs knew the way, of course, because only the day before they had come the three hundred miles from St. Anthony. They were in good shape and eager to go back.

Storm made no attempt to move. He was untied but didn't even know it. Walter made sure his dogs were far behind Storm. He knew—as I had yet to learn—that they would attack a strange dog if they got to him.

Storm stood, facing away from the other dogs, his tail down between his legs.

"Your dog all right?" Walter asked.

"I think so."

"All right, start him. I'll release the brake, and we'll go." Walter was poised ready to pull the brake.

"Storm! Go! Go, boy!"

Storm paid no attention to my voice. He didn't move an inch. I yelled again.

Storm acted as if he had not heard me. He stood looking sheepishly back, as if begging me to get him out of there. He was headed in the right direction because I'd put him there, but he wouldn't take one step. His eye kept darting from me to the barking dogs behind him.

Walter released the brake. The twelve dogs took off, but Storm didn't move. In those brief seconds before they reached my dog, we both sensed the danger. Walter had his whip out and snapped it fiercely, but they had already piled on top of Storm. The whip came down on the dogs, hitting them at random. They yelped. His whip came down again, again, and again. The dogs barked and howled, yet despite their fear of the whip, they seemed determined to tear Storm apart. Walter kept the whip going, all the while yelling for them to stop attacking Storm. As the whip rained down on them, Storm was hit as well as the other dogs. Walter's strong voice finally prevailed, and they backed off. Even as they whimpered and backed away, Walter hit them yet again.

The dogs backed off, but Storm lay on the snowy trail. His body was bleeding in several places, mostly from his belly, a vulnerable thin-haired area. Fortunately, the dogs hadn't torn holes through Storm's hide, which they easily could have done if Walter had not been quick with his whip.

Storm raised his head and looked piteously at me with his one eye. I petted him and said soothingly, "There, there, boy, it's all right."

By then Dr. Curtis had disappeared over the horizon, and we had forgotten about him. I looked around—my first chance to do that in the daylight. I realized we were on the edge of town and there were no other houses and no other dog teams.

"I guess we'd better let Storm follow," I said to Walter. "He sure can't go ahead of them."

Shock and fear were engraved all over that dog. He just stared with his good eye and whimpered. I unharnessed him and took the trace that he was supposed to use for pulling. I put it on as a leash, tying one end around his neck and the other to the back of the sled.

"I think we're all right," I said to Walter.

He nodded. The sled started. The leash drew tight and pulled Storm by his neck. Down he went. He didn't resist, walk, or try to run. He lay on his side as the sled dragged him along.

Walter then turned and saw what had happened. He swore as he pulled up his team and yelled at his dogs to slow down. They had just felt the whip and were anxious to go faster. Somehow he got them stopped. Storm lay quiet and unmoving, exactly where he had stopped. I hopped off the sled and ran back to my dog. I lifted his head, patted him, and spoke in my most soothing tones. "Everything's going to be all right, Storm, old boy," I kept saying.

I untied the leash from the back of the sled. "This isn't going to work very well," I said to Walter. "Can you drive your team slowly for a little while, so I can walk along with him?"

To the credit of his self-control, Walter didn't say anything, and he did what I asked. With a loose leash, I coaxed Storm to get up, and he started to walk with me. We gained thirty yards or so, and finally he walked on his own without my having to pull him. I tied the leash to the back of the sled again so that we wouldn't go off without him. I hoped that he would trot along.

"Walter, I know this will slow you down a little, but Storm will come if you can drive slowly enough."

He shook his head and said, "I'll try." To keep the dogs walking slowly, he left the chain on the front of the sled and drove them as if they were pulling a heavy load. Sled dogs like to go as fast as they comfortably can.

By trotting fast, they make the sled slide more easily. When it moves slowly, they have to put more muscle into it. Once they build up momentum, the sled glides along the trail. The dogs kept straining, trying to go faster. Walter held them back, as I kept calling, "Come on, Storm. Come on, boy, come on, boy."

Storm moved forward. He was beginning to limp, but there was nothing I could do for him. As time wore on, the limp increased. But we went slowly enough for him to keep up.

Far up ahead, Dr. Curtis wondered where we were. Finally, out of concern, he and his team waited at a village until we caught up. I explained what had happened, and he listened patiently to me. Then he wondered out loud, "Do you suppose we could leave the dog at a village and try to pick him up in the summer?" That would be the next time I returned to Deer Lake.

"Gee, Dr. Curtis, I wouldn't like to do that."

"I suppose you're right," he said. "Let's see if we can get him going."

We started again. Storm managed a slow trot. Fortunately, it was an easy trail. We had the previous night's light snowfall on the trail and no serious problems.

Because of the delay with Storm, we knew we would not reach the village where Walter had planned that we would spend the night. (It was the middle of the next morning before we reached that village.) That first day we only made ten miles in eight hours. Normally, a good sled team makes five miles an hour. The two teams had expected to make the three hundred miles to the hospital in no more than eight days. I didn't like to think how much Storm and I were slowing them down.

By dark, we couldn't go on any longer. Dr. Curtis pulled up at a log cabin in the thick of the woods, a place used by mail carriers to rest between villages. No mail carrier had been there for several days; normally they traveled only once a week into the rural area. Four feet of snow had drifted around the front door.

By the time our team arrived, Dr. Curtis was already "on the shovel." I paused long enough to tie Storm to a tree not far from the door. The other driver handled both teams of dogs while Walter helped Dr. Curtis shovel.

I learned for the first time why the door of a log cabin must open inward. Dr. Curtis, who reached the doorknob first, pulled the rope, which lifted the inside barrier. That released the pressure on the door, and it opened inward. Covered with snow, we fell into the cabin. Immediately, Dr. Curtis turned around with the shovel, scooped the snow up, and threw it out.

Once inside, one of the men hurriedly gathered twigs and started a fire. The room warmed quickly, and only then did we take off our heavy clothes. That's when I learned not to take off my heavy clothes when I first enter an unheated cabin so as not to cool off too quickly.

Like all the other cabins in that part of the country, this one was small with a low, seven-foot ceiling. It was about fifteen by fifteen feet. Single bunks lined three walls, with a stove along the fourth. The bunks were so wide that three or four men could sleep in the same bed.

One of the men took the melting pot and packed it tight with clean snow. He packed it tight because snow has a huge volume for the amount of water gained. He melted that snow and hurried out for more. By the second melting, we had enough water to "cook" the meat and potatoes, both of which had been previously fried. Food was always fried at the hospital before the teams went out. This was done so that they could still eat even if they couldn't get a fire started. Of course, the food would be frozen or at least very cold.

Before going to bed, I checked on Storm. He had eaten his supper, a sign that his wounds weren't going to overpower him.

Then it was time for bed. Both Dr. Curtis and I had sleeping bags, so we rolled them out on the bunks and climbed inside them. I was dead tired from my previous restless night and the trail trauma with Storm. I went to sleep quickly.

The next day we started out slowly. It didn't take long for Storm to realize that he had to come with us. He moved a little faster. The second day we made between fifteen and twenty miles. Storm's limp persisted, but it didn't worsen. The second night we stayed at a village, and I tied him up outside, separate from the other dogs. On the third day, I let the leash go, and he padded along on his own. He never would come up to the sled, always staying just a little behind us. Normally, Storm would approach and smell other dogs, but not these dogs. He had been frightened, and he wouldn't get close to them again.

When I saw another team approaching from the opposite direction, I would jump from the sled and go back and walk beside him. I did this not only because Storm was frightened, but also because I wanted to make sure the other team didn't charge him.

On the third day, we were beginning to pick up a little speed. Storm often lagged so far behind that at times I couldn't see him. In the early afternoon, as we approached the crest of a hillock, a team from the opposite direction was suddenly on top of us. It was too late to help Storm. I yelled at the driver, "Loose dog!"

"I don't care!"

As Walter later explained, the other driver thought I was warning him of a dog up ahead that might attack him.

Fortunately, nothing happened to Storm. I imagine he ran off the trail when he saw the sled coming.

➤

Everywhere we stopped, the people wanted the doctor to sleep at their houses. Dr. Curtis usually stayed at the home of the man in the village who had caught the most fish and was, therefore, the town's wealthiest and most influential citizen. Each time he arranged for me to stay there, too.

While in the villages, Dr. Curtis ministered to the people. On that trip he wasn't able to do any surgery, but he handled minor illnesses and many damaged hands.

Staying in the homes of the natives was quite an experience for me. As winter approached, they would close the master bedroom and the husband and wife would sleep on the couch or on a bench in the kitchen where it was warm. The kids would have to sleep in their own bedroom. Upon our arrival, they would usually light a fire in a little stove inside the closed-off bedroom where we slept.

Walking into these bedrooms was like walking into a cold shower. The walls, ceiling, and floor were covered with frost. Soon the heat melted the frost, and the walls, curtains, bedding, and floor became wet. It was horrible, yet not so horrible that we would refuse the room. But we hated to take off our clothes. They would be damp in the morning.

One big problem I faced was spitting. All the Newfoundlanders I met spit constantly. I had been brought up to believe that spitting around others was impolite and something well-bred people simply didn't do. If people had to spit, they went into the bathroom or did it in private. In those houses, all around the stove and the woodpile, I found evidence of spittle—and it wasn't from chewing tobacco. Tuberculosis—what they called "consumption"—was rampant, causing the people to spit phlegm incessantly. It took a little getting used to for me to be in such unsanitary conditions.

The Newfoundlanders didn't bother to build outhouses to protect themselves from the weather or from public view. If they needed to defecate, they simply went behind the woodpile, which they kept near the doorway. Afterward, dogs came and cleaned up almost everything, leaving only paper strewn everywhere. They wiped with the pages of Sears and Roebuck catalogs or whatever was available. Sometimes they settled for twigs, branches, or grass.

Everybody used the same dipper when they drank the water. Naturally, being a properly brought up New Englander, I didn't like that. When offered water, I said, "I prefer tea." I love water but I couldn't bring myself to drink it. The water came from wells, if they had them, or from melted snow. It was a lot of work to melt snow, and more work to find clean snow. Actually, clean snow didn't exist around their cabins. When the people went outside for snow, they usually got the snow closest to the door. This snow was dirty, containing wood chips and other debris, as well as waste from the dogs.

As bad as this sounds, and as much as it took for me to get used to the conditions of Newfoundland, I adjusted quickly. *This was adventure.* I loved it. I kept thinking of all the wonderful tales I would share with my friends back home.

➤

During those eight days of travel, Walter taught me a lot about dog driving. Storm got better at keeping up. Near the end, we increased our daily mileage, doing more than fifty miles on each of the last two days.

When we arrived at St. Anthony, I followed Dr. Curtis to his house, a plain two-level, clapboard house. He gave me my own room. After the primitive conditions I had endured in Labrador, I couldn't believe I had a room all to myself.

Everyone at the mission loved Dr. Curtis. I felt privileged to be living at St. Anthony. When students came, they knew they would do the grunt work around the hospital. Although they usually had several students at any time during the summer months, it was highly unusual to have one stay during the winter. I was the only young person from the States to work the rest of that winter. Everyone treated me well. I liked the work and the schedule.

As for Storm, he never did pull a sled in Newfoundland. He was just a large, one-eyed dog who kept away from the other dogs the entire time.

Four

"In loving memory of Watch, Moody, and Spy, who gave their lives for mine." The words I read on a plaque at Dr. Grenfell's house intrigued me, and I wondered who those three men were. Grenfell's house, much larger than Dr. Curtis's, had a porch all the way around the two-story structure. The bronze plaque, on the wall near the front door, stood out so that it was hard for anyone to miss it.

When I finally got to meet the legendary doctor, I wanted to ask him about those three names, but I was too much in awe of him. I remember Dr. Wilfred Grenfell as graying and mustached, of medium weight, at least six feet tall. He wore a jaunty sea captain's cap and dressed in working clothes, which should have made him look like anybody else who lived on the Labrador coast. But he looked different. The way he walked, even the way he stood, gave him the bearing and dignity of a commanding officer. As I learned in my months there, he was a quiet man, but his alert eyes made it obvious that he was aware of everything going on around him.

He stuck out a long hand and shook mine. "I heard you had come, Norman. Glad you are here. Do you like it?"

"Oh yes, sir," I said. "I like it very much."

"I am so pleased you could be with us," he said.

That was the total conversation, but even in that brief exchange, he put me at ease. Yet he also had a reserve about him that didn't invite us to become friends. That was fine with me; I had come to be one of the grunts.

Since I hadn't asked Dr. Grenfell about the plaque, I decided to ask Dr. Curtis. That evening when we relaxed before bedtime, I mentioned having seen the plaque. "Impressive, isn't it?" he said.

"Who were those three men? How did they give their lives for Dr. Grenfell?"

"Quite an interesting story," he said, laying his head back in the chair. "Would you like to hear it?"

Of course I did. As well as I can remember, this is the story Dr. Curtis told me that December night in 1925:

Dr. Grenfell received a telegraph message that a man had accidentally shot himself. He had been out on the trail crossing a fallen tree when the gun went off. The bullet went through the back of his knee. Dr. Grenfell knew only that the bleeding had stopped. Sanitation in Newfoundland villages approached zero. Grenfell set out alone on his sled, pulled by nine dogs. Because there was no evidence of a spring thaw, he assumed the ice was solid, and so Dr. Grenfell planned to go directly across Hare Bay. Otherwise, he would face an additional ten miles of travel—about two hours by dog sled.

Just as he reached the bay, a man came off the ice with a small sled and waved him down. "Doctor, go around the bay," the man yelled. "This has become dangerous. The ice is breaking up, and you might get caught."

"But you came across, didn't you?"

"Yeah, but I'm not sure you can get across with your heavier sled."

"A man's life is at stake," Dr. Grenfell said. After the two men conferred another minute or so, the doctor said, "I'm going to go across."

"I wish you wouldn't," the man said, then continued on his way.

The doctor started across.

When the man reached his village, he told everyone about meeting the doctor. One of the men in the village expressed concern. He went out to check whether the wind was still on shore. If so, the ice would be safe. While he was outside, the wind shifted. The villager became gravely concerned.

Dr. Grenfell was a little beyond the halfway point when he heard a cracking sound. He knew he had made a serious mistake. Now he found himself and his dog team on a large sheet of ice that had broken off. Small sections continued to tear away from the big float he was on. This left him on a fairly small ice pan. Sensibly, he got in the lee of the sled, and the dogs huddled around him. A high wind rose and the bay ice broke into pieces. The water whipped against the ice pan as it floated in the middle of the bay. It threw water into the air that stung the doctor's face and wet his outer clothing. Grenfell turned the sled over and put his back against it while sitting on his food box. Soon the continuous spray soaked through his clothing. Grenfell prayed for help as he sat helpless and alone.

In the meantime, the people waiting for the doctor, in anticipation of his arrival, had started fires along the shore. They would burn all night long or until he arrived. The people knew that Grenfell was coasting out to sea. From his island of ice, he could see those fires burning. He knew the people were at the end of the bay, the place he had tried to reach, and that they were thinking of him and praying. But his ice pan continued to move farther out to sea. Before long, a chill had thoroughly penetrated his body.

As Dr. Grenfell prayed, a message "came" to him, telling him that the only way he could save his life and six of his dogs would be to kill three of the animals, skin them, and wrap their skins around his wet back. In deep agony, he chose three dogs. Being a skilled surgeon, he did his work rapidly and efficiently. All the while he worked, he realized it was getting colder and the wind-swept spray was numbing his body. When he finished, he wrapped the wet skins around his back and crouched down behind the sled. He felt immediate relief, but he still wasn't rescued. He continued to pray, feeling assured that God would somehow save him. He undoubtedly would have died if it hadn't been for the protective skins of his three dogs.

A short while later, a miracle happened; the wind shifted direction and began to blow toward shore. Now he could see that he was heading toward the banks of the bay. As they got closer to shore, the dogs jumped onto the next ice pan and then the next and the next. Soon the ice all crunched together. He and his remaining six dogs moved onto the land.

When the doctor reached the village, the man he had started out to help was alive. The bleeding had stopped, and the villagers had wrapped a dirty burlap sack around his injured knee.

After Dr. Grenfell did everything necessary for the wounded man, he sledded back to St. Anthony, going the long way around the bay.

I never forgot that story. Two years later, when I went to Antarctica with Admiral Byrd, I took along three brother dogs that had come from St. Anthony. They were beautiful, wonderful huskies, two of which were white, the third brown. I named those dogs in memory of the three who had been sacrificed to save Dr. Grenfell: Watch, Moody, and Spy.

➢

After my first night at St. Anthony, I fell into a routine. Every morning I got up early and went with Walter to the woods to cut down trees and bring back a load of wood for the hospital furnace. We started in the dark and reached the trees at daybreak. We drove the sleds about ten miles, and it took most of two hours to get there (and a little longer to return with our firewood). Once there, we put on snowshoes so that we could move around and cut the trees. We went to work with our axes and loaded up the sleds.

Walter taught me how to ride a loaded sled. Even more important, he showed me how to drive dogs across the tundra over unmarked trails. After a few days of this, I was able to drive my own team. I carried a much lighter load than Walter did because I had fewer dogs, usually six or seven. Walter drove at least fifteen and sometimes as many as eighteen dogs.

Each morning between ten and eleven o'clock, we returned with our loads of wood. Walter and I would then sit down and enjoy a full, well-earned breakfast in the hospital kitchen.

The hospital itself was a simple wooden building with a good operating room, ten beds for patients, a large dining room, a kitchen, and a wood-burning furnace heater.

During the afternoons, I assisted in the operating room of the hospital. I was the swab man, doing what they call today scud work. My job was to use forceps and pick up swabs from the floor. In those days, doctors didn't place their sponges in receptacles, but just dropped them on the floor. Somebody then had to pick them up.

After surgery was over, I did anything they asked of me for the rest of the afternoon. Today they would say I was a gofer.

Even now the memory of my first day in an operating room is vivid. They had already anesthetized the patient with ether. The odor permeated the room, but I tried to ignore it. They had to amputate a man's left foot, but they were going to save the heel as a cushion for a prosthesis. I watched Dr. Curtis cut through flesh and bone, and then sew up the stump in a lengthy operation.

The next thing I remember is waking up in the hallway. I stared at the nurse through fog-filled eyes. She smiled as she said, "It's nothing serious, Norman. You fainted. It was the ether, but you'll get used to it." She hovered over me until she was certain I was all right. "Now you're ready to come back inside." She left me and went back into the operating room.

I waited until I was breathing normally before returning to the operating room. I never fainted again. And I found I liked watching the surgery.

➤

St. Anthony's hospital owned two steamers. I shoveled coal a few times on the *Strathcona*, which was more of a luxury cruise ship that carried both freight and people. Dr. Grenfell traveled on this one. They called the smaller mission boat the *Wop*. (In those days, they called all workers like me wops, with no intended slur.) The *Wop* supplied mission stations and carried supplies to St. Anthony.

In early April 1926, Dr. Grenfell planned to go north on the *Strathcona* to make medical visits to the villages along the coast for two months. He went down the Labrador coast just as early as he could, in spite of the ice. He tried to get in as much work as he could during the summer months because he couldn't return there until the following April. He felt a particularly strong sense of mission toward the fishing settlements. He genuinely loved the people and they loved him.

As the doctor traveled the coast, he saw fishermen from larger Newfoundland seaports who had journeyed north to anchor along the coast while they set out their nets. On his trip, Dr. Grenfell would visit the people on boats as well as those on shore. He did whatever he could for the sick, and he seemed to have time for anyone who needed his services. Everybody loved Dr. Grenfell and eagerly awaited his visits.

He had become a legendary healer. Many of the people were convinced that if Dr. Grenfell medicated them, they would get well, no matter how sick they were. A few sick people seemed to improve just from shaking his hand.

➤

In the spring, other students, most from prep schools but a few from colleges, arrived to work until they returned for fall classes. One of the things they did was to go after sand for the new hospital that the mission was building. Newfoundland is a sandless island, so the *Wop* had to transport it from the Labrador coast. By April, the frost was gone, and they could pour cement. The *Wop* had to make repeated trips to Labrador for more sand.

One day, Dr. Curtis said to me, "Do you like to sail?"

"Yes, sir, I love to sail."

"Excellent," he said. "And do you like the captain of the *Wop*?"

"Yes, I do," I said. I had met him and found him a friendly man.

"The captain says his mate is sick. He needs a replacement. The captain has a lot of confidence in you and has asked specifically for you. He told me he believes you will do exactly as he says no matter what it is. Is that true?"

"Yes, sir, I will." Just the thought of working on the *Wop* excited me. And who wouldn't feel good to hear that the captain wanted him?

So it was agreed that I would become the captain's mate on the next trip for sand. Once we started out, the captain told me, "My bunk is right behind the wheelhouse. Mainly you'll steer the boat when I'm asleep. You'll travel according to the course I set." He explained that he slept fully dressed. If anything went wrong, I had only to knock on the wall, and he'd be out on the deck in seconds.

This is great, I thought. Here I am just a kid, not yet twenty-one, and I'm a captain's mate. The round trip for sand from northern Newfoundland across the Strait of Belle Isle was a five-day journey.

As we sailed across the strait, the ocean was rough. The St. Lawrence River was swift, pushing everything out to sea through the Strait of Belle Isle. It was tough going, and the captain said it would take us all day to get across to the Labrador coast.

The crew members were all Newfoundlanders, but we also carried six students who had just arrived. I didn't know any of them, which made the situation seem strange to me. The students were the deckhands, and I was their new mate.

After we crossed the Strait of Belle Isle, trouble started. The engineer was supposed to shovel coal to keep up the steam. He came down with pneumonia, and soon he was so sick he couldn't get out of his bunk.

The captain approached me. "Boy, we're in tough shape. Will you go down and be the engineer?"

"Yes, sir."

"You'll have to keep the boiler fired up. Do you think you can do it if I show you and keep you posted on what to do?"

"Yes, sir."

I didn't mind the temporary demotion. I stayed below decks all day and kept the steam up. When we reached the harbor, we couldn't get close to the dock because of ice. Strong winds pummeled the tug. Even if we could have landed, we couldn't have shoveled sand. We anchored in the middle of the harbor, waiting for the ice to move enough for us to reach the dock.

That night, I was going to sit down to supper when the captain called me.

I raced up the iron stairway. His face told me that he had another problem.

"I need your help," he said.

"Just name it. Anything."

"Crane's gone berserk," he said. Crane was the cook.

"What do you mean berserk?"

"He's out of his head, yelling and screaming and not making any sense. I've had him locked inside the cook's quarters."

Now I waited. He hadn't called me up to the main deck just to share this information with me.

"The cook's gone berserk," he repeated. "Just plain crazy. Now that we've anchored, you can let the boilers cool down. So, Vaughan, will you be cook?"

"Yes, sir," I said, "I'll do that."

So I became cook on that tug for all those people, including the six students. Meanwhile, the real cook was kept locked up in his cabin because the captain was afraid he would hurt someone, or himself. And the engineer was sick. I had to laugh. I had begun as mate. Then I became engineer. Now I was a cook. One demotion after another.

I didn't mind being cook, but I had one problem. I had never cooked a meal in my life. But, as I learned, none of the students had either. Breakfast wasn't a big deal. I cooked oatmeal, and we had plenty of canned milk and sugar. For lunch, I opened whatever cans I found on the shelves. We had no bread because I didn't have the slightest idea how to bake bread. But I did know how to make pancakes. So with every meal, I served pancakes.

Before I served my first meal, I said, "If anyone criticizes the cooking, that man becomes the new cook. Now eat up."

Nobody complained, but then nobody complimented me either.

On the fifth day, the wind let up and the ice separated enough that the captain felt certain we would be able to reach shore the next day. That news lifted our spirits. We hadn't been working during the five days, so we would be rested and ready for shoveling sand.

Then something else happened to lift our spirits even further. A local fisherman had been out in his tiny boat and jigged some cod. He came up alongside us and gave us part of his haul as a gift. I should have baked it or put it into a codfish stew, but I didn't know how. I fried it.

"Best codfish I ever had in my life," said one of the students. He stared at me in a way that made me think he didn't mean it.

Still, others echoed him. No one complained. Oh well, I thought, that means I'm still the cook.

➤

In April 1926, Dr. Curtis made his final sled dog trip of the season around the northern part of Newfoundland. The two-hundred-mile round trip would take him up the east coast to the tip of the Strait of Belle Isle and then westward down the west coast of Newfoundland, and finally around Flower's Cove. Of course, at each of the villages where he stopped, he cared for the sick.

Dr. Curtis approached me. "Norman, I'd like you to drive the team." That meant Walter was not going, and I would drive the team of eighteen dogs. It was a heavy responsibility, and I was pleased.

"Of course," I said. "I can do it easy."

"Do you think you can control all these heads?" he asked, referring to the dogs.

I assured him that I could and would.

A few days later we left.

Before we entered the first village, we had to go over a small hill. Dr. Curtis was riding on the sled and I was in front, steering and guiding the dogs by voice. We started down the hill, and I put the drag chain out to slow the sled. Suddenly a cat ran across the trail in front of us, then down under a house. Like all houses by rivers in that part of the world, it was on log piles, or stilts. Because it was almost summer, the stilts were at least three feet above the snow.

The dogs, all on individual traces, didn't stop when I tried to brake them. They followed the cat right under the house, wrapping their traces around the piles. They barked and snarled and became a tangled mess.

Dr. Curtis, not waiting for me to stop the sled, hopped out and went into another house. People were waiting, probably everybody in the village, and he was eager to do what he could for them. As I had already learned, when the doctor arrived, everybody became sick, and they all needed a personal medical conference.

While he was inside, I tried to get the dogs untangled. No one came out to help because they weren't interested in me or the dogs, not with the doctor in the village. It was such a mess that I had to take one dog at a time and lead him away from the house. Then I secured him and went back for the next one. I had eighteen animals to contend with, all tangled up in each other's traces. As I got one dog untangled, another would move and tangle the lines again. It took me nearly two hours to pull all the dogs out from under the house and get them ready to go again. After crawling around and dragging those dogs out, I just wanted to sit and rest. I had been on my hands and knees most of the time, working in a crowded space, and it had worn me out. I dropped onto the sled, but within two minutes Dr. Curtis bounded out of the house.

"Glad you had a chance to rest up," he said, unaware of what I had been doing. "I'll need you inside at the next place."

Not one to admit I was tired, I carried on.

At the next village, he had to excise a cancerous growth from the outside of a woman's nose. His skill impressed me more then than at any other time. And I could say that I assisted in the surgery, even though it was still the lowly job of picking up the swabs that he threw to the floor. (In this case, a kitchen floor.)

The woman never complained or moved as he cut out the growth. He made an incision like a flap, put in two stitches on either side, and left a big loop. He cut around the outside of the growth and eventually picked it off with a pair of forceps. After he cut out the growth, he pulled the thread tight. Then he dressed her face. She was a young woman, so he told her that in two days she had to make the half-day trip herself to the hospital, where the nurses would take out the stitches and redress the wound.

Traveling with Dr. Curtis was exciting for me. Just by being with him, I felt as if I were making some contribution to the healing of others. Whenever we stopped at a village, I felt the people's respect. They often called me doctor, too. I heard remarks like, "Doctor, this is fine that you came along." "Doctor, we're glad to see you."

Naturally, I didn't discourage it.

Five

"NORMAN, YOU CAN HAVE THEM IF YOU WANT," DR. CURTIS SAID, KNOWing how much they would mean to me.

"I'd be pleased to have them," I said, aware that my words failed to convey my gratitude to the good doctor.

It was the spring of 1926, and he had given me three Labrador huskies. I think it was in appreciation for the work I had done during the 1925–1926 academic year. I had worked hard but I had enjoyed myself immensely. Even though I could have gone home in May, I continued working through the summer. But then, as the first of September approached, I made plans to crate my three puppies, pack up my few belongings, and leave. The time had come for me to return home. Fall term at Harvard was less than a month away, so I couldn't delay my departure any longer.

It was no problem to ship the dogs on the train with me. As I neared home, my thoughts were not on Harvard or academic work, but on my dogs. In addition to the three puppies, I still had Storm, as well as Eddie Goodale's Fido. That made two dogs and three pups. By fall, the puppies were large enough to be part of a sled team.

My family thought keeping five dogs was crazy. I don't recall specifically what my brother or sister said to me, but I do remember my father saying to my mother, "I will not stop him from having dogs, but he'll have to take care of them and keep them out of everybody's way."

"I'll feed them and keep them away from the house," I promised. "And I'll arrange for someone to take care of them while I'm at college." That would be no problem. An older man who lived nearby often did odd jobs for the family and ate many of his meals at our house. When I asked him, he was happy to take care of my dogs.

In the fall of 1926, I returned to Harvard with no academic restrictions except a promise to my parents to do my academic work. When I came home for Christmas vacation, I intended to put my dogs on the trail. I had missed dog sledding, and I missed being with my animals. I made plans to go for a week with the dogs. By then Eddie Goodale had acquired a second dog, so that would give me a total of six dogs to take out. Unfortunately, we didn't get enough heavy snow in our area, so I decided to go north where there was plenty of snow. I thought of going to Wonalancet, New Hampshire, to meet a man named Arthur Walden, who was known as a sled dog racer. He had once delivered mail in Alaska by dog sled. If I could talk to him and watch what he did, I figured I could learn more. Traveling all that way, spending the night, and then turning around to come home again would make a wonderful winter trip, I decided. As I worked out my route, I was well aware that I would be gone over Christmas. Being young and thoughtless, my quest for adventure was too strong to let time with the family get in the way. I decided to leave on December 20 so that I could get to Wonalancet and back in time for the first day of college. Eddie couldn't go with me because his family had a reunion over Christmas that he couldn't get out of. My family wanted me home with them, but I felt it was more important to be off in the woods. I was told I'd spoil Christmas for everyone if I went away, but I didn't listen. Selfishness ruled.

The morning of my departure, I had a little trouble getting the dogs ready to travel. Instead of leaving at noon as I had hoped, it was midafternoon before I called Eddie. By now, he had his own car. He helped me tie my sled on top of his car. The six dogs piled inside. "We're off!" I yelled. And the dogs barked in anticipation.

Eddie drove north. It was late at night when we finally reached a part of New Hampshire with plenty of snow. When we both agreed that there were no more dry spots on the road, it was time for the adventure to begin. Eddie dropped me off in a field, said good-bye, and headed home. I still had 175 miles to go to reach Wonalancet. By mushing twenty-five miles a day, I would be there in a week. I planned to spend one night, then make the journey home. The rest of that first night I slept in my sleeping bag, curled up inside the sled, the six dogs huddled around me. I was scared, wondering whether somebody would come and want to know what I was doing there. Would they call the police? What would happen if the weather got worse? What would I do in a blizzard? I didn't have a tent or any extra equipment. I had planned to make the whole trip by sleeping outside each night.

All the while I was on the trail, the dogs and I never encountered any big storms. Still, I did get a lot of snow, and I had trouble sleeping in open fields. Because I had not learned about windbreaks and brush shelters, I was cold all the time.

To lighten my load, I carried no food. I assumed I would beg along the way. In those days, people shared food and water much more readily. Of course, I also had to get food for my dogs. I stopped at the local butcher shop in Rochester, New Hampshire, to ask for fat and bones. When the butcher found out why I needed them, he couldn't give me enough. After that, I supplied my dogs by going to the nearest town and asking the butcher for bones. With the bones came a lot of meat.

Feeding myself demanded an entirely different strategy. I never worried about getting food because I had faith in human kindness and trusted my ability to make a good case for myself. As mealtime approached, I would start looking for a house where the occupants might be kind enough to feed me. I couldn't explain the kind of house I looked for; I simply trusted my instincts. And my plan never failed me.

The first morning, I got the dogs going as soon as it was light. We traveled for two or three hours. By then I really wanted breakfast, so I stopped at a farmhouse. I left the sled and the dogs staked in plain view and walked up to the door. When a smiling woman answered, I said, "May I have a drink of water?"

"Well, of course you may," she said, and invited me inside.

Once inside, I mentioned—as casually as I could—that I was going as far as Wonalancet. "I've got a dog team, as you can see." I made certain that she saw them from the window. "I'm just getting along the best I can." Then I added, "I can't carry any water, and I get awfully thirsty."

"Have you had any breakfast?" the woman asked.

"No, I'll get some somewhere."

"You don't want to go on the road hungry like that. We've got leftovers. Would you like that?"

"Why, that would be nice," I said, flashing her my biggest smile.

After a hearty breakfast of leftover corn muffins, which I loved, and six strips of bacon (and making sure I got plenty of water for my dogs), we were on our way. That's the method I used every day I was on the trail.

When I got hungry, I stopped, and nobody turned me down. People were generous to my dogs as well.

I decided to stay on roads that weren't heavily traveled, so that I would have plenty of snow. On Christmas, I was traveling a back road. It was a pretty wild area, and I saw few houses. By one o'clock in the afternoon, I was beginning to wonder if I would find a place to stop for food.

Finally I saw a house. As I got closer, I saw three kids playing in the yard. Instinctively, I knew that was the house where I would eat Christmas dinner. I paused, waved, and said, "Hello! Merry Christmas."

"Where you going with all those dogs?" asked the youngest child.

"Just going along the best I can." I was delighted they had responded. I stopped and introduced my dogs to them.

Their mother stared out the window. Then she came outside.

"Ma'am," I said after I had greeted her, "could I have a drink of water?"

While she was getting the water, the father came out of the house and started talking to me. "Where are you going?"

"I'm going up to Wonalancet, up the line, with my dogs."

"What's at Wonalancet?"

"I'm going to see some dog drivers, and then I'm going back home. I've been on the road since December twentieth." We had a friendly chat. I finished my water and acted as if I were ready to move on.

"Had anything to eat?" the husband asked.

"No," I said.

"We've got plenty left over," said his wife. "I'll warm it up."

"Would you like a little Christmas dinner?" he asked. "Seems a shame not to have a big dinner—"

"I'd love it," I said, letting them take me inside. While I sat by the stove, the mother heated a variety of vegetables, including sweet potatoes, and brought out pieces of turkey. She finished by serving me two kinds of pie. As I ate Christmas dinner, my hosts, even the children, seemed enraptured to hear about my trip, and about my year in Labrador. I added how happy I was to be eating their wonderful food.

After my meal and treats for my dogs, I was again on my way. I still had twelve miles to go to make my twenty-five for the day. Another twenty-five the day after Christmas would take me to Wonalancet.

On the afternoon of December 26, I reached Arthur Walden's place. I introduced myself and mentioned several mutual friends. Because he was a dog man, and I was obviously one who shared his passion, he accepted me without hesitation. I was barely inside his house before he said, "Norman, I'm delighted you came to visit." Arthur was a short man with weather-beaten features, maybe fifty years old. "And I'm pleased to see somebody who is out doing something."

Walden said that his greatest times had been living in Alaska. It took no prompting to get him to tell me one of his many stories about gold prospecting in the Yukon Territory, how he carried mail to the miners, and how he often hauled gold back to Dawson on his return trips.

Walden invited me to eat with him. I didn't refuse, of course. Nor did I tell him that I had been counting on his hospitality. He brought out food for my dogs and showed off his dogs. He had developed a new breed called Chinook, the offspring of a German shepherd and an Eskimo dog. He had already started successfully breeding a line of sled dogs that were strong and yet gentle around people.

I explained that I had wanted to meet him, but that I soon had to go home. As a sled dog driver, he needed no more explanation. He invited me to spend the night inside, but I had earlier observed an open shed, so I said, "No, I'd rather sleep outside near my dogs, in case one breaks loose."

"Fine, fine." The dog man understood.

The next morning, I packed up and left before Walden stirred. Seven days later, when I reached the area with insufficient snow, I met a college student. I was sitting by the side of the road, my thumb out and my dogs staked out of sight. The college student and I chatted for a while. I told him about my trip, and then I persuaded him to drive me and my dogs back home. He laughed about it all the way.

Six

THE FIVE-WORD HEADLINE OF THE *BOSTON TRANSCRIPT* FOREVER ALTERED THE course of my life. In September 1927, I was a student at Harvard again. One night while studying with my four roommates, I had opened the paper and read these words: "Byrd to the South Pole." Although I didn't know how I was going to do it, I immediately knew that I *had* to become part of that expedition.

Richard E. Byrd was already one of my great heroes. The previous year, he had made a historic first flight over the North Pole. Now he was leading an expedition to Antarctica, intending to stay on the virtually unexplored continent for fourteen months. Besides doing scientific and geological exploration, he would fly over the geographic South Pole.

After reading the article several times, I lost interest in my studies. Instead, the very next morning I went to Byrd's home in Boston. An officious maid wouldn't let me inside to talk to him. But I wasn't ready to give up. Next, I went to the office of the *Boston Transcript* and found W. A. MacDonald, the reporter who had written the story. Using him as an intermediary, I made Byrd an offer: I would leave college and work for Byrd for a full year without compensation, training his dogs to go to Antarctica. After a year, he could decide if he wanted to take me. But there was no obligation for him to do so.

Two days later, MacDonald phoned me. "Commander Byrd has accepted your proposition."

Of course, I was ecstatic. I had gotten my foot in the door with Byrd. Now I faced one more big obstacle: I had to get my parents' approval. They had allowed me to drop out of Harvard for a year to go to Labrador. When I returned, they assumed (and so did I) that I would complete my studies and go into business after graduation. Now I wanted my parents' permission to drop out of Harvard a second time and go to Antarctica.

The next day, I left Harvard and drove home to talk with my parents. After I explained about Byrd's expedition, I said, "Father, I want to go. I must go. It's the most important thing in the world to me. I know I'm a disappointment to both of you, but it's something I must do."

When my father realized how strongly I felt, he consented. However, being thoroughly businesslike and sensible, he asked me questions about financial arrangements. Then I made a mistake. When Father asked how much Byrd was going to pay me, I said, "Don't worry, Father. Commander Byrd is going to take care of me." All the time I had been in school, they gave me what was then a generous allowance of $25 a week. I counted on using that to provide for myself the year I was working for Byrd without pay.

"Then we won't need to send him his allowance anymore," he said to my mother.

I couldn't back down and beg them to continue, so I agreed. Of course, Byrd had promised nothing, and I had no idea how I would provide for myself. Yet I knew I had to go on that expedition. I would find a way to eat and live.

➤

Arthur Walden was, according to the newspaper, in charge of assembling the dogs for the expedition to Antarctica. I decided that if I waited for a formal invitation from him, I might not get it. The sensible thing for me to do—or so it seemed—was to show up at his door and announce, "I'm here to help you get the dogs ready for Antarctica." When I had visited Walden the day after Christmas, he had said nothing about the expedition, so I assumed he had not known about it himself. He had liked me, so why wouldn't he want me there to help? After all, it wouldn't cost him anything but my room and board.

I unexpectedly arrived at Walden's door without food or much money. My arrival shocked him because he had not yet heard from Byrd about me. Walden gave me a place to stay—outdoors in the gazebo. The gazebo offered little more than a roof for protection, and I would be there through the winter. But I didn't mind. In fact, I thought it was exciting sleeping outside with the animals chained nearby.

Walden and his wife, Kate, operated a small inn that catered to the wealthy who came for winter sports. Unfortunately, they had turned the kitchen and dining room over entirely to the cook. I arranged with the cook, who was a hard, demanding woman, to let me be a waiter in the dining room. In return for my services, I received no money, just leftovers from the guests' plates. She would not allow me to have leftover food that had not been served because it had to be saved for the next day. So I got what would normally have been garbage. But I didn't mind. I had wanted adventure, and I felt this was part of it.

The first night on the job, I devised a few tricks so that more food would be left on the plates. When I brought first helpings, I gave each guest extremely small servings, knowing that it would not be enough and that they would want more. When they asked for seconds, I heaped on the food. That usually ensured generous leftovers for me because they couldn't eat all that I had given them. Once guests caught on to my strategy, they asked for more food than they planned to eat, leaving large portions. They were really good to me.

When I realized how great it was going to be on the expedition, I telephoned my best friend, Eddie, to come with me. He gambled by leaving Harvard and joining me. After two weeks together, we said to each other, "We want Freddie Crockett with us." When we called him, Freddie hesitated at first, but then he signed up. We three promised each other that we would go back to Harvard if Byrd didn't take us.

When I was not serving in the dining room, I trained dogs for the expedition. Working with the expedition committee, I took on the responsibility of figuring out what equipment and food we needed for the dog sleds. Ninety-seven sled dogs were going to Antarctica, so such preparation demanded a lot of calculating. How much seal meat could I count on being available once we reached Antarctica? What kind of food would the dogs need apart from seal meat? I worked with a national dog food company, which is still in business today. With the help of Milton Seeley, a New York chemist on a leave of absence from his business, we worked out a formula that guided the company that eventually contributed forty tons of dog food. They followed our meat–cereal formula, and we fed it to our dogs in Wonalancet. After two months of feeding the dogs with great success, we gave final approval, and the company manufactured forty tons.

Calculating dog food should have been Walden's job, but he wasn't very good at estimating amounts and making long-range projections, so I did it. That was my first big mistake in my relationship with Walden.

Even though we were gambling that Byrd would take us, my two friends and I had a wonderful time. We worked with the dogs and served in the dining room. I taught them my tricks for getting more food. Somehow enough food was left on plates that we always had plenty to eat. We slept all winter in the drafty gazebo. We could have grumbled, I suppose, but instead we chose to use the primitive living conditions to toughen ourselves physically and mentally.

After eleven months, we met Byrd. He liked us and appreciated our work. He agreed that all three of us could go on the expedition with him, which I had never doubted. Byrd dubbed us the Three Musketeers, and other members of the expedition picked it up. (At the end of the expedition, he would name a mountain for each of us.) Along with Paul Siple, who represented the Boy Scouts of America, we were the youngest men on the expedition.

➤

We went on the Norwegian whaling ship *Sir James Clark Ross* from Norfolk, Virginia, to New Zealand to get through the tropics as quickly as possible. The other expedition ships would have been too slow. Also, the big wooden decks on the whaler were fine places to walk the dogs. I volunteered to work below decks for the six-week journey. As a member of the "black gang," I stood a regular watch and shoveled coal into the ship's three boilers and raked out clinkers. The heat was so intense that we wore only three items of clothing—a wide type of jockstrap, a large neckerchief to wipe away perspiration that continually ran down our foreheads and into our eyes and mouths, and wooden-soled sandals that lifted us a full inch above the steel deck to protect our feet from the inevitable red hot clinkers that landed all over the steel flooring. Although it was the most physically demanding work I have ever done in my life, I loved it.

We had shipped most of the donated dog food to Dunedin, New Zealand. The rest went on board to feed the animals. The first time we gave it to the dogs, we discovered that it made them sick. After examining the food, we learned that someone had thrown in the sweepings from the floor, containing everything from pieces of rope, dust, and pebbles to nails and wire. We had eighty thousand pounds of useless dog food. But we had to have provisions for the dogs. We scrounged rice, cornmeal, powdered milk, cod liver oil, and meat scraps from the ship's supply.

During our month of layover time in Dunedin, we put the dogs on Quarantine Island at Port Chalmers. I volunteered to take care of acquiring new food for the dogs. Again, Walden should have done that because he was the man in charge of the dogs. But he lacked initiative and didn't seem to have any idea how to provide so much food in such a short time. I went to the stores in Dunedin, where I borrowed ingredients that consisted of fish meal, meat meal, beef tallow, wheat germ, molasses, and cod liver oil.

A chocolate factory allowed me to use their mixing equipment at night after their workers left. I slept on top of flour bags during the day and worked twenty straight nights by myself mixing the food. When the factory workers arrived at seven in the morning. I had to have everything cleaned up and ready for them. The night watchmen alerted me at four o'clock so that I could stop working and steam clean the large mixing machines and paddles. I had to leave them spotless and sanitary. Those nights of work proved to be quite a strain, but again I thought of the fun and adventure I was having.

For my meals, I ate leftover products from the chocolate factory, such as doughnuts and biscuits. After a day or two, the workers realized that was all I had to eat and brought me good food from their homes.

We fed the new mixture to our dogs, and they liked it.

Only one person marred the trip: Arthur Walden. I became increasingly aware of his sullenness toward me. The episode with the dogs' food had widened an already apparent breach between us. Had I been more sensitive, I would have tried to get along better with him. But I was young and impulsive. I thought I could walk right by Walden—and that's what happened. I figured he was the one who had the problem. Soon his resentment began to show more openly. A month after we established our base camp at Little America, Walden's favorite dog, Chinook, disappeared. We assumed the dog wandered off to die. Walden was so attached to that animal that he grieved about it for weeks. That added to his depression. I often wondered if somehow he blamed me for the death of Chinook.

In early April, we lost the sun and did not see it again until its first rays reached us on August 29. During the period of the "long night," Walden became more sullen and withdrawn. It would not be many days before he made me actually fear for my life.

With the perspective of years, I'm a little more understanding of his feelings. During the year of preparation at Wonalancet, I had become a little cocky, and I knew Arthur Walden had begun to resent me. Although he was good with dogs, he was not the kind of man who knew how to solve larger problems. His experience had been mostly in Alaska twenty years earlier. Thinking that I knew more about dogs than he did, I constantly upstaged him. It was stupid and arrogant of me, but that's who I was. I say this because of what happened between us once we were on the ice.

On Christmas 1928, our ship reached the Bay of Whales in the Ross Sea. All crew members landed and immediately started to unload equipment. One of Commander Byrd's first responsibilities was to establish a base that he had decided to name Little America. Within minutes after our landing, Byrd wanted to go inland to select the site himself. He walked up to me and said, "Vaughan, hitch up a team." Then he added, "You're going with me."

I was thrilled by those words. We would be the first ones to go inland. I wanted to see and do everything. This was the true beginning of the expedition I had dreamed about for more than a year. But it was to make things even worse between Walden and me. I can now imagine the jealousy that must have inflamed him. Rightfully, he should have been the one to drive Byrd to the initial site. That had been his original position. But as far back as our days at Wonalancet, his indecisiveness and uncertainty had hurt his chances for recognition.

In all honesty, I didn't give much thought then to how Walden felt. I was having the time of my life. It was like having the Harvard football coach call for me to replace a starter in the big game against Yale.

Byrd often asked me to do things that should have been Walden's job. When he wanted to know about the general condition of the animals, their food supply, or their shelter, he asked me. Byrd didn't intentionally try to hurt Walden. Had he disliked him, Byrd was the kind of leader who would have ordered him to board the ship and return to New Zealand.

Although Walden began to withdraw and become sullen toward us, he still continued to do his job well during the unloading period. Only after we stopped our demanding work and he had more time to brood did he become worse. He showed obvious hostility toward me, but I was too busy enjoying myself to care.

When Byrd announced that the Three Musketeers would go with Larry Gould, the second in charge, on his geological expedition, it was probably the worst news Walden could have heard. He had been pushed aside.

Several Norwegians were on the ice with us as part of the expedition, and I learned from them that Walden was out to get me. They also warned me that he had started to carry a gun. Whenever Walden and I saw each other—and it was difficult not to have contact since we were all in one building with tunnels leading to our barracks—he refused to speak to me. He only gave me sullen stares. I began to stay in the barracks until after I knew Walden had eaten.

He slept in the other barracks with the Norwegians. Later, some others took his gun away from him. Even so, I feared he would find a way to kill me. His carrying a gun made me realize how deeply he hated me and how easily he could sneak up on me in the night when I was defenseless in my sleeping bag. So every night I began sneaking outside, going only about fifty yards to avoid getting lost. I dug myself a place to put my pup tent. Then, fully dressed, I climbed into my sleeping bag. Most nights the temperature dropped to forty degrees below zero. On our coldest night on the ice, the temperature reached minus seventy-three. No matter how cold it became, I decided I could always find a way to get warm. But I wasn't sure I could find a way to protect myself from Walden. I was genuinely afraid for my life.

>

On August 20, 1929, the first rays of the sun returned to Antarctica. Each day we enjoyed a few more minutes of light. The sunlight would continue to increase until we had no night, and then slowly, over a period of six months, it would recede to total darkness again.

Finally, in October, Byrd decided it was time for the geological team to leave. And we were ready. On October 29, 1929, six men, ten sleds, and forty-six dogs set out on our expedition. We did not reach the South Pole, but that had never been our intention. We were doing geological exploration. If Byrd had trouble on his polar flight, we would become his search-and-rescue unit.

On November 29, Byrd flew over the South Pole. En route, he buzzed over us and dropped us messages and food. After he reached his polar goal, he returned to Little America. We went eastward into unknown territory. It was thrilling.

On December 21, we reached our destination in the Queen Maud Mountains, which we called Supporting Party Mountain.

Larry Gould wrote in his notebook:

> *We are beyond or east of the 150th meridian, and therefore in the name of Commander Richard Evelyn Byrd claim this land as part of Marie Byrd Land, a dependency or possession of the United States. We are not only the first Americans but the first individuals of any nationality to set foot on American soil in the Antarctic.*

➤

Two days before Christmas, we started back toward Little America because our dogs could not continue. They had worked hard, some were limping, and all were showing the physical strain. We had not brought enough food for the animals to continue inland. Gould had not planned to reach the Pole, but he had hoped to find answers to a number of geological questions. He had not found everything he wanted before we turned around, and he was disappointed.

On the Axel Heiberg glacier, however, his disappointment vanished. There he found pieces of yellow sandstone. The sandstone was part of a large mass of rocks that topped the larger mountains. This proved that the mountains were actually gigantic blocks of the earth's crust that had been pushed up from sea level to as high as fifteen thousand feet. One of the men who had been with British explorer Sir Robert Falcon Scott had discovered sandstone two hundred miles west. This discovery confirmed that the Queen Maud Mountains were a continuation of the mountains on the western borders of the Ross Sea and that we stood on the largest mountain fault system in the world.

Excited by his discovery, Gould sent a radiogram to Byrd:

> *No symphony I have ever heard, no work of art before which I have stood in awe ever gave me quite the thrill that I had today*

when I reached out after that strenuous climb and picked up a
piece of rock to find it sandstone. It was just the rock I had come
all the way to the Antarctic to find.

To add to his excitement, Eddie Goodale found lichens, a symbiotic
association of fungi and algae. This was the farthest south anyone had ever
seen such plants.

➤

One of my most powerful memories is of Christmas night. We discovered the cairn of my hero, Roald Amundsen. He had left a five-gallon
gasoline can, a waterproof package with twenty small boxes of safety matches,
and a tightly sealed tin can. Inside the can, Amundsen had placed two pages
of a notebook with the names and addresses of his men. Dated January
6–7, 1912, it stated that they had reached the South Pole and that they
hoped to get back to camp alive. If, however, the crevasses opened up and
swallowed them, he wanted the king and citizens of Norway, as well as the
rest of the world, to know that he had reached the South Pole on December 18, 1911. Amundsen and his men, the first to reach the pole, did survive. They beat Sir Robert Falcon Scott by thirty-one days. Scott and his
men perished on their way back to their camp.

Although it was written in Norwegian, Gould copied Amundsen's note
word for word. He left the copy along with a note explaining what he'd
done, and took Amundsen's original. Years later, the Norwegian College
of Academics honored Dr. Gould with a prestigious award, and Larry Gould
handed King Haakon VII Amundsen's original note. It is displayed today
in an Oslo museum.

On January 19, 1930, we returned to Little America. We had covered
more than fifteen hundred miles in eighty-seven days.

After we returned, Arthur Walden was somewhat less morose, but he
still didn't speak to me or acknowledge my presence. As much as possible,
I avoided him until we left Little America.

➤

Once we reached New York, we were all honored as great heroes. My mother and other relatives met us when our ship docked in New York. Father stayed at home to prepare for the arrival of the fifty-four dogs that I brought back from Antarctica. It was a wonderful, exhilarating time for us.

The next day we were honored with a ticker-tape parade. I rode with Eddie Goodale and Freddie Crockett in the first car behind Byrd and Gould. As our car crept along, I looked up at an amazing sight. Between the tall buildings, paper floated down in such wild abundance that it looked like a snowstorm.

We were home. It was the end of an adventure of a lifetime. That thought depressed me. I didn't think I'd ever have another experience that would come close to my time with the Byrd Antarctic Expedition. I am happy to report more than sixty-five years later that I was wrong. But in 1930, I didn't yet know that.

Seven

"IT'S OVER, NORMAN," ADMIRAL BYRD SAID AS HE STOOD ON THE DECK AND gazed at the mushed-over trail. I had just brought him by dog sled back to the ship from Little America, where he had lowered the flag. He said just those few words, but they conveyed more than any of us could say. It was a few minutes before nine on the morning of February 19, 1930. We were leaving our home of the past fourteen months and going back to the United States.

I wondered if I was the only one who hated to see the expedition end. Most of the men looked back, a silent farewell to the ice-covered continent. I couldn't do that; I didn't want to look back. It had been my home. I was happy there and didn't want to leave.

Byrd turned toward me. His eyes met mine, and he smiled. "Norman, we did it. Now we must celebrate our victory."

"Yes, sir," I said, mustering as much enthusiasm as I could. I just didn't feel like celebrating.

The others, however, did celebrate. Some were cheering, already speaking of Antarctica as a thing of the past. I had to get away by myself. I knew I was going to miss that barren land.

➢

Upon our arrival in New York, Wall Street celebrated with us. Symbolically, it was a victorious homecoming for all of America. We had gone to the unknown continent and claimed a portion of it for the United States. People cheered and paper floated down from the skyscrapers. Reporters from newspapers, magazines, and radio asked questions, eager to know everything about the trip. The April 1930 issue of *National Geographic* devoted itself almost entirely to the Byrd expedition.

And then it was over.

➤

When I returned to Hamilton, Massachusetts, I had fifty-four dogs left from the expedition. We had offered dogs to any members of the expedition who wanted them. Some men chose dogs and took them to their homes. Father, who had fenced in part of the farm for the dogs, allowed visitors to come and see the animals. A few weeks later, Eddie Goodale took the dogs to his family's farm and advertised that visitors could see the dogs that had gone to Antarctica. He charged 25 cents for a visit, or 50 cents to stay and watch the dogs' daily feeding. For an additional 50 cents, they could feed the dogs themselves. For several months, Eddie made a tidy profit from his show business. Eventually, Eddie and I placed the dogs in good homes.

Then it was time for me to return to Harvard and to start making plans to earn a living. When I left for Antarctica, there was no question that I would return to Harvard. Father expected me to be enrolled for the fall semester of 1930. Returning to the campus, I walked around Harvard Yard, feeling restless. Attending classes seemed boring. I had changed too much. I decided I couldn't go back and sit in classrooms.

I hated to tell my parents, but, of course, I had to. I couldn't stay at Harvard. I knew I was a terrible disappointment to my parents, particularly Mother, but I couldn't go back. I simply wouldn't fit in. I tried to explain my feelings, but I knew that my parents didn't understand how I had changed.

The decision dismayed my parents, but they respected my wish. "Well, Norman, then what do you plan to do?" my father asked. The pointed question was his way of saying that he didn't approve.

"Work," I said. As a matter of fact, I had already taken a job before I came to see them. I would sell advertising space in both *Time* and *The Sportsman* magazines. Although I was unenthusiastic about the work, I did fairly well. I liked being with people, and selling wasn't difficult, but I needed a greater challenge, stimulation, something to help me adjust to the real world. Through contacts with friends, I got a fine opportunity with N. W.

Ayer and Sons of Philadelphia. At that time, N. W. Ayer and Sons was the largest advertising agency in the world. They were impressed enough to groom me for a management position.

I accepted their offer, hoping it would provide the challenge I needed. It didn't. Boredom and depression still tugged at me. I tried to ignore those inner feelings. After all, I had just returned from one of the greatest adventures of the twentieth century. Feeling let down was natural. Now I had to force myself to get in step with the world around me.

No matter how relentlessly I pushed myself, I never did manage to get in step. I tried a number of diversions. In the fall, I played semiprofessional football while I worked for N. W. Ayer. My department manager, however, horrified that I would risk injury, insisted that I could not continue to play and work for such a prestigious company. So I gave up football.

Shortly after I went to work for N. W. Ayer, I met a lovely young woman named Iris Rodey. We started dating, fell in love, and were married in 1931. Two years later, we had a son, whom we named Gerard Gould Vaughan. His middle name was in honor of my friend, a man I still deeply love, Dr. Laurence M. Gould, who had been second-in-command of the Byrd Antarctic Expedition. He later was to see Jerry under unusual circumstances.

Unfortunately, our marriage had little chance of success, which was mainly my fault. Although I loved Iris, I wasn't ready for marriage to anyone. No matter how hard I worked at it, I remained a bad fit for a conventional lifestyle. In 1938, when Jerry was still very young, Iris and I separated and divorced. She knew—perhaps even better than I did—how the spirit of adventure constantly pulled at me. Iris, by contrast, wanted to be a good mother and homemaker. We were simply incompatible as husband and wife. Despite the divorce, as long as she lived, we maintained a friendly relationship. She raised our son very well and didn't prejudice him against me.

During this difficult period of my life, sports and recreation remained my true source of pleasure and the only way I knew to relax. I played a little polo in the summer and went duck hunting in the fall. When winter came, I had two diversions that temporarily enabled me to forget my misery. First, I skied. I could totally abandon thoughts of my work-weary world when I glided down mountain slopes. I also enjoyed giving nightly ski lessons at the Winchester Golf Club in Winchester, Massachusetts.

Skiing became increasingly important to me, and I took advantage of every opportunity to get to the slopes. In 1936, I published my first book, *Ski Fever*, the first book written in the United States on skiing. It was a how-to book that illustrated techniques approved by Sigman Buchmayor, the first European ski instructor brought to the United States by Katherine Peckett.

The second thing that gave me enjoyment was, of course, my dogs. I drove dogs as often as I could. I remained one of the most active members of the New England Sled Dog Club. Each year, the club sponsored eight weekend races in different towns. They were great fun, and I went to them all.

In the winter of 1932, we learned that the New England Sled Dog Club would hold an important race. The winner would represent the United States at the 1932 Olympics in Lake Placid, New York. Members of the New England Sled Dog Club were hardly world-class dog men. For us, racing our dogs was reward in itself, although race sponsors did present trophies to the winners.

Twenty-six teams entered the two-day event, which took place in Wonalancet, New Hampshire. Teams raced fifteen miles on both days. Drivers could hitch up as many as twenty-five dogs. I ran with twelve—and won!

When the impact of that win hit me, I could hardly contain my enthusiasm. *I had qualified for the Olympics.* I felt as if I had come alive again, even though I was too young to appreciate what the Olympics really meant.

I reveled in the challenge of getting ready. By the time I had qualified, the Olympics were less than two weeks away. I needed to get my dogs and sleds to Lake Placid and spend the remaining time in training. I went to Lake Placid by train, sleeping in a freight car with my dogs. I placed them in slatted crates with wire on one side so that they had plenty of air. I also took extra harnesses and an extra sled in case one broke.

By the time I reached Lake Placid, I had only three days left to train before the race. It was too little time to do much good, but I didn't dwell on the odds. I was there to enjoy myself and trusted my dogs to do their best.

The dog sled race was an exhibition event that didn't count in the medal tally. Even so, the race followed strict Olympic rules. We of the New England Dog Sled Club had been enthusiastic proponents of dog sled racing as an Olympic event. And since 1932, I have urged Olympic committees to include it as an official event, but to no avail so far.

I competed against eleven other teams in a seventy-five-mile race. With so little training time, I didn't expect to win, but I was thrilled to be part of the event. My dogs and I hadn't gone seventy-five miles in three days all winter. Moreover, I had no handler, which meant I had to do everything myself.

A Canadian won the event, and my team came in tenth. I was elated anyway, and it was an exhilarating experience. That year was the only year the Olympics featured dog sled racing.

➤

Through most of the 1930s, I found little adventure in life. One event did energize me for a time. Early in 1932, Admiral Byrd phoned to tell me that he planned a return trip to Antarctica the following year. *And he wanted me to go with him.* He asked me to solicit equipment for the expedition. This I did with Victor Czegka, who had been the master tool maker and mechanic on the Byrd Antarctic Expedition.

Byrd's plan was to begin much as the earlier expedition had, establishing living quarters at Little America. When winter came he planned to extend his observations to the Queen Maud Mountains. No one had ever spent the long winter night in the interior of Antarctica. He intended for three men and eight or nine dogs to stay with him in the interior. For six months, we would live in total isolation, four hundred miles from the others. The best part of the news came when Byrd said, "Norman, I would like you to be one of the three men." I was elated.

Byrd said one other thing that touched me deeply. "Norman, I would never have asked you if I didn't have absolute faith in your ability." My life had not been particularly good for the previous two years. At the time he asked, Iris and I were still married—barely. I had lost much of my self-confidence, largely because my work did not excite me. Even though I was successful on the job, I felt like a failure in my family relationships. My parents never rebuked me, but I felt I had failed them too. I needed to hear Admiral Byrd say those words.

Because Byrd was an international hero, the N. W. Ayer and Sons company gave me a leave of absence to work with Byrd and go to Antarctica. For nine months I worked closely under Victor Czegka, soliciting funds and equipment. The United States had still not recovered from the Great Depression, and we had a difficult time getting donations for this expedition. Even so, new energy seemed to flow through me. My depression lifted. Life became fun for me once again.

Somehow, Victor and I were successful, and Byrd had his equipment. The financial contributions were not as generous as five years earlier, but they were adequate. In-kind support was easier to get than cash.

Then came the blow that took me a long time to get over. Byrd and I often walked together along the esplanade around the Charles River in Boston. In May, only months before the expedition was to leave, Byrd said in a remarkably casual tone, "Norman, I've been thinking about something."

Accustomed to these walks when the admiral did his thinking aloud, I didn't say anything. We continued wordlessly down the path in the summer sunshine.

"Norman," he finally said, breaking the silence, "I've decided we don't have enough time to establish a camp at the Queen Maud Mountains." I could tell from the tautness of his features and the sound of his voice that he was under stress. He was trying to tell me something. I knew what he was getting at, but I had to hear him say it.

"I've had to revise my plans," he said.

"Oh?"

After another lengthy silence, he added, "I won't be able to take you out to the Queen Maud Mountains. I'm going to go out there and spend the long winter night on the ice barrier alone."

Until that morning, I had no doubts that I would be living in isolation with Byrd. I don't remember saying anything. Shock temporarily prevented me from feeling the rejection and the pain.

"Norman," he went on, "you are going to be my second-in-command. You will be in charge of Little America while I'm away." Without giving me the opportunity to protest, he hurriedly outlined my position. As I listened, I knew he had been thinking of this for days, possibly weeks.

If this had been our first trip to Antarctica, the offer would have elated me. In those days I had been just a dog driver. But we had been close since our return. I didn't know anyone I admired as much as Byrd. He was my mentor and personal hero. And now I began to feel the rejection.

We finished our walk, and I left. His change of plans, I knew, had nothing to do with limited time. It took me several days to figure out the real reason. If Byrd took three of us to live with him, he would get far less publicity than if he did it alone. Living alone near the South Pole would make him even more of a hero to the world. It was his "grab for glory."

His decision hurt me deeply. I didn't want to settle for being second-in-command. I faced a serious decision. Should I continue with Byrd or withdraw from the expedition? I had never faced a more difficult decision. I wanted to return to Antarctica, and I wanted to be part of the expedition that I had helped put together. But what was most important was to be at the advance base at the Queen Maud Mountains.

Finally, I went to see my father and told him everything. A practical man, he understood my dilemma. Since my return from Antarctica, we had become closer. Or perhaps it was simply that I had felt closer to him. He wasn't affectionate or open with his feelings. But I had carried his watch around my neck during my first trip to Antarctica. I felt bonded to him, and I trusted his advice.

Father had the ability to look objectively at a situation. On the one hand, he pointed out, it would be a valuable experience. It would help me make a name for myself as an explorer. Possibly it could even provide job opportunities.

On the other hand, he said, "If you don't go to the advance base, you'll return without having done anything new." How well my father knew me. It would not be a new adventure for me, but only an attempt to re-capture the old one.

Then he spoke of the practical aspects of my going. "You won't return with any greater ability to earn a living. You can't go on exploring all your life because there is no money in that vocation." Ever the practical father, he said, "You now are married. You must think about your finances and your future."

In May 1933, four months before the admiral left for Antarctica, I voiced my father's concerns about my future as an excuse not to go.

As I remember, Byrd didn't comment. Soon thereafter, he wrote me a letter. It said, in part:

> It is imperative from every angle that I consider your connection with the expedition first and above all else from the standpoint of your future. We have reached a crisis in your life, and have a big decision to make, and my job is to encourage you to do the thing that will add most to the contents of your life. As to what decision will do that, no one but the good Lord can tell.
>
> If we do go, and you returned handicapped in business, as you think you will be, it seems to me that for your best good,

*you had better accept one of the business offers you now have. In
saying this, I am not considering the expedition, which, of course,
cannot replace you. I do not know just what we will do without
you, but that is not the point.*

I decided not to go.

I did, however, continue to work with Byrd as he made his final preparations. At the time I withdrew, he still did not have all the funds he needed, and I would not stop working until he had everything. On the day of his departure, September 25, 1933, I drove to the Boston Navy Yard and watched as my hero, Admiral Richard E. Byrd, sailed on the *Bear of Oakland.*

My life felt as if it were over. Nothing could excite me or make me want to go on. I didn't become suicidal, but I had to force myself to go to work each day, to simulate enthusiasm for my job. It was, I believed, the lowest point of my life.

Eight

I FIND IT DIFFICULT TO WRITE ABOUT THE 1930s BECAUSE THEY WERE THE most unsatisfying years of my life. Just enough adventures and opportunities came my way to give me hope, but they were mixed with enough boredom to keep me slightly depressed. I kept trying to fit into a conventional lifestyle, but I never quite made it. I have never been able to live the tranquil life.

Following the breakup of my marriage to Iris, I went to work for the Homelite Company, selling pumps and generators. It was a fine company, and I did reasonably well with them. I stayed with that company until World War II was imminent, and then I joined what was then called the United States Army Air Corps.

Romance did return to my life. In 1938, while I was dog driving, I traveled to Peckett's Inn on Sugar Hill just outside Franconia, New Hampshire, where I met an attractive young woman named Rosamond Lockwood, from the back bay of Boston. She had brown eyes, brown hair, and a nice figure. She was two years younger than I. We liked each other the first time we met and got along well. She was athletic and interested in sports and the outdoor life. Soon after we met, I gave Rosamond a ride with my dog team. She liked it very much, and the next day she went with me for another ride.

During the following weeks, we got to know each other well. She came from a prominent family in Boston. I was single, with the same social background. Invitations to parties came to me constantly, especially for coming-out parties for debutantes. Prominent families gave the dances to introduce their daughters to society. The coming-out mania was rampant in those days. At one time, I was attending an average of two such events a week. I didn't like them too much, but I've always liked being around people, especially single, attractive women.

After I met Rosamond, I began seeing her at parties and weekend skiing events. Sometimes she would accompany me when I drove my dogs. I fell in love with Rosamond and married her that same year. The marriage survived for the next twenty-seven years, but it wasn't always a happy relationship for either of us. I take the blame for it. Years later, I would say, "I love women, but I'm just not very good at marriage."

We married in Providence, Rhode Island. The next day we went by train to New York, where we would board a cruise ship to Bermuda. When we got off the train, I ran into one of my friends. His nervousness made it clear that he was distressed.

"Norman, I've got something to tell you," he said. "Something quite embarrassing."

"What's wrong? What is it?"

"Iris is going to be on the same cruise ship."

"Oh, really?" I said. "That's going to be exciting."

"On the *same* ship you're taking."

"Yes, I heard you. I'm sure I'll meet up with her."

My friend was dumbfounded, but I hadn't exaggerated my nonchalance. Iris and I had parted on good terms. She had previously met Rosamond, and no enmity existed between them. Since then, Iris had gone to work for the United States Navy. She had Jerry with her and was on her way to start a new job in Bermuda. She planned to make Bermuda her permanent residence.

It was an interesting three days' travel on the cruise ship. I stayed in one cabin with my wife. My son was in another cabin with his mother. Several times I went into Iris's cabin to see Jerry. I loved to see the startled expressions of the other passengers when I introduced them to both my present and my former wives.

➤

Two years after her move to Bermuda, Iris called to tell me that she had met a wonderful Bermudian who worked for the police force. She loved him, and he had asked her to marry him.

"I'm happy for you," I told her. I would see less of Jerry, but Iris was a wonderful mother who deserved a good marriage, and now Jerry would have a stable environment.

Then tragedy struck Iris's life. She had returned to the United States to make final preparations for her wedding in Bermuda. The day before she was to return, she received word that her fiancé had gotten sick and suddenly died of pneumonia. She wanted to reach Bermuda as quickly as she could for the funeral. She could catch a plane in New York, but she had no way to get there. She called me for help.

"I'll drive you to New York," I said. In those days, driving from Boston to New York meant driving all night. "I'll take Rosamond with us and we'll motor down there, spend the night, and you can catch a plane in the morning."

Rosamond and I picked Iris up in Wellesley, where she was staying with friends. She left Jerry with them because she would be flying back again in a few days. With Rosamond in the car, the three of us drove as far as Hartford. We decided to spend the night and continue to New York the next morning. We rented one room, which raised eyebrows, but I didn't bother to explain.

The next day, we put Iris on a plane for Bermuda.

➤

Beginning in 1938, I made a number of mountain rescues with my dog team. A volunteer, I was unofficially on call for years. Whenever a plane went down or people were lost in mountainous areas, officials asked me to take my dog team to the accident site. I was always ready for rescue work if they needed my help. At the time, I was the only one known to have both experience and a dog team ready to go. I found it exciting to think that newspapers, police forces, and other civil organizations saw my dog team as a way of rescuing people.

One early rescue operation that stands out in my mind is the call I got to go to Mount Washington, the highest mountain in New Hampshire, well over 6,000 feet high and site of some of the worst weather in the world. Before I arrived, I knew only that we were searching for two lost people. I traveled from Boston, a distance of 150 miles, towing my dogs and my sled in a trailer. When I reached the site, the father of one of the young men had already arrived. I was told that three college students had started a climb. It was early winter, and they had been poorly dressed and ill prepared. The weather had turned cold and windy, and then a storm blasted the mountain. They had not begun with the intention of scaling the peak. But one of them had suggested they climb to the top, and another had agreed. It's likely that none of them realized that Mount Washington is treacherous because it juts into the lower jet stream and thus has sudden severe weather changes.

Eventually, one of the climbers made it back down and reported the other two as missing.

My dogs and I went up the mountain to search for them. Partway up, we met some rescue climbers who had gone up ahead of us. They were bringing down one of the bodies—dead. We put the body onto the sled, and I turned around. It had been a difficult climb going up, and it was even harder going down. The sled wanted to go faster, and I couldn't keep it upright without help. Four people followed, each using ropes to help hold back the sled. We didn't turn over, but by the time we reached the bottom, we were exhausted.

When the waiting father saw the sled carrying a passenger completely covered, he ran across the field to meet us. He lifted the brown canvas sled sheet. "Oh, no," he groaned, staring at the face of his son.

An ambulance was waiting. Two men took the corpse from us, and I moved away from the grieving father. I was given two cups of coffee and four doughnuts, not good trail food, but all that was available. Then it was time to start back up the mountain. This time, however, I didn't get very far before I saw a party of rescuers approaching with a second victim.

Both young men had died from hypothermia—exposure. Although neither of them had blood on their hands, they had literally worn their fingers down to the bone. They had lost their mittens but continued climbing on the icy rocks in the storm. Having lost all feeling in their hands, the flesh tore off their bones.

By the time we reached the bottom, the ambulance had returned to take away the second victim. I heard muffled crying from the crowd. They had been waiting, hoping that the last climber would still be alive.

My job was over. With a heavy heart, I unrigged my sled and dogs and prepared to return home. The father of the dead climber had gone, but he left $50 for my gasoline. This touched me deeply. Later I corresponded with him.

> ➤

By early 1941, most Americans sensed we would eventually enter the war in Europe. I knew that even if war came and they drafted soldiers, my age—thirty-five—and my marital status—married and the father of two children—would probably exempt me. Of course, at that time, most Americans assumed that even if we did enter the war, it would last only a year or two at most.

I still worked for Homelite Company, which manufactured generators, pumps, and blowers. In October 1941, the company sent me to observe the war games of military personnel on maneuvers at military bases in both North and South Carolina. I went as a civilian observer to watch my company's blowers as they filled balloons. Called "barrage" balloons, after being filled, they floated upward over the housetops, still anchored. The idea was that if the enemy invaded, the barrage balloons would prevent their airplanes from flying in low over a city. The cables anchoring the balloons would entangle any planes that tried to fly lower than the balloons. In the war games I observed, the Army Air Corps used the balloons as signals to ward off the airplanes attached to enemy units.

Six weeks later, on December 7, 1941, the Japanese attacked Pearl Harbor, and the United States entered the war. Immediately, young men eighteen to twenty-six were being drafted. Although I was ten years above the draft age, I felt I had to find a way to get actively involved in the war. This push came from both a strong sense of patriotism and a lust for adventure. I wanted another chance to live fully again.

In February 1942, after I had talked with several people in Washington, I volunteered for service in the Army Air Corps and asked for a commission. I was accepted. Because of my age and the fact that I had been at Harvard, they commissioned me first lieutenant.

My one regret was leaving my family. Our daughter, Jacqueline, had been born in March 1940. I can still remember having her christened in an Episcopal church. As I held the tiny child in my arms, I realized how much I loved her and how proud I was to be her father. I loved my son, too, and I thought about how fortunate I was.

Nevertheless, I wanted to go into the service. Given those perilous times and my own personality, I could have done nothing else. I was ready to begin a new life—military service. This left Rosamond with two young children to raise—Iris had sent Jerry from Bermuda to live with us because she felt he could get a better education in the States. Even though Rosamond and I later divorced, I never questioned the outstanding job she did of parenting both children. I've always been impressed that she showed no favoritism toward Jackie, that she treated Jerry no differently because he was her stepson. When Rosamond passed away, she left the two children equal inheritances.

Nine

IT WAS A PROUD MOMENT IN MY LIFE WHEN I BECAME AN OFFICER IN THE U.S. Army Air Corps. Never had our nation been so united against a common enemy. Some have called it "the good war," and many believed it was the war to end all wars. And I was going to be in the middle of the action!

Upon my induction, I received a uniform but no training. Immediately, I was shipped to Presque Isle, Maine, for temporary assignment. I did mostly grunt work, and it wasn't exactly the kind of action I had wanted or expected, but I didn't complain, because I got to know the base and to understand operations. Besides, it was only a temporary assignment, and I knew they would attach me permanently or maybe even send me overseas.

After a week, I received orders to report to Holton Air Force Base—as the commanding officer. That title sounds more important than it really was. Holton was, as we called it in those days, a "small contingent." Only a few miles from Presque Isle, it was an alternative landing base for planes that couldn't get in. Each day I reported by telephone to the commanding officer at Presque Isle. He told me what to do, and I carried out his orders.

My command lasted seven days. At the end of one week there, I was ordered back to Presque Isle for further assignment. I spent the night at the base and flew out the next day to Goose Bay, Labrador, the first American officer to go there. My job description said that I was to "establish the American presence." That meant I opened the American section of the base. (The Canadians had been there for several months.) The Air Force assigned eight enlisted radio men and one officer, Second Lieutenant Bill Knapp, to my crew. Bill, who came from North Dakota, was in his early twenties, a graduate of a college ROTC program. He was short but strong. I liked Bill because he cooperated without hesitation and was a good man to have around.

The Canadian ground troops lived in underground bunkers in case of invasion. We called them the underground contingent, because their armament was underground all around the triangular-shaped airport. They had sandbags above the deep holes where they lived. We ate in the Canadian mess, which was aboveground, and Knapp and I walked from our temporary office building over to meals. It was rather a long walk, but it enabled us to get to know each other well.

Instructions regularly came to us from Presque Isle, which made it easy for me to command my eight men. They did their radio work, and a highly qualified sergeant supervised them.

Before long, aviation into Goose Bay intensified. Soon, so many planes flew in and out that we had trouble keeping up with our portable radio system. We had to stay in touch with the planes coming in and clear the runway for them to land. Finally, I explained the difficulty we were having and asked for a control tower. The answer came back: "We will send you one as soon as possible."

In those days, a DC-3 was the biggest thing in the air, and no plane could carry the weight of a steel platform. So I doubted that they could send us a tower. Five days later, however, we received a new message: "Control tower being sent your station."

Their communiqué explained that they had made the tower out of timbers and erected it in Presque Isle. They used bolts and no nails. When they took the tower apart, they marked each piece, so we only had to follow simple instructions to reassemble it.

The tower came in one load aboard a DC-3. We were excited to have a real control tower. Aside from greater efficiency, having our own tower would give us a psychological boost. We had the feeling that we were becoming a big base. Once we erected the tower, we would move the radio equipment into it. We understood we would have space in the tower for reading charts, and two people could work there at one time—one on the radio and one to observe and act as the control tower operator.

Knapp and I worked with the other eight men to unload the pieces. Because the plane landed late in the afternoon, by the time we finished unloading, it was too late to attempt to construct the tower.

"We start construction at 0800 hours," I said. I also informed the men that, except for one man at a time who would be waiting for emergency messages, all of us would participate in the construction. Everyone was delighted to be involved.

After breakfast the next morning, we returned to where we had unloaded the DC-3. We were stunned. The wood had disappeared! At first, I thought I was at the wrong corner of the triangular airport. To satisfy ourselves, we searched all around the airport. We found no wood nor any evidence of the control tower.

We huddled for a few minutes in utter amazement, trying to figure out what had happened. In the short time I had been at Goose Bay, I had never heard of anybody stealing anything. We found no tracks that might indicate what had happened. Naturally, I asked the Canadians, the only other occupants of the base, and they assured me they knew nothing about any missing lumber.

With deep chagrin, I contacted the officer in charge at Presque Isle, who had sent the load. "I'm sorry, sir," I radioed, "but the wood is not here. I mean, it has been stolen." I tried to explain, but it only made me sound incompetent. But the truth was that the lumber had disappeared, and we had no clues whatsoever.

Presque Isle, following the usual line, insisted on an investigation.

"Come over and investigate all you like," I said, "but I just told you what happened. We have searched everywhere. The lumber is not here. It is gone."

After a day or two of confusion, they decided not to investigate but to build us another one. When the second shipment arrived, the pilot handed me a written order that I was to "secure the material for the tower and see that it did not get stolen."

That night I posted two men to guard the lumber for the tower. The wood was still there the next day.

Soon we had erected a control tower, and it functioned just fine.

Seven weeks after the erection of our new tower, I received a dinner invitation from the commanding officer of the Canadian underground contingent who had reported to Goose Bay only a few days earlier. Instead of eating in the aboveground mess hall, I went underground to their quarters.

And there was the wood we had lost. The markings were still evident. Obviously, the Canadians had made a midnight requisition. They had used our lumber to bolster walls and floor and keep sand from washing in.

"Nice quarters you have here," I said to my host.

"Yes, I think so," he said, "in view of the conditions under which we live."

"Well constructed," I said.

"Yes, we have several handy soldiers here."

I made no further comments. I didn't report my discovery to Presque Isle or tell the Canadians I knew. Months later, I finally told my commander. By then it was too late to do anything about it. Naturally he asked why I hadn't reported it.

"Then you would have had to report it to security," I said, "and security would have had to conduct a big investigation. What good would that do? By then we had another control tower. And they are our allies, aren't they?"

"Close allies," he said and laughed.

➤

Early in my management of the Goose Bay Air Force Base, I received a wire that read: "Unidentified aircraft landing your station tomorrow morning. Lend every courtesy." The message implied that a VIP was flying in, but we had no idea who he would be. I alerted everyone on the base, and we all showed up at the landing site. I wouldn't have minded having VIPs visit, but we were still under construction. We had nothing in which to transport passengers except a Fordson tractor and a flatbed trailer with side boards.

Almost on schedule, a four-engine aircraft appeared on the horizon. The plane was painted black and carried a Russian insignia. It taxied up to us, and we stood at attention. The wait seemed endless. Finally the nose of the airplane opened, and a long ladder dropped to the ground.

The first man appeared. He stood at silent attention for a minute. None of us even looked at his face; his stunning fur boots mesmerized us. Covered in fur, they went up to his knees. The man moved, in solemn military fashion, down the steps and stopped. He rested one hand on a rung of the ladder.

As commander, I walked up to him and extended my hand, but he ignored it. Later I wondered if he had been testing the rungs of the ladder. He turned back toward the plane and said something in Russian. Another man came down. Again, I offered to shake hands, but he ignored me and stood beside the first man. Neither man said a word to me. Four more men came down. All of this took place in silence. All wore similar beautiful boots and black uniforms under field jackets. As I saw no insignias, I finally assumed they were enlisted men.

After the sixth man had come down and stood beside the ladder, I looked up to see an older man appear in the doorway. He wore a flight jacket with a gold insignia. At last, the VIP himself, I thought. Once his men were lined up, he came down. I stretched out my hand once again. He took it. He looked around, but he didn't say anything. Hovering immediately behind him was the interpreter, who greeted us in English.

I acknowledged him and extended our greetings. Then I asked the interpreter, "Who is this gentleman?"

"Comrade Molotov." (He was, after Joseph Stalin, the most powerful man in the Soviet Union.)

I caught on to the use of *comrade* and said, "Welcome, Comrade Molotov," because I thought that was the right thing to do. I introduced myself (I was then a captain), and then added, "How do you do?"

Instead of answering, Molotov turned slightly and his eyes went up the ladder. As if they had heard his silent gesture, two women appeared, Mrs. Molotov and their daughter. Both were stout, sturdy women and neither particularly pretty. They came down the ladder and then silently stood beside Molotov. For several seconds, no one moved.

Not sure of protocol and tired of standing around, I said to the interpreter, "Could I take you to breakfast?" We still ate our meals at the Canadian mess, and I had arranged for them to feed the visitors.

"Yes."

"Will you tell these people that all I have for transportation is a flatbed trailer?" I pointed to it. I chuckled to myself, as I thought of the wonderful reception I was giving *Comrade* Molotov and his family.

"Very good," he said, then he explained it to the Russians.

Without dissenting, all of them climbed aboard. They stood on the back of the trailer. I made a slow start. Through my rearview mirror, I could see that they were holding on to each other to keep from falling. We went over rough roads, but none bad enough to bounce them off.

I assumed that after a long plane trip, the first thing they needed was to go to the toilet. I said to the interpreter, "I am sorry, but the only place to go to the toilet is in the outhouse."

The mess hall had been built with a lot of glass windows. It was nice to sit inside and stare out over a typical Labrador landscape. Because they were all males, the Canadians had placed their outhouse only twenty yards in front of the window, near the entrance. The outhouse door had long ago blown away and no one had bothered to replace it. Nevertheless, the two women, who went first, handled the situation very graciously. Mrs. Molotov entered the outhouse while her large daughter stood in the doorway. She more than adequately prevented anyone from seeing in. Then they switched places. A few minutes later the two women returned to the mess hall, quite nonchalant and without any sign of embarrassment.

The Russian men then lined up at the outhouse and accomplished their mission quickly.

By the time they returned, breakfast was ready. I thought it would be a gentlemanly gesture to offer my place at the head of the table to Mrs. Molotov. I motioned to her as graciously as I knew how and pulled out the chair for her. She started toward me, but just then Comrade Molotov stepped in front of her and took the chair. He sat down, pulled his chair in, and said nothing, not even a grunt of thanks.

Confused, I turned to the interpreter, but he said in clipped English, "Mrs. Molotov and daughter are not to sit with him. They will sit at the next table."

The enlisted Russians took places at the second table with the two women. I sat down next to Molotov and the interpreter sat opposite me.

During breakfast, I decided to make conversation, asking brilliant questions through the interpreter, such as "Did you have a good flight?" "Did you have any snow?" "It is a beautiful day here today, isn't it?" Although I didn't ask where he was going, I did ask when he was going.

"As soon as we can refuel."

Our people were already refueling the black phantom.

After they'd left, I realized there was another question I'd wanted to ask: "Where can I buy boots like those?"

➤

The second control tower was big enough to do the job—for a while. But as the war escalated, so did the flow of planes. Before long we had to have another, larger, control tower. They built a replacement, but this time they sent it by ship, along with a construction crew. Soon we were receiving P-38 bombers. Before long, it seemed as if the entire Air Force was passing through Goose Bay.

By June 1942, I had been promoted to major and then relieved of command. "We've got to replace you with a flying officer who wears wings," my commander said with regret in his voice. "It's regulations that plane crews must be commanded by pilots."

"I understand, sir," I said. I didn't mind, for I welcomed a change. They sent me farther north to Chimo, Canada, to a place the military designated Crystal-1. (There was also a Crystal-2 on Baffin Island.)

At Chimo, where I stayed for eighteen months, the Air Force was just starting to build an airport. It was summer, with beautiful, balmy weather. I had under my command sixty-eight enlisted men and twelve officers. We maintained radio communication with planes that flew over, gave weather reports, and did what we called housekeeping tasks for arriving and departing planes. Our weather reporting was important because much of the weather blew past us on the way to Presque Isle.

It concerned me that the men at Chimo didn't get enough physical exercise, so I decided to make exercise part of their daily routine. I put out an order of the day that read something like this:

> *Beginning tomorrow morning at 0600 hours, all enlisted men and all officers will hereby trot when they go from one building to another except under the following conditions. . .*

Then I listed the exceptions. If the ground was icy, they didn't have to "dogtrot." If they were in military formation, they didn't have to dogtrot. If they were with visiting personnel or a high-ranking officer, they didn't have to dogtrot. Otherwise, everybody dogtrotted. When they went for chow, to the control tower, to the dispensary—they dogtrotted. To set an example, I dogtrotted at all times.

Eventually, I could boast that my men were in excellent shape.

Ten

On July 15, 1942, EIGHT PLANES MADE A FORCED LANDING ON THE EAST COAST of Greenland. The squadron, two B-17s and six P-38s, was part of what was known as Operation Bolero. It had passed through Goose Bay, Labrador, and was to join the Eighth Air Force in England. On the flight to Iceland, it ran into bad weather, and the two B17 captains decided to take their P-38s back to Greenland. During the return, the planes ran low on fuel and the ranking P-38 pilot decided to make an emergency landing on the Greenland ice sheet.

The crews radioed that they were all alive, but bad weather prevented searchers from locating the planes. Three days after the forced landing, search planes were deployed. By parachute, they dropped food, sleeping bags, whiskey, and medical supplies.

The details started to form a story. Colonel Crocker Snow, the commanding officer of operations of the North Atlantic Division of the Air Transport Command, was responsible for routing, reporting, safety and navigation, and aircraft operations to each base on the North Atlantic routes to Europe. For over a year, Colonel Snow had urged headquarters to allow uncoded weather reporting for our plane movements. But Washington insisted on coded weather reporting. This insistence led to the loss of eight battle-ready airplanes at that critical time in the war.

The eight planes had been two separate units, Tomcat Yellow and Tomcat Green, each composed of a single bomber and three P-38s. On July 14, the units were on the western shore of Greenland, at a base that was designated BW-8, when they were told to prepare for takeoff. Both B-17 navigators received weather decoding cards. The cards explained how to interpret the coded information they would receive that day while airborne.

The planes flew eastward toward Iceland. The B–17s navigated because the P–38s had no navigation capabilities; the P–38s followed their mother airships.

About two hundred miles from Reykjavik, the planes encountered bad weather. Visibility was less than a plane's length. Ice built up. Unable to raise anyone on the radio, the pilots decided to set a course back to BW–8. They turned 180 degrees and headed back the way they came. Then they got a coded message. BW–8 was closed in. A few minutes later they learned that BW–1 was open, but now they were off course and on the other side of Greenland, several hundred miles from their objective. Years later, Colonel Snow determined that the weather at BW–8 had been *clear*. The mixup occurred because the decoding cards that had been issued to the B–17s were for July 14, the day before the planes took off.

Unaware that he was decoding the weather report with yesterday's card and could land at BW–8 after all, Captain Brad McMannus said his tanks were nearly empty and that he had to land. He assumed the squadron could all land safely on the hard surface of the glacier. The bombers could then radio the base for fuel.

McMannus's P–38 descended with its wheels down. When he landed and decelerated to about fifty miles per hour, his nose wheel dipped into the snow and stuck, flipping the plane forward onto its back. The other P–38 pilots thought McMannus was killed. They flew around and around, trying to figure out what to do. They saw smoke coming from the overturned plane. Then they saw McMannus. He had freed himself from his harness and slid open his window.

They realized they had to land with wheels up, which they did, skidding to perfect landings. They were safe and the last two planes didn't even touch their props to the snow. Finally, with all six P–38s on the ground, the men all came out of their planes and waved to the two B–17s still in the air. The two bombers soon landed.

Once on the ground, the men quickly converted two planes, *Do-Do* and *Big Stoop*, into a survival camp. Someone cut off the propeller tips of *Do-Do* so that they could run the engine and keep the batteries charged for communication with BW–1 and BW–8. Then bad weather struck. For two days, search crews went out, but didn't have enough visibility to spot them.

Meanwhile in Washington, the Air Force brass didn't know how to rescue the men. "How can we get them off the ice?" they asked each other.

"We don't have any ski aircraft," someone said.

"Then let's get ski-equipped aircraft from somebody else."

They approached the Canadian military and private sectors, but they didn't find one that could be taken apart, put in a transport plane, and flown to Greenland. They tried the private sector in the United States, but failed there, too. Frantic action continued in Washington for three days after the crash. By then, the men had been sighted.

Planes from BW-1 had dropped supplies to the men, including food, sleeping bags, and medical supplies. They received a message from the men on the ground: "Don't send any more toilet paper. Send women."

➤

I didn't learn about the planes until July 16.

Because I had a lot of experience in rescue work in snow, my commander, General Smith, sent for me to come to Goose Bay for a conference. At the time, I was stationed at Crystal-1, nearly one thousand miles away from Goose Bay. When I arrived, it became obvious that the Air Force had no idea how to rescue the twenty-five men. They considered sending personnel to Greenland to rescue the men, but they were unsure how to go about it.

After listening to suggestions by several officers—and there were not many ideas offered—I finally said, "I think we can get them out by dog team."

"Dog team?" asked General Smith. "How can you rescue twenty-five men with a dog team?"

"Of course, one at a time," I said. Actually, I didn't know if we could do it or not, but it was the best idea so far.

"How are you going to do that?"

"I don't know, but if we can get a dog team up there, we can do it. We can send someone up with a sled and dogs and lead them out on foot." I explained that since they were only about ten miles from the coast, a ship could be waiting.

General Smith nodded and said nothing. He told me later that he was laughing inside, thinking it was a foolish idea. "Gee, I don't know about this," he finally said. But as a good officer, he reported to his commander in Washington that Norman Vaughan, who had experience in snow country, thought the men could be brought out by dog teams. General Smith explained that I had a dog team in Boston and that I could get the dogs easily. He didn't expect a positive response.

Within hours, General George, commander of the Air Transport Command, sent back a terse message that read something like this: "Send Vaughan to Greenland. Have him hire Eskimos and their dog teams. Go get those men!"

"Read this," General Smith said.

"Sir, this is impossible," I said. "Can't be done that way."

A perplexed general stared at me and asked, "Why?"

"Because, sir, Eskimos won't go up on the Greenland ice cap. The deep crevasses represent grave danger for them. They don't travel up there, and you can't hire them to go into that dangerous region. They travel with their dog teams only along the coast on the landfast ice."

"Then how do you think you can go up?"

"Sir, I don't know, but I have had crevasse experience in Antarctica, so I know something about traversing such treacherous, uncharted areas." I wanted him to know that I was just as scared of crevasses as the Eskimos. "The only thing to do is to get my dog team and try."

"All right, Vaughan," he said. "Do it your way."

I prepared to leave for Boston to get my dogs and gear. As I was getting on the plane, with General Smith there to see me off, a thought hit me. "General," I said, "a good friend of mine, Freddie Crockett, is on the east coast of Greenland, but he's in the Navy. He's a good dog driver and was with me in the Antarctic. If we could get the Navy's permission to use him, and have him get his dog team down the east coast of Greenland, I could rendezvous with him. Then we could go in together to rescue those men."

He didn't answer me.

I tried once again, "Sir, if you can get Crockett to do it, he'd be a good man for the job." With those words, I saluted and boarded the plane for Boston.

The general made it easy for me to move quickly in Boston. In 1942, America had started gas rationing. The general arranged for a military truck to meet me and drive me home to Hamilton. Unfortunately, I had no time for anything but a hurried conversation with Rosamond and a peek at baby

Jackie. For the next four hours, the four military men who had come with me helped me search the barn for the sled, harnesses, sleeping bag, dog food, chains, ropes, stoves, snowshoes, rain gear, tent, sled bag, feed pans, pails, shovels, tools, repair wire, wooden cooking and eating utensils—all the equipment I would need. I decided to take six of the twenty dogs I had. The best leader, Jeddo, was actually Rosamond's leader, but she was glad to send him on a mission to save lives.

After loading gear and dogs and having a hot meal that Rosamond prepared for us, we hurried in the truck back to Boston, where I caught a C-47 transport. We flew directly to Presque Isle, then on to BW-1, the southernmost American base in Greenland. I unloaded everything, including the dogs, and was taken aboard a Coast Guard boat named the *Comanche*, which had been waiting for us. I had not slept for a while, so I got some rest on the boat.

I soon learned that General Smith had gotten the Navy's permission to borrow Freddie Crockett. He had collected his dogs, boarded a boat, and already landed. He did the right thing: Instead of waiting for me, he had started up the glacier to the planes.

The ten miles from the coast to the stranded airmen was over many crevasses, mostly running perpendicular to the planes. Because cracks in a glacier are easily spotted from the air, Naval Lieutenant Attebury, flying a Catalina flying boat very slowly, guided Crockett through the crevassed area. He kept flying back and forth over the rescue party, zooming them, when necessary, to change directions to circumnavigate the crevasses. Crockett flagged his route so that the return journey would be made over a solid trail. It took him seventeen hours to reach the planes. Crockett later told me that he had to zigzag through the crevassed area, just as we had done in Antarctica. Consequently, it was an eighteen-mile journey, although the straight distance was only ten miles.

Upon reaching the crew, he announced, "You have one hour and then we leave." He told them he was going to take them to the Coast Guard boat. After a few miles they began to discard their extra clothing and other personal items. Some men had turned a piece of engine cowling into a sled, but they couldn't drag it easily, so they abandoned it. Crockett used a small boat to ferry the men through the pack ice to the larger Coast Guard boat. All twenty-five men survived the ordeal.

After Crockett returned to his station at Angmassalik, I thanked him by radio. The Air Force brass were delighted. I was given thanks for having "supervised or coordinated" the rescue, and Crockett was given his proper credit. The rescue of those twenty-five men turned out to be the largest rescue of stranded airmen in World War II.

That should have been the end of the story. It might have been except for one small detail—a bombardier's lapse of memory. His lapse involved America's second most secret weapon of World War II.

Eleven

WASHINGTON WAS ELATED WITH THE RESCUE OF THE TWENTY-FIVE AIRMEN. Officials decided to debrief the survivors of what had come to be called the Lost Squadron. They sent a general from public relations to meet the crew members at BW-1. By then, the men had had a chance to rest and eat. I, too, received a summons for a critique. Freddie Crockett had gone back to his base and couldn't attend.

"You," the general said to an officer, "you tell the complete story. After you finish, each man in turn will speak up, give his perspective, and add any details until I have heard everything. Do not retell the story. Just give us additional information."

The first man told the story well. The next man added an insignificant detail or two. When the first bombardier's turn came, he stood up and said, "General, sir, I have one thing to add. When I knew we were going to be rescued, I went to my B-17 and blew up my Norden bomb sight."

Next to the atom bomb, the Norden bomb sight was the United States' most secret weapon of the war. This bomb sight enabled us to strike targets accurately at night and through rain, snow, sleet, or clouds. Its success gave the Allies the opportunity to send one thousand planes on a strategic target. One plane with the sight flying with four other bombers off each wing tip make a great offensive weapon. All nine planes could release their payloads at the command of the middle plane. The enemy had not been able to capture this instrument because of the security that had surrounded it.

"You did the right thing," the general said. "Have you anything else?"

"No, sir." He sat down.

They went on, adding a detail here and there. Finally, the second bombardier stood up. "Sir, I have something terrible to tell you. I did *not*, repeat, did *not* blow up the Norden bomb sight on my plane."

Silence filled the room. For a long time, nobody spoke. The poor fellow was chagrined by his failure. He had sworn on his life to guard that bomb sight; he had only to push a red button to activate the self-destruct mechanism. In the confusion of the rescue, he had overlooked the bomb sight. It remained inside the plane.

The information about the surviving Norden bomb sight reached General Smith and Colonel Snow in Goose Bay. I received a direct order from General Smith: "Go to the B-17 and bring back or destroy the Norden bomb sight."

The opportunity to use my dogs delighted me. I had the chance to single-handedly win the war, or so I thought.

Within minutes, I was ready to go.

➤

It concerned me that the German submarines off Greenland's east coast could see the airplanes, which were 2,700 feet high on a glacier that sloped all the way to the sea. The Germans could look right up the glacier and see the eight planes. If I followed Crockett's trail, I would be in full view of the Germans.

Had I been commander of one of those subs, I would have either gone out myself or sent a party to investigate the presence of eight enemy airplanes. I would at least have wanted to make certain they wouldn't fly again. I would have destroyed them and taken the guns and ammunition and then would have discovered the sight.

Had they already done that? If not, would they? No one knew, but going after the bomb sight, I faced the serious possibility of enemy interference. Consequently, I decided that I would not go directly from the coast to the plane, as Crockett had done. And I made another decision: I wouldn't go alone.

I believed that Max Demerest was the best skier in the Air Force, and I asked if he wanted to go with me. Max, who was from Cambridge, Massachusetts, was in his late twenties, dark, thin, very agile, an excellent camper, and a good companion. He immediately said yes.

Max and I planned to go by Coast Guard boat, disembarking fifty miles short of where Crockett had landed. From there, we would head due west into the interior for fifty miles, then north for another fifty miles. Thirty miles farther east we would reach the planes. I estimated the trek would take a total of eight days round-trip.

We landed at the base of an ice face at Comanche Bay. The captain there assigned fifteen men to help us move our sled equipment and dogs to the top of the ice wall. By moving carefully and making two trips, we eventually got most of the gear to the top.

Next came the dogs. We tied a rope to each one. They were harnessed, but their traces were unattached. By pulling on the rope from the top of the two-hundred-foot ice fall, each dog was able to stay on its own feet and follow the pull of the rope. One dog lost its footing partway up, then made no attempt to get back on its feet. We could have released the dog and allowed it to slide back to the bottom. Instead I said, "Keep on pulling." As long as we avoided sudden jerks that might hurt its neck, the dog would be fine. The haul rope was actually tied to the harness, so the pull wasn't directly on its neck. We pulled slowly, and the dog stayed on its side and didn't struggle until it reached the top. It survived the pull.

Finally, we pulled up the empty sled and bags that contained a tent, food, dog gear, and skis. All in all, it wasn't a particularly dangerous operation, but we certainly could have fallen. I don't think anyone would have been seriously hurt, but a fall on the hard glacier would have banged us up a little and caused us to slide back to the bottom.

Once at the top, Max and I thanked the men from the ship and shook their hands. The crew cautiously went back down while we prepared to start inland. It was late in the afternoon. We had spent most of the day getting from the boat to the top of the ice. As I paused to watch the departing boat, I noted how small it appeared as it moved out into open water. I waved, reminding myself that I would see the men again in eight days.

At least I hoped I would see them again. None of us would have it easy. While waiting for us, the captain had to navigate the same ocean shared by the German submarines. He would not stay in a harbor where a submarine could easily attack him. Rightly or wrongly, he believed that the Germans wouldn't attack a single small ship if it kept moving. Thus far, none of the Coast Guard boats had been attacked by the submarines.

Once the Coast Guard boat was out of sight, Max and I proceeded on our course. We wanted to get out of sight of the coastline. We went about two miles and then made camp.

Within an hour after setting up camp, we were pounded by a freezing rain. The storm pinned us down all night. In the morning, it raged on, so we made no attempt to start. The dogs began to whimper in discomfort. We were camped on a relatively flat area, and as the wet snow became sludgy, we found it difficult to move around. As we walked, we had to lift our feet and place them down carefully, so as not to walk into a hole and have our boots fill with water. The first day I did stumble into a small water hole; I made certain I didn't do it again.

We fed our dogs that night, but it was not a happy meal. They ate, even though they weren't hungry. In the morning, they defecated where they were tied. They were not in harness, but rather on a picket line—a long chain with neck lines every few feet—that we had anchored from our sled to an ice ax. Although we could rotate the ice ax cable 180 degrees, it didn't make much difference, as it was as wet one place as another.

The dogs stayed outside that first night, and we stayed inside our small tent. After twenty-four hours, our sleeping bags had absorbed a lot of moisture from the wet tent floor. Our tent provided protection from the wind and rain, but the wet snow came in on our boots no matter how carefully we brushed off. Soon, just about everything inside the tent was wet.

By the second morning, the storm had not abated. The conditions were now seriously affecting Max and me. We had nothing dry to wear. Our stove was wet and we couldn't get it started to heat water for tea. The oatmeal, crackers, and bread were wet. Everything else had to be cooked. For three days we ate nothing but butter and sugar.

By the second day, Max and I were so wet, even inside the tent, that we would frequently wring out our gloves and then put them back on. In below-freezing temperature we didn't dare go barehanded. It was better to wring out the gloves and put them back on. At least they retained some of the heat escaping from our wet hands.

We had no letup from the weather. When puddles began to form on the tent floor, we stuck a knife through the floor to drain it. But water began oozing back into the tent. Outside, the steady downpour continued, and we saw no sign of it ending. We couldn't detect much difference between day and night, except that it was a little darker around two in the morning.

On the third day, the dogs' whining increased. I knew they were suffering, but there was nothing we could do for them.

We worried about high winds. If such a wind suddenly struck, we could lose our tent. To counter this, we cut a hole in the side of the tent and pulled the front end of the sled inside with us. This took quite a while to accomplish. The sled was as wide as the panel of the tent.

Putting the end of the sled inside served two purposes. First, the sled gave us something to sit on and enabled us to get off the wet floor. Second, we were able to get some sleep, although not much. One at a time, we would climb onto the sled. We weren't afraid of dying, because we knew the storm would eventually blow over. But we were damned miserable and dehydrated.

"You know," I told Demerest in an attempt to lighten our spirits, "I know of only one persistent rainstorm in the history of the world that never stopped."

"Oh? Where in the world is that?"

"Right here."

He was amused. Our attempts at lightness did make the situation more bearable. Outside, however, the dogs continued to whine in a pathetic monotone.

Finally, I brought the most miserable dog into the tent. We had no place for her on the sled, but she tried to get onto it anyway. Eventually we tired of fighting her off the sled and left her alone. She managed to get onto the sled, so we had to move her around from time to time.

The other dogs were still whining, but there wasn't room for more than one at a time in the tent. We didn't change dogs because we felt this dog was suffering worse than the others.

We made it through the third night, and just before morning, we saw a break in the weather. The storm slowed and finally stopped. The black clouds disappeared. The sun came out before nine. Soon we felt a drying wind from the west, and we began to shed water inside the tent. To speed up the drying process, we took down the tent, shook it, and put it up again without the fly. The surface snow began to dry out, and we knew that after another windy night, the saturation would be gone, we could walk better, and the sled would slide without getting stuck.

But we were still uncomfortable, and our food was still wet. For breakfast and lunch on the fourth day, we again ate butter and sugar.

My biggest concern was that we had lost three days' traveling time. We had to move quickly if we were going to make our rendezvous with the boat. On the fourth morning, we dried out as quickly as we could and started on the trail.

We didn't get very far that day. The snow had not dried out enough, and the ground was still mushy. We couldn't ski, but we could walk— slowly. It exhausted us to push on this way. We estimated that we made a little more than a mile before we decided to conserve our energy and make camp again. This time, we didn't even put up the tent. The snow was drier than before. No one would suffer more from the weather.

Max and I rested by half sleeping and half leaning against the loaded sled. We could have taken the food box off the sled, making room in the front for one person to sit. But we were just too tired.

About three o'clock in the morning on the fifth day, we were both wide awake. "Let's go," I said.

"We'll make good time today," Max said with more enthusiasm than I had heard since we arrived in Greenland.

After a lengthy stop, it always takes a long time to get started again. We had to put the dogs back into harness and on the gang line. Finally we were ready. Max went in front to lead the way, and I drove the dogs from behind. We hadn't gone more than a hundred yards before Max said, "I think we can ski."

We put on our skis, which made the going much better than trudging through wet snow. By late morning, we were doing better and gaining altitude with every step. Everything was drying out, including the snow. The compass worked, so we glided toward the fifty-mile mark, where we turned north toward the planes.

At the end of that day, we discussed our position. The three-day delay had fouled up my plans.

"We can't make it back by the eighth day, can we?" Max asked.

I shook my head. No matter how hard we pushed, it was now impossible to reach the plane, take out the Norden bomb sight, and return within the eight-day limit. "I think you'll have to go back and ask them to wait," I said. I didn't like going on alone, but we both knew one of us had to return to meet the ship on the eighth day.

"Of course, that's logical," he said.

Max could easily reach the ship by the eighth day and tell the captain that it would be another three days before I could get there. If he didn't turn back and alert them, the Air Force would start searching for us—an unnecessary risk for the pilots. It was still the beginning of the war, and there were few planes available. I didn't want any of them diverted to search for us when we weren't lost.

We had brought along markers, or "wands," four-foot bamboo poles, to stick in the snow to mark the trail for our return. Markers have always bolstered my confidence that I was on the right trail. When we made a change of direction, we put down three wands, to one of which we added a flag. On my return, I would easily see the wands and know where to turn.

Max said good-bye, and I went on alone with the six dogs. I put out wands about eight to a mile. The next day, I reached a dangerous area filled with crevasses. As they were snow covered, they were not easy to detect. I knew that if I fell into a crevasse, I would never come out. For protection, I tied myself to the front of the sled. If I did fall, I reasoned, the dogs would stop me before I reached the bottom.

Psychologically, it was a great comfort, but practically, it wouldn't have worked. Afterward, when I thought more about it, I realized that if the sled had broken through into a crevasse, I could not have released my line before the force had dragged me over the edge and into the crevasse, too. Fortunately, I never had to find out whether it would work.

Once we had passed through the danger zone, I skied next to the sled, constantly reading the snow ahead for crevasses or sastrugi—long, wavelike ridges of hard snow formed perpendicular to the direction of the wind that are common in polar regions. On the seventh day, we turned ninety degrees to the east. After we had traveled two or three miles, I saw dark spots on the horizon. They had to be the planes.

Excitement filled me, and automatically I speeded up. Then disturbing thoughts filled my mind. What if the Germans had already reached the planes? What if they had stolen the bomb sight? What if they were there *right now*, and I fell into their hands? What if I got there and then they came? As I moved forward, I fought off these fearful thoughts. Yet they were all very real possibilities.

Twelve

THEY WERE LESS THAN A MILE AWAY—ALL EIGHT PLANES. ALTHOUGH SNOW had lightly dusted them, I had no trouble recognizing them by their shape. New strength surged through my body as I hurried forward. As I neared, I saw no indication that the Germans had come, only the old tracks of the American crews. Inside inverted steel helmets, which they had discarded, the men had made fires for heat and cooking. Soot from the fires was everywhere.

I put on the sled brake, tied down the dogs, and hurried over to the first bomber. Once inside, I found that the Norden bomb sight had been exploded by its self-destruct mechanism. As I ran to the other bomber, my eyes searched the seaward horizon. The Germans had not come, but were they on the way right now? What if they came today, while I was still here? Even though I didn't want to think such thoughts, I couldn't get away from them. Perhaps they were merely investigating eight abandoned warplanes. Surely they didn't even know about an undestroyed bomb sight. Being sailors, they had probably never heard about such a device.

Just before I left for the assignment, I had heard a widely circulated rumor that the Germans had misdirected the fliers and caused them to make the forced landing. The rumor was rampant that the Germans had broken the code and sent the pilots a message that said: "You are about to reach a point of no return. Reykjavik is closed. Go back to Greenland."

True or not—and it turned out that the pilots had received no messages from any unidentified source—the possibility of German interference intensified my fear of encountering them at the plane site or on the way back. For the moment, I pushed such thoughts aside and climbed aboard the second B-17. I immediately spotted the Norden bomb sight, which was about sixteen by sixteen by twenty inches and looked like a compressed telescope. I estimated that it weighed twenty-five pounds. I searched for one of the two wrenches I had brought with me. Because I had been concerned about losing the special-sized wrenches, I had strapped one of them to my body and put the other in my tool kit. En route, my sled had tipped over once, spilling the tool kit, but I had been able to retrieve it.

While I removed the bomb sight, I began to feel like a bank robber. I saw myself inside a bank, breaking into a safe. As I released the bomb sight, a thrill went through me.

Within minutes I had eased the bomb sight from its hold. A constant rattling and banging filled the plane. A howling wind hammered against the rudder and ailerons. All of this caused movement inside the uninsulated plane.

Once I got the bomb sight out of its hold, I laid it on the floor of the plane. My immediate task completed, I began to feel hungry. I peered out the window, scanning the horizon, but detected no movement. I took my stove from the sled. Because of the rain, I had not been able to get it started. This time I was successful, so I melted snow for tea. Along with the tea, I ate crackers and cheese. Not a very substantial meal, but it refreshed me. I especially needed the fluid.

Although anxious to get away from there, exhaustion overcame me. If I stop now and rest for two or three hours, I thought, I'll make better time. The dogs were sound asleep outside. Except for my fear of the Germans, there was nothing forcing me to push on. Once again, I paused to stare toward the sea; I could see a long way. Nothing seemed to be moving out there.

I took my sleeping bag into the bomber and cleared a space near the door. I found something to use for a pillow and covered myself with the sleeping bag. I shut my eyes, eager to drift off to sleep.

Crack! Bang! Dozens of noises I couldn't identify pounded my ears. My mind envisioned German troops at the door of the bomber. I got up and crept to the window, but I saw nothing unusual outside. My dogs were still resting. Reassuring myself that I was in no danger, I again tried to sleep. A short time passed before another unidentified noise disturbed me. I investigated, but detected nothing unusual. A few minutes later, it happened again. I discovered that the rudder was moving in the wind and the slack cables were hitting the side of the plane.

By now the mental pressure had become intense. I couldn't stop thinking about the Germans. They had to know about the planes, and if so, surely they would investigate—wouldn't they? But I saw no evidence of them, I reminded myself. So I lay down, determined to sleep. Then another strange battering sound echoed through the plane. A peek outside convinced me that I had overreacted. I've got to get some sleep, I kept saying to myself. I can't keep jumping up and peering out the window every three minutes.

Yet as soon as I closed my eyes, I envisioned Germans surrounding the plane. They were all heavily armed. I've got to protect myself. If I go to sleep and the Germans close in, they'll come up the ladder into this plane and shoot me. I took my rifle, loaded it, and pointed it toward the door. I checked to make sure my side arm, a Colt .45, was loaded. Then I lay on my back, gun in hand, ready to shoot at the first provocation.

In my exhausted state, I couldn't think clearly. I simply felt I was doing the right thing. With the loaded rifle and handgun beside me, I began to relax. I compared myself to a soldier caught in the trenches. It was, in part, exciting, and I found myself wondering how many of the enemy I'd be able to shoot before they got me. Maybe I'd get them all. Above all, I told myself, if Germans came, I would be ready.

Then I had a terrible thought. What if Max meets the ship and then comes here on skis? What if Max comes up the ladder, opens the door, and I shoot him? I snapped to a sitting position. What a tragedy that would be if I fired at Max. Sleep was now utterly impossible. Yet I was still exhausted. I unloaded the rifle and put my side arm back in my holster. Then I crawled to the door and down the ladder. I saw no Germans, but I also saw no value in staying and being tormented by every sound. My only chance to sleep was to put distance between the planes and me. Just the thought of getting away gave me peace.

I had not yet taken the bomb sight out of the plane. I picked it up and started down the ladder. Just then I spotted a Colt .45 on the floor. Obviously, one of the men had left it behind. My gun was old and had been issued to a hundred officers before me. This one looked new, so I picked it up and took it with me. Once outside, I put the Colt on the sled and strapped my old one to the outside so that I could get at it in a hurry.

As I hurriedly relashed the sled, my thoughts continued to revolve around the Germans. Then another danger struck me: *polar bears*. Fear swept over me. A polar bear was the only animal that could smell me, track me, kill me, and eat me.

For two hours, I moved toward the first turn, thirty miles away. I had gradually ascended a glacier, which put me higher than the planes. They were between me and the sea, and I could still see them. This, I decided, would be a good time to sleep.

I lay down beside the sled. I was so tired I didn't bother with the sleeping bag. My parka kept me warm enough. The gentle snowfall didn't bother me, as it wasn't wet enough to melt underneath me. I *had* to get some sleep, even if only for a short time. I figured I would be able to sleep for only a couple of hours, because by then the cold would penetrate my clothing. Right then I didn't care about the cold; I was too tired to care about anything. I must have fallen asleep as quickly as I closed my eyes.

Two hours later, I awakened, feeling better. I had no sense of danger. The snow had stopped, and the sun shone brightly. A light wind blew from the east. The snow was probably three-quarters of an inch deep, making a great cushion for the dogs' feet. Travel conditions for the dogs were ideal.

By the time I was fully awake, I realized it was midday. I got out more crackers and cheese from my sled and snacked on them. That small amount of food refreshed me, and I felt ready to travel. The dogs and I started out again. We made excellent time, and by nightfall, we had covered thirty miles and reached the first turn. I fed the dogs, cooked a meal for myself, put up my tent, and slept through the night.

As I traveled the next day, I realized how foolish I had been in the plane. Every noise had startled me, but the dogs had not barked once. If any person or animal had come close, the dogs would have howled. I was so tired, I hadn't thought of that. Now I laughed at myself as I mushed onward.

Near the end of the second day after leaving the plane, I spotted a figure on skis. I knew it was Max, just by the way he moved. After being alone with just my dogs for a few days, it felt wonderful to see another human—and a friend at that. The dogs and I speeded up, and Max flew toward us.

I had told Max that after he explained to the captain that I needed another three days, he should come out and meet me. He had done that and had made a good run on skis. Of course, he didn't have a sled behind him to slow him down.

Together, Max and I traveled back without incident. We made it to the coast by the evening of the eleventh day, which demanded long marches near the end. At times, we had to force ourselves to keep going. When we reached the coast, both of us were worn out, but we were also excited to have completed the assignment.

We found the ship waiting in the little harbor. As we got closer, we saw that several crew members had climbed the ice face and were waiting at the top for us. They greeted us warmly, and it was a joyful time for us all.

Then came the work of getting down off the ice face. We reversed everything we had done to get up. I made sure that we eased the sled down because the bomb sight was strapped on; if it broke away, it could roll into the water. Of course, the crew had no idea what the sled contained.

The dogs didn't want to go down. Again we used a rope to ease them down. Sailors took one end and stood at the bottom. I took the top and cautiously, gently eased them down. No problems arose, but it still took an hour and a half to lower everything.

After the captain gave us an enthusiastic welcome aboard, the boat lifted anchor and headed back toward BW-1. I fed the dogs and settled them down for the night.

The captain invited Max and me to sit at his table for dinner. He asked numerous questions about the trip. At one point, he said to Max, "You know, I would like to have been with you when you reached the plane. I'll bet there were some abandoned guns. I've always wanted a Colt .45."

"I didn't get to the plane, so I don't know if Norman saw any or not," said Max.

"Did you see any guns?" he asked me.

"Yeah, I saw some," I said. "Too bad you weren't there."

The conversation then skipped to another topic. I thought to myself, this captain risked his life for us, so I'll give him the new Colt. I excused myself, saying something about checking on the dogs. I went to the sled, found the gun, came back, and laid the Colt .45 on the table.

The captain's eyes bulged.

"Present for you," I said.

He picked it up. "Why, it's a brand new gun! The leather hasn't been tanned with grease. Looks as if it just came from the factory."

"It's yours now."

He was delighted, and I felt pleased to be able to do something for him. We didn't say much more about the gun, and in fact I forgot all about it.

Forgetting about it was a mistake.

➤

We returned to BW-1. I turned the Norden bomb sight over to the commanding officer. "Will you take charge of this bomb sight," I asked, "and release me from this responsibility until you send it back to the Air Force?" Of course, he agreed. The bomb sight eventually got back to the repair facility at Warner Robins Air Force Base in Georgia, where it was checked and repaired. The bomb sight was later installed on a B-24 for service in North Africa.

When I returned to BW-1, the crew of Operation Bolero was long gone. I was the last person there who had seen the planes. This was wartime, and no one thought about going back to rescue the planes. They would stay on the ground for another forty years before anyone made an attempt to salvage the Lost Squadron.

➤

In September 1988, United Technologies Norden Systems invited me to Atlanta, where they presented me with a citation for getting the bomb sight out of Greenland. They handed me a miniature Norden bomb sight (which now sits on my desk at home). On the outside, it reads:

World War II Bomb Sight
Presented to Major Norman Vaughan (Ret)
"For always being on target."

A full year later, General Smith called me into his office. "What is this about your giving away government property?"

"Sir, I don't know to what you're referring." I searched my memory, but I could think of nothing that would prompt the question.

"I have received a report from Washington that you were giving away government property. They are quite upset about it, so I need an explanation from you."

"Yes, sir, but to what property are you referring?"

"I'm referring to a pistol you gave the Coast Guard officer after returning from the mission in Greenland."

His words were a shock, and I had to think about it. It had not been a big thing to me, and I had long forgotten about giving him the gun. Then

I remembered. "Yes, sir, now I remember that very well." I told him the story. Apparently someone had inspected the Coast Guard ship, found the gun, realized it had not been issued to the captain, and demanded an immediate explanation.

After I explained, General Smith smiled and said, "I would have done the same thing. Nevertheless, I must make a formal report."

Together we drafted a lengthy explanation to the inspector general. I never heard another word about this situation.

➤

Just before I left BW-1 after recovering the Norden bomb sight, the commanding officer called me into his office. "Vaughan, we have a secret mission, and we need your dog team." He didn't say he needed me, just the dog team.

"Yes, sir," I said.

"The mission is as follows: Up the east coast of Greenland is a German encampment. This is fairly well known. The Air Force has decided we should learn all we can about this camp. We have hired a man who is an extraordinary skier, hunter, backwoodsman, dog driver, and trapper. He has been hired to act the part of a trader and to take a dog team so that he can travel along the coast and spy on the German encampment. He will not shoot them, only gather information. To accomplish this, he needs your team of dogs."

I didn't know the man, who was Finnish, but the commander said all the right things about him. He was telling me what he'd been told, however, not what he knew.

At first, I had to push away disappointment. After rescuing the bomb sight, I had built myself up as the great heroic spy of the war. In my fantasy, I had already won the war. But now I could do another heroic deed: I could lend my team, my sled, my tent, my cooking equipment—everything would go except me. "Anything that will help win the war," I said.

"I thought you would feel that way," he said.

I went back to my base at Crystal-1. One month later, I received a lengthy letter of explanation from the general at BW-1. The Finn had come shortly after I departed. He packed up the things I'd left and started overland, crossing the southern tip of Greenland. He then began to work his way up the east coast. He intended to buy skins from the Greenlanders in the town of Angmassalik. With skins in his possession, he could convincingly tell everyone he met that he was a trader. He carried no radio, in case the Germans searched him. The first night he reached the ice cap. On the second night, he was making camp when a storm blew in. Although snow was falling, the wind was the worst part of it. He tied the dogs to the picket line—a cable line running from the front of the sled to an ice ax. Attached was a short chain that kept the dogs from fighting or breeding but allowed them to turn around. Dogs turn around a few times and then drop into holes that the driver is supposed to have dug for them with a shovel. Unfortunately, the Finn he didn't make holes for them because he wasn't the experienced driver that the C.O. said he was. After he fed them, they each curled into a ball, with their noses tucked under their tails. He had supper himself and got into his sleeping bag for the night.

The wind rose during the night—an unusually cold summer storm with temperatures around zero and winds at more than sixty miles per hour. (When the gusts are that strong, people cannot stand.) The wind weakened the tent pegs and whipped the tent. Unless you've been inside a tent in those conditions, it's impossible to imagine the feeling, the horrendous sounds. The walls flap furiously, and the floor rises and falls if you haven't put snow on the skirt. The tent shakes unceasingly, and there's nothing you can do. When I've been in such conditions, I could only hope that the next gust wouldn't tear the tent apart.

Finally, the wood stays broke and the tent blew down. The Finn held on to the cloth to keep the air from ballooning the tent. Everything was in a terrible state. Time dragged interminably, and the storm raged on. Then, abruptly, the wind died down. The Finn was able to relax his grip on the canvas and crawl out of the collapsed tent. He went to check on the dogs. None of them were moving.

Every dog had frozen to death during the night, all because he had failed to dig small holes for them. This is mandatory when dogs are not in soft snow. His failure to do this indicates that he was not a real, experienced dog driver. The fault was his, but I also blamed the Air Force for not knowing the man's limitations.

I received the report, but not a single word of regret about the loss of my dogs. It deeply saddened me, for those dogs should never have died.

Especially sad was the task of writing Rosamond and telling her that Jeddo, her leader, had died in this terrible fashion. She, too, felt the loss deeply.

At the same time that my dogs perished, Max Demerest went out on another rescue mission. A B-17 had gone down. This time, instead of skis, he traveled on a newly acquired apparatus called a snowmobile. It was made up of skis mounted on a sled and powered by a motorcycle engine. The rider sat on a short platform in the middle of the sled. Upon reaching the B-17, he started to drive the snowmobile around the plane and under the wing to refuel it from a gas tank there. Just then, a bridge over a crevasse opened and swallowed Max and his snowmobile.

His death was a terrible loss to the Air Force, and I grieved the loss of a good friend.

Thirteen

ON APRIL 15, 1943, I RECEIVED A REPRIEVE FROM MY ROUTINE WORK AT Crystal-1. A message arrived that a plane had been found on the coast of Labrador. My orders from General Smith were to go from Crystal-1 at Chimo to Labrador to investigate and retrieve the bodies. After commandeering a small plane at Crystal-1, I went with a Lieutenant Holmes and a Lieutenant Norton in an AT-7 and landed at Hebron, the largest town on the north coast of Labrador.

Here, I met an Eskimo who had discovered the tail of the plane sticking out of a snowbank. The rest of the plane was under snowdrifts. He had made his observation on April 9, while traveling with his dog team across Cape Saglek, twenty miles north of Hebron. His report said he had seen no life around the plane. The illiterate Eskimo had managed to copy down the large numbers on the tail of the plane: 41-17862. He knew that was our way of identifying aircraft.

Our people matched those numbers with a B-26 that had been lost months earlier. It had left for Narsarssauak (BW-1) on December 8, 1942, and soon thereafter a bad storm struck most of the west coast of Greenland. All planes except one landed safely.

Upon my arrival at Hebron, I hired two dog teams and their drivers. Each driver wanted to take twenty dogs, and I agreed. It was a large number, but we would be bringing back quite a load. If we found them all, we would have eight bodies.

Early the next morning, Lieutenants Holmes and North said good-bye and returned to Crystal-1. I was set to leave when I realized that the two drivers' wives, who had been helping us get ready, planned to go along, too. "What is this?" I asked one of the drivers.

"Wives. They go with us."

"But they'll slow us down."

"No. Will not," he said, ending the discussion.

He was right. When we got into difficult places, the wives went ahead of the dogs and broke the trail. I had never seen women doing this before, and their fortitude impressed me. They certainly didn't slow us down.

We traveled along the shore toward Cape Saglek. Just before we figured to reach the plane, we stopped for the night. The two men searched for the right snow with which to build igloos. I watched them in utter fascination. They would stick their knives deep into the snow until they felt a place where it was even and not crusted underneath. Even snow meant that it would hold together; crusted snow would break apart. Finally they found a spot that satisfied them and started to build the igloos. We needed two because there were five of us.

I had never slept in an igloo before, so it was going to be quite an adventure for me. Unsure about sleeping arrangements, I waited. One of the husbands said to me, "You sleep with us."

"That's fine with me," I said.

First, it was time to eat. I thought I had made it clear to the Eskimos that they were to bring their own food with them. I got out my stove and prepared to cook for myself.

One of the men walked over to my sled and asked, "Where our food?"

"Didn't you bring your own food?"

He shook his head.

I had brought enough to feed myself for five days. What else could I do but share it? I took what I had and divided it with the four Eskimos.

A few minutes later, the same man asked, "Where dog food?"

I stared at them in total disbelief. Not only had they brought no food for themselves, they had brought none for the dogs. I never did figure out why they would leave on such a perilous journey over sea ice without food for the animals. We had been out all day and had covered perhaps twenty miles. The dogs had worked hard and were hungry.

"I didn't bring anything for the dogs," I said. "What are you going to feed them?"

He shrugged.

"What would you feed them if you were home?"

"Seal meat."

"Where's your seal meat?"

"In shed. Home."

I sent one of the men back home to get the seal meat. With his dog sled, he went back twenty miles, changed his dogs, and fed the fresh ones before he returned. He brought back a whole seal, which he then chopped up for the dogs. By the time he arrived, it was very late at night. Despite the long hours of daylight, the sun was going down.

The dogs that had not gone back to the village, of course, were ravenous. They fidgeted, whined, and snarled, as they waited for their driver to chop up the seal meat. If he had cut the meat outside, the dogs would have caused a terrible ruckus, so he went into the completed igloo to chop the frozen meat. Outside, the dogs knew what was going on. They could certainly smell the seal.

While one man was inside chopping seal meat, the other man and the two women were building the second igloo. Judging by the earlier construction, I knew it would take them about an hour and a half to construct a whole igloo.

I decided to go inside to watch the man cut up the seal. To prevent the dogs from entering while he cut up their dinner, he had blocked the entrance to the igloo with a slab of snow. I removed the slab and carefully replaced it. Inside, I watched as chips of seal meat flew around the igloo. Some of the smaller bits stuck to the walls. I thought that this might not be a good place to sleep tonight with all this mess in here. I'd better stay outside. By now, the dogs were getting worse. Their whines and barks grew louder. They all knew that the seal meat was coming.

The Eskimo motioned for me to go outside because he was nearly ready to feed them. I was supposed to push the slab door from the inside. But the dogs, beside themselves with hunger, were swarming around the igloo entrance, snarling and fighting with each other. In their food frenzy, they banged against the igloo. Suddenly, I heard a thump and the wall caved in, unblocking the tunnel entrance, and a pack of howling, squealing, pushing dogs charged inside.

The dogs forced the Eskimo away, attacked the carcass, and tore apart the seal. Within minutes, they had eaten everything—bones, skin, and fat. At least they got fed, though not evenly. Yet this was the way of life in that part of the world, and I couldn't change the people or the culture.

The igloo was so badly torn apart that the four Eskimos quietly built another. Afterward, it was time to eat again. The returning Eskimo had brought caribou and bread. We ate together again, and then it was time to sleep. I went inside one of the igloos, and one of the Eskimos followed me. He threw a polar bear rug on the floor of the igloo and pointed out where he wanted me to lie. I dropped my sleeping bag on top of it.

None of the Eskimos spoke more than a few words of broken English. But my host said, "Not need," and pointed to my sleeping bag.

"It's all right," I said. "I'll sleep on top of it if I don't need it."

Underneath the polar bear rug, he had smoothly laid out harnesses so that they didn't create lumps. (They took off the dogs' harnesses so that they wouldn't eat them during the night.) Because the rug was large and thick, I didn't feel the harnesses underneath. To my surprise, they brought in a second polar bear rug. This one was for a covering. Now I understood what the man had meant by not needing my sleeping bag.

They took off their outer clothes and got into bed. I put my sleeping bag to one side and also got under the covering. There wasn't any conversation, just sleep.

In the morning, we started the day with my tea and bread for breakfast. They harnessed the dogs, and we set off. By midmorning we had reached the plane.

When I saw the tail protruding, I inwardly prepared myself for a long, unpleasant job. I set about the initial task, which was to locate the bodies and to learn whatever I could about the accident. Using a shovel, I began to dig under the wing of the plane. That's where I discovered what had been the men's last home. Everything was black and sooty, including their faces. Even in an "empty" plane, there's enough residual fuel to light a fire. As evidence that they had used airplane fuel for a fire, I found an upturned helmet that contained a few discolored stones and two small wrenches.

As I learned later from a diary, all eight men had been alive when the plane landed. Yet I found only four bodies. They died of starvation under the wing of the plane. They had used their B-4 military bags to make the walls of a primitive room. Within that small space, they had lived and finally died.

The plane's captain, First Lieutenant Grover Hodge, Jr., kept a diary, which I found on his chest. In the diary, he wrote that the plane had tried to return to Greenland but had gotten lost, run out of gasoline, and made a crash landing. No one was injured. The only obvious damages were the torn and sprung bomb bay section and eight broken propeller blades.

Sadly, no one had taught them about arctic survival. One basic rule is to light a fire at noon—every noon—until rescued. They had gasoline to do this, and they could have burned the plane's rubber tires. Had they started a fire every noon, they would have attracted the attention of the Hebron Eskimos. At that time of the year, the Eskimos hunted seal all through that area and had a shelter eight miles down the coast.

I especially remember reading an entry in Hodge's diary, written the day after the crash, that began something like this: "Thank God we won't die of starvation here because there are so many seals." When they landed, seals were everywhere, and they could have easily shot them from the plane. But no one thought to shoot one or two of them at that time. They decided to wait until they needed them for food. They assumed the seals would be there when they needed them. But the weather turned colder, and the seals moved on, farther offshore, as another diary entry noted.

A sad story came to light afterward. Before the men left Presque Isle, they went to the base PX. A young woman who worked there had a lengthy conversation with one of the crew members. Even though they had just met, she said, "You're such a nice guy, I'd like to give you something as a good-bye gift." She gave him a large jar of peanuts. He opened his B-4 bag, stashed the jar in an outside zippered pocket, and forgot about it.

When I pulled his body away from the wall of their hovel, his back was against his B-4 bag. Inside was the unopened jar of peanuts. Had he remembered them, he might have survived a few more days. With that extra time, they might have been able to kill a caribou or a bird.

➤

Another entry in Hodge's diary explained what happened to the missing four men. On December 23, thirteen days after the crash, four of the men left in a rubber boat, headed south for Goose Bay. They never made it, and their bodies were never found. Here are Hodge's last two entries:

26 January (Tuesday)
Overcast but fairly calm. Each day we don't see how we can last another day, but each time we manage to go on. We all smoke a pipe of tobacco. This morning Galm really got sick, and I felt pretty bad, but we came out of it pretty well.

3 February (Wednesday)
Spent a solid week in bed. Today Weyrauch died after being
mentally unbalanced for several days. We are all pretty weak,
but should be able to last several more days at least.

When he made that entry, they had already survived nearly two months
in freezing temperatures. The men, according to Hodge's diary, knew they
were about thirty miles north of Hebron, but they apparently thought it
was just a spot on the map. Had they walked just eight miles down the
coast, they would have found the trail from the shore that led to Hebron.
Within twenty-four hours, they would have been picked up by Eskimos.
But they had been instructed that in case of a crash, they were to stay with
the plane. They followed those orders.

➤

I had to take the bodies out of the plane and put them onto the sleds.
By custom, the Eskimos wouldn't touch dead bodies, so they didn't help
me pull them out from under the wing or lash them to the sleds. Because
of the snow that had built up and drifted during the intervening weeks, I
was actually working inside a poorly lighted cavern under the plane. After
tying ropes around their arms and legs, I pulled them out, one at a time.
Finally, they were all out of the plane and securely lashed to the sleds.

An arm of one of the men was frozen perpendicular to his body. I
couldn't lash him to the sled that way, so there was nothing to do but break
the arm. Although he had been dead for weeks, it was a grotesque experience, and I felt as if I had mutilated his body.

Once all four men were tied to the sleds, the Eskimos and I headed
back to Hebron, arriving there on April 22. Back at Crystal-1 we selected
the top of a nearby hill, where we buried the men. Every man in camp
attended the service. As the four men were committed to the earth and to
God, I remembered that when I found them, each man had either a Bible
or another religious book over his heart.

Fourteen

"TWENTY-TWO PEOPLE HAVE GONE DOWN IN EASTERN CANADA ON A B-24," General Smith told me. "They are all civilians, except for one Army sergeant."

My assignment was to find the plane, and if its passengers were alive, to rescue them. I flew to Mingan Air Base on the north shore of the St. Lawrence.

Government-employed civilians had left Greenland on their way back to the States when their pilot lost his bearings. He reported being lost over eastern Canada. It was after midnight when he ran low on fuel and made a forced landing on one of Labrador's many frozen lakes. That was the last word from the converted four-engine transport.

Day after day, our search planes had tried to find the downed plane. I flew on a number of those missions. Mostly, though, I coordinated the search. Finally, one of our people located the downed plane. He also detected movement near the plane and believed that someone was alive. We needed a ski-equipped aircraft to get them out, so we rented a ski plane from a Canadian bush pilot.

I was confident we could make the rescue, because the lake was large and offered good landing conditions. But how could we get the B-24 out? That four-engine plane was a huge bomber that had been converted to carry cargo. I figured the only way to get the plane in the air was to construct a firm runway. But how? I thought about it and finally figured out a plan. The snow on the frozen lake was three feet deep. If we pumped water onto the snow from the lake underneath, the snow would turn to slush. The slush would then freeze. Bingo, a runway, I hoped.

When I explained my idea, one of the top officers shook his head and yelled, "Vaughan, how are you going to turn that lake upside-down?"

"I know how to do it," I said. "But I'll need six portable pumps." Since

I had sold those pumps for years before the war when I worked for Homelite, I knew exactly what I wanted. "Give me three-inch pumps. Then we'll just have to dig down, cut a hole in the ice, pump the water out, and the watery slush will freeze. That simple."

"Will it work?" I was asked.

"I think so," was the best I could answer.

Nobody had ever tried it, so nobody could say it wouldn't work. I got the pumps and other equipment from my old firm in Boston. The Canadian bush pilot agreed to fly me in with my pumps. This "mission" turned out to be one of the hardest assignments I ever had.

We had trouble locating the lake, even though we knew approximately where the search pilot had seen the plane. It was midwinter, and about as cold as it gets in that part of the world. With a lot of snow and fresh storms coming practically every day, we just couldn't see the plane. We searched almost all day for three days.

Several times the pilot had to stop and refuel. He kept a storage place in the bush where he cached five barrels of fuel. He had a worn-out, single-engine plane, and every takeoff felt as if it would be the last. Every time we landed, the ski fastenings broke, and he had to refasten them with baling wire. He spent enormous amounts of time just repairing the broken skis.

On the morning of the third day, we located the plane. It took us two tries to land with two of the six pumps aboard. Other pumps would come with Gail Lemoine, the district manager of Homelite and my former boss. He was ready to join me, but he couldn't fly in until my pilot returned and told him exactly where we were.

The downed plane was on the edge of the lake, which we began calling Lake O'Connor after the captain of the plane that went down. The people from the plane knew they had been spotted several days before, which had helped keep up their spirits. They had long ago run out of food, and none of them knew anything about outdoor survival. The search plane that first found them had carried no supplies.

Upon landing, I saw that they had a poor imitation of a fire going. On top of a smoldering pile of ashes, they had placed a pot filled with water. Inside was the carcass of an owl that one of them had shot with a rifle. They balanced the bird inside the pot by running a wire through its eyes. Staring at that awful, unappetizing thing, I realized that they had already eaten the meat off the owl. They were drinking the water from the kettle.

I surveyed their attempts to survive and saw nothing that impressed me. They had taken everything they could out of the plane and piled it on the shore. They showed no camp management. The captain, a good man, was no outdoor leader. He didn't take charge. Instead, the survivors acted individually, and little was done to make the wait easier.

Fortunately, we had brought them food. After they ate, the next thing we did was to teach them to cut and split wood. Before long, we had a snapping fire blazing away. The fire warmed not only their bodies but their spirits as well. Everybody expressed gratitude, even though snow continued to fall.

Once the bush pilot returned and reported our location, Northeast Airlines pilot Hazen Bean flew a ski-equipped DC-3 out of Mingan Air Base. No skis had ever been put on a DC-3 before. Workers at the H. J. Heinz plant in Pennsylvania, however, volunteered to make skis for the plane. Working night and day, they replaced the wheels with skis.

Bean landed on Lake O'Connor, and the joyous civilians gathered around the plane. A sergeant, the only noncivilian on the downed plane, volunteered to stay behind to work with me and get the downed plane into the air. Bean flew out all the civilians and left the sergeant and me on Lake O'Connor.

Two days later, Bean returned with six men. They brought food, tents fuel, and a small tractor with a front plow. We spent the next day trying to plow a runway on a lake that now had three feet of snow. We eventually gave up the idea as impractical.

By then, Bean had brought in Gail Lemoine, the Homelite manager. I went to him and said, "We'll pump out six streams of water right from the plane to the middle of the lake." With each pump we could wet down an area fifty feet wide. "That should make it long enough for a runway," I said.

Gail, my former boss, did whatever I asked. He didn't know the capability of the pumps under those conditions or whether my theory would work, but like me, he was willing to find out. The first pump started off very well. We had a suction hose that went down into the lake and a discharge hose twenty feet long. We sprayed water on the snow as if we were using a garden hose, moving the hoses often to keep from soaking just one area.

My theory went like this: Wet, warm snow has a temperature of twenty-eight degrees F. Cold snow has a temperature of ten degrees. Water in the lake had a temperature of about thirty-four degrees. When the water hit the snow, it would cause the snow to melt, and then the cold air would freeze the slush into a solid runway. So we began pumping water from just under the lake surface. After pumping four or five hours, with all six pumps going, we still had no melted snow. The water went down through the cold porous snow to the surface of the lake and started to spread out over the surface of the lake. It was like spring overflow.

"We're all right," I said to Gail. "The water will eventually melt the snow. Then it will freeze because the water is on top of ice."

We kept on pumping and spreading the water. But it wasn't working. Soon we were wading in water, with no indication that the water would freeze. On paper, my theory was fine; on the lake, it didn't work. The cold air wouldn't penetrate the snow and freeze the water. The snow was a protective blanket.

"So what do we do?" Gail asked.

"We've got to freeze the water. That's the only way to fly this plane out." After thinking about it all day, I came up with my second idea. "Let's lay out a runway, a short one to be sure, but a runway long enough so we can fly the plane off. We'll dig trenches around the perimeter of this runway. Then we'll make an ice wall in the trench and fill inside with water. It will freeze, and we'll have an effective runway."

"Do you think we can do it?" Gail asked.

"Absolutely." This time I knew we could do it. "We'll mark off the runway and then start digging the trench with shovels."

We dug an open ditch, about two feet wide and a thousand feet long. Then we started the hoses and put a light coat of water into the entire ditch. By the time we finished—six hours later—the water in the ditch had frozen. Then we did it all over again, pouring water on top of the new ice and letting that freeze. We kept doing this until we had filled the ditch with ice. Working night and day, it took us a week. Of course, water leaked all over the place, but we had accomplished our task. We now had a walled-in space. Then we put all the pumps to work filling the inside with water. It was about zero degrees and everything froze well. Then we had to wait another two days until the ice was solid enough to hold the plane. Once we were sure it was solid, Bean brought in a pilot and a mechanic, who revved up the engines that had been idle for thirty days. Everyone boarded the plane except the sergeant and me. Slowly, the plane moved onto the man-made strip, picked up speed, and took off. "They've made it!" we yelled as they ascended. It was an exciting moment. We could hear them inside the plane, yelling, "We've made it." The next day Captain Bean returned to get us and fly us home.

The bomber suffered no great damage and was back in action a week later. The sergeant who stayed with me was given his choice of any station in our command. He chose to stay at Presque Isle.

➤

One morning in the summer of 1943, I received a phone call saying that one of our planes had exploded and then taken a nosedive onto the top of Camel's Hump in Vermont. No one knew the cause of the explosion or if anyone was still alive. I received an order to try to rescue the nine crew members.

I asked for Captain Shearer from our Presque Isle search-and-rescue outfit to oversee this operation. He and his crew drove the two hundred miles to Camel's Hump. We assembled at the base of the mountain. A truck containing four mules arrived from Maine. The idea was that we would bring out on mule back any wounded or dead we could find. Mules did quite well in those mountains, and I had used them on previous rescues.

We took off for the wreck site. Captain Shearer and his men had no trouble locating bodies. There had been no fire, just wreckage strewn around the top of the mountain. But we could find only three engines. After an extensive search, we located the fourth in the bushes two hundred yards from the wreck. Apparently, it had separated from the fuselage before the plane hit the ground.

When we counted the bodies, including one wedged high in a tree, there were only eight men. Yet we knew there had been nine on board. Again we searched but found no clues. With only ten people to search the mountaintop, we couldn't do a thorough job. We wanted to believe that the ninth person had survived the crash and had tried to get down the mountain. There was nothing to indicate that he had survived, except that we couldn't find his body.

I sent a junior officer down the mountain to the nearest town to ask for the Boy Scouts or other volunteers to help us. Because it was summer, I was confident we would have no difficulty getting volunteers. In the meantime, of course, we sent the eight bodies down the mountain by mule.

Scouts, scout leaders, and several other volunteers began to arrive at sunrise. "We need your help," I told them. "There is one man still left up there. He may be alive."

They were eager to do whatever they could. "Start at the top," I told them. "The first man will start three feet from the top. He will circle the mountain counterclockwise and blaze every tree on the downhill side about head high. The second man will start blazing trees about three feet down from the first, and so on. When you complete your circle, drop downhill to the last man and go around again." In this manner we could cover every square yard of ground.

Eagerly, they went to the top, a climb of about two thousand feet. Because it was midsummer, flies and insects buzzed everywhere. It was hot, grueling work, but no one complained. The volunteers were just as determined as the military people. "We have to find that last man," was the message in all our hearts.

Some time later, the scouts found the ninth man. He was alive—barely.

They found him on the edge of a snow patch, where he had fainted from exhaustion. He was badly frostbitten, especially where his body lay in the melting snow. Apparently, he had crawled from the wreckage to the snow to get water. The snow that he ate helped keep him alive, but he was unconscious and in shock. Someone covered him, and the scouts waited for instructions.

We called for a mule and a stretcher. With everyone's help, the stretcher-bearing mule worked its way through the woods, onto a trail, and down to a waiting ambulance. The man was taken to a local hospital for survival treatment, then on to the air base at Presque Isle.

The man was in such bad shape that surgeons had to amputate both hands and feet. As a quadruple amputee, he remained in the hospital for several months. Everyone remarked about his upbeat spirit. No complaints. No self-pity. He was just thankful to be alive. He became an inspiration to the staff, patients, and visitors.

In a nearby ward lay a soldier who had lost a foot. His terrible attitude bothered everyone. He grumbled constantly about everything from the food to the nursing staff to the weather. He was angry with the doctors. He blamed the Air Force for his condition. Understandably, nobody wanted to be around him.

Then one day the commanding officer of the hospital said, "Move the amputee into the ward of the footless soldier. Let him see a man who really has something to complain about."

Both victims were now in the same ward. The belligerent one started his ranting. Then he noticed the new man at the far end of the ward, who smiled back at him. He was shocked at the newcomer's cheerful appearance. He thought, this man is worse than I am, yet he's happy. How can he feel that way? For several days he watched the new man in the ward. Not once did the quadruple amputee complain. When anyone moaned from pain, he was the first one to call out words of encouragement.

The complainer finally stopped grumbling. He admitted to a nurse, "Maybe I'm better off than I thought I was."

"Maybe you are," she said.

The two men, who were eventually moved to adjacent beds, talked and became good friends. The longer the footless man was around the other amputee, the nicer he became. When he received his prosthesis and was discharged from the service, he went home a different man.

Eventually, the Air Force transferred the quadruple amputee to a hospital in Philadelphia, his hometown. He fell in love with the nurse who was his primary caregiver, and eventually they were married.

Stories of this man's indomitable courage stirred the public, and the *Philadelphia Inquirer* ran a series of articles about him. The publicity led to a campaign to raise money for him. With the contributions, the couple was able to build a house with ramps and specially adapted apparatuses.

I kept track of the man for several years. Every year, on the anniversary of the accident, he would fly over the Hump and drop eight wreaths, saying, "Because I remember you guys." Then he would add, "I'm the lucky one."

Fifteen

WHAT HISTORY HAS TERMED THE BATTLE OF THE BULGE WAS ONE OF THE
bloodiest battles in Europe. In the winter of 1944–1945, General Eisenhower
prepared to strike along Germany's Rhine River. On December 16, 1944,
the Germans launched a surprise counteroffensive against a thin section of
the American front in the Ardennes. They used three armored reserve units
against small, sometimes-isolated American units. Eisenhower rushed in the
U.S. Third Army and an airborne division to attack the south shoulder of
what became known as "the bulge." Reinforcements gathered on the north
shoulder. During the month-long battle, the Germans lost more than 100,000
soldiers.

During the heat of battle, I learned, Americans conscripted German
prisoners to transport wounded men on stretchers through the deep snows.
Using four prisoners for each stretcher, they carried the injured from the front
to motorized transportation behind the lines. The work exhausted the prisoners and upset the wounded. The prisoners, lacking decent footwear for
sloshing through wet snow, suffered badly. After carrying a wounded soldier
to the waiting ambulances, they resisted returning to the front.

I thought the Allies needed help getting the wounded away from the
front. The evacuation process seemed slow and laborious, and I questioned
the wisdom of entrusting our wounded to captured enemy soldiers. The
prisoners couldn't have been the best of workers. We could certainly do it
more efficiently with sled dogs.

I radioed my commander, General Smith, and suggested that we transport the wounded by dog team. "With dogs," I said, "we can move much
more quickly and efficiently."

General Smith, long used to my unorthodox ideas, took only one day to think it over before sending a message to Washington. He said that we, the North Atlantic Division Air Transport Command, could efficiently move the wounded back from the front. He explained the concept, adding, "We are specialists in the handling of dogs."

Some people in Washington didn't think much of the idea. Many of them were afraid to take chances or to approve anything that sounded different.

Some of our own people opposed the idea. They asked, "How can you go to the European front and leave the North Atlantic Division Air Transport Command without the rescue facilities you yourself have championed?"

"American soldiers are dying every day because they don't get medical help quickly enough," I said. "Can't you see how this would save lives?"

I persisted in spite of the opposition. Maybe it was the spirit of adventure, maybe it was stubbornness, but I saw how much help we could offer with our dogs and sleds. I knew it was an obvious and logical solution. And I had faith that eventually I would get approval. After all, it made sense.

I started preparing as if we would receive the okay. To every base commanding officer of the search and rescue group, I sent a directive: "Get the following men ready. [I named them.] They are going to the front. They may be killed, but they're going to the front. Each of these drivers will have nine dogs. You select the dogs, but inform me which ones they are by name."

I figured we would leave a few teams behind. I hoped that would be enough for emergencies. They could be flown wherever they were most needed.

Once I sent out the order, I learned that the drivers were eager to go. Each would take along nine dogs, two sleds, dried food for a month, harnesses and other equipment, plus a tent and a sleeping bag. Once we got to the front, my plan was for Captain Bill Shearer to lead eight men and me to lead the other eight. Including replacements for sick and wounded dogs, I had orders cut for 209 sled dogs and 17 drivers. The only thing I left out of the orders was a departure date. All we needed now was approval.

Unknown to me, another event was unfolding. The war was nearing its end, and Allied leaders of the "big three"—the United States, Great Britain, and Russia—were making preparations for a secret meeting. President Roosevelt would meet with Joseph Stalin of the Soviet Union and Winston Churchill of Great Britain. Known as the Yalta Conference, it was to be held at a Ukrainian seaport on the Black Sea.

In the middle of our preparation for the Battle of the Bulge, I received secret orders that President Franklin D. Roosevelt was going to a conference by an as-yet-undetermined route. None of us in search and rescue knew his ultimate destination, but we did know the three possible air routes across the Atlantic Ocean. The Air Force would not notify the appropriate personnel until the day before the president's plane was due to leave Washington, D.C. In the meantime, the bases on all three routes were to be on ready-alert. The three routes were to Goose Bay, Labrador, then to Greenland, Iceland, Scotland, and into Europe; to Gander, Newfoundland, then directly across the Atlantic to Europe; and to Bermuda, the Azores, then to North Africa, and on to the ultimate destination.

My role was to prepare for possible search and rescue along each route and to provide a B-17 with a lifeboat to follow the president's plane. Crash boats were put on alert, but having three routes to cover meant that a one-day notice would not be enough to move them into position. We had eight crash boats, seven of which I deployed for the president's flight. The B-17 with the lifeboat was already standing by. We also alerted mountaineers along the route. Without revealing that it was the president, we said *an important person* would possibly be flying over their area. In case of a crash on land, we would need all personnel. Consequently, none of them could take leave until further notice.

The orders that set everything up came from President Roosevelt's aide. His name happened to be Colonel Harry Vaughan. Every message, of which there were many, bore the signature of Colonel Vaughan. Everyone in military authority knew of him, even if they had never met.

Although I was involved in preparation for the conference, I was more personally involved in the plan to move dog teams to the Battle of the Bulge. While waiting for approval, we modified our plans several times. Eventually, the request to use dogs reached the general who was the most involved in the Battle of the Bulge—George S. Patton. We both came from Hamilton, Massachusetts, so I knew him well. The very day he heard of my plan, he sent back a terse message: "Send the dogs." Now we could go forward.

That very afternoon four C-54s, our best four-engined cargo aircraft, were assigned to transport us. They picked up men and dogs from the various bases and took us to BW-1 on the southern tip of Greenland. There, I met a friend, Commander Norman Von Roseninge, who had been the Danish consul in Boston and was now in the Coast Guard. We had a delightful, albeit brief, reunion. He didn't know my mission, but when he saw that I had come with so many dog teams, he knew it was important and that we would be involved in the war in Europe.

Norman and I had a lovely dinner together. Just before I left, he handed me a bottle of whiskey, even though he knew I didn't drink. He explained that it was the only thing that he could buy on the base that he could think of to give me. "Take it," he said. "You're going to the front and this might be of some value."

I thanked him, put the bottle into my B4 bag, and forgot about it. I had no idea how handy that bottle of whiskey would be later on.

Just before we took off from BW-1 to Keflavik, Iceland, the orders came through for route A, the northern route for Roosevelt's trip. His plane would touch down at a base at Prestwick, Scotland, commanded by a Colonel Montague. I knew him well. A full colonel, he was a proud, ego-tistical man. It was well known that he wanted to retire as a general. Every-thing I knew about him indicated he manipulated matters to call attention to himself.

In the meantime, no longer involved with the president's itinerary, I was flying with my men and dogs to save lives on the Continent. We were supposed to land in Iceland; however, bad weather forced the pilot to climb to twenty thousand feet. He never told us, and without oxygen masks, ev-ery passenger, including the dogs, passed out. When we awakened, we all had splitting headaches. The pilot and crew had inhaled oxygen, but they didn't give us any or even tell us they had it. I thought it was a dirty trick.

We didn't stop at Reykjavik, but continued on to Prestwick. The fol-lowing message from operations had been sent in code to both Iceland and Prestwick: "Colonel Vaughan and 209 VIP animals coming your station. Lend every courtesy." Colonel Montague jumped at the name of Vaughan and made a wrong assumption. As for the "209 VIP animals," 209 was approximately the number of people who could travel on four C-54s with the president. The C-54s had fifty seats each. When Colonel Montague got his message, he flushed with excitement and cried out to his aide, "My God! The president of the United States is coming my way. I must cer-tainly greet him with my best."

Colonel Montague rushed to send messages all over Great Britain. He secretly invited everyone he considered important to come to Prestwick, making it known that President Roosevelt would be there within twelve hours. He targeted top officers from the Royal Air Force, the Royal Canadian Air Force, a variety of diplomats, and prestigious Americans in the British Isles. No one turned down his invitation.

When we reached the coast of Scotland, it was rainy and windy, and I wondered if we could land there. The pilot contacted the tower at Prestwick. Along with instructions to instrument land, the pilot received an odd message: "The commanding officer sends the following message to the first plane to land. Wait until the other three planes land before proceeding to operations or the parking ramp."

It was night and we had to land by instruments, which was hard in those days. It took twenty minutes before we were on the ground. Then we idled a full hour, waiting for the other three planes. It had been a long flight, we were tired, our dogs needed to relieve themselves, and my head was aching badly.

I went to the cockpit and peeked out the front window of the plane, but I couldn't see the operations tower for the fog and rain. When the last plane landed, we received orders that Colonel Vaughan's plane was to go first and the other three were to taxi behind it.

It was now late at night and raining heavily. On the approach, I could make out some black objects in front of the operations building. Something didn't look right, but I couldn't figure out what it was. As we neared, I saw one man making a steady, repetitious movement. Then the lights came on, and we could see a man beating a large drum. Military people were lined up at attention in the rain. All wore dress uniforms. They had not worn their coats, and they were getting soaked.

"Damn peculiar behavior," the pilot muttered.

I agreed, wondering why they would have a band and all the military brass out there to meet us. And why all this at such a late hour in the pouring rain? Were we really so important?

Just then a jeep approached with a ramp jutting out over the driver's cab. From the front of the plane, I couldn't see them place it flush against the side of our plane, but I figured out what they were doing. They had built the ramp to fit perfectly, under the assumption that Roosevelt would come down the ramp in a wheelchair. Then I noticed that they had spread out a red carpet, and that two MPs in white helmets stood at the bottom of the ramp.

We opened the cargo door, and several dogs surged toward the opening, eager to deplane. As I was the first one at the door, I stared into the face of the commanding officer who stood below me. "Greetings, Colonel Montague!" I said. I was about to salute, but I saw that he was clearly in shock.

"Norman!" he said, astonished. Then he turned his back to me. "I've been skunked," he said to the crowd and marched off.

At once the dignitaries knew that Montague had blundered. Obviously, these were not the president's planes. By now the dogs were barking and demanding to get off the plane. We were no longer of interest to anyone. The next thing I knew, the red-carpeted ramp disappeared and the band left. During all this, no one said a word to us. We were still inside the plane, staring down at this bizarre scene.

Since they had taken away the ramp and brought nothing to replace it, we had to get down on our own. It was a ten-foot drop to the tarmac. I had two men drop to the ground, and then I lowered the dogs, holding on to their harnesses. The "catchers" put the animals on the ground. Someone else tied them to trees on the grass lawn. Soon we had picket lines stretched from tree to tree. The other three planes unloaded their dogs and did the same thing.

Once we were all down, one of the men at Prestwick rushed up, horrified that we had staked our dogs on the lawn. "Sir," he said, "one week ago, Colonel Montague had new grass planted here. He has intended it to be a showplace for those who land here." Too bad, I thought, and smiled at the thought of what the lawn was going to look like when we left. Once our dogs felt soil under their paws, they scratched and squatted. It was still raining, and the ground was thoroughly soaked. Some of the mud got thrown against the windows of the operations building. They would later have to hose them down to get rid of the mud. I thought it was rather funny.

The big shots were furious with Montague. For his part, the colonel did not show us one bit of courtesy. He made no attempt to house us. All the beds at Prestwick were taken by the dignitaries he had invited. My men had to sleep on the floor and on the counters of the operations building. About one o'clock in the morning, when the last dog was tied up, I returned to the plane to catch a little sleep. We used the plane's ladders to climb in and out.

Just then, a man wearing a black derby came over to the plane. He called to me, "Excuse me, but I am looking for a Colonel Vaughan. Can you help me, please?"

As soon as I saw him, I suspected he had something to do with quarantining imported animals.

"I'm Vaughan," I said. "What can I do for you?"

He said his name was Mr. Murphy and that he'd heard that a contingent of dogs had arrived. That's all I let him say before I interrupted. "Why, hello, there, Mr. Murphy. You are just the man I want to see."

"Oh, really?"

"Yes, come aboard. Up the ladder. It's safe." It was raining quite hard now. From the look of the poor man, he must have been asleep when he got the call—from Montague, of course.

"You know, Colonel, we have to quarantine—"

"Let's talk first, Mr. Murphy. Let me show you around." I took his hand and shook it profusely. "Have you ever been inside a C-54 before?"

"Oh, no, certainly not," he said.

"Let me take a few minutes to show you. Nice plane, isn't it?" I took him forward. I made him sit in the pilot's seat. He asked questions, and I explained everything in detail. I illustrated my points with stories. I wasn't a pilot, but neither was he, so he had to accept whatever I said. When he asked me about the instrument that connected to the Pitot tube, I went on to explain in detail how the Pitot tube worked. I was trying to use up time while I figured out some way to stop him from quarantining the dogs. Then I had an idea. I opened my B4 bag and took out the bottle of whiskey.

"On a bad night like this, we both need a good, stiff drink," I said. I opened the bottle and passed it to him.

He hesitated only a second and then took a long drink. I put the bottle to my lips, pretended to drink, and passed it back to him.

Then we went back to questions and answers about the plane. I told him a few stories about flying, pulling out every fact I knew or suspected about aviation. He seemed fascinated. I kept passing him the bottle, which helped make my stories even more exciting. I probably could have started repeating myself, because he was beginning to feel the effects of the whiskey. He never turned the bottle down when I passed it to him. By the time the bottle was half finished, his speech had started to slur. Now I knew things were going to be fine.

At half past three in the morning, he was still sitting inside the plane, mostly, I suspect, because he couldn't have walked straight. With slurred, hesitant words, he asked, "What am I going to write on my report? I have to write something, you know."

"It's easy enough, Mr. Murphy. Just say 209 sled dogs were driven off course. They remained at Prestwick overnight and took off the next morning."

"Sounds like a capital idea," he said—his words weren't very clear. He tipped the bottle again. Had there been a real argument about it, of course, I would have had to give the dogs up. It would have been a disaster. Scotland had a six-month quarantine law.

I made a comfortable spot for the inspector on the floor of the plane, right beside the freight door. Once he was asleep, I started getting ready for departure. I called my sergeant and told him to have everybody on board at daybreak so that we could take off for Paris.

Finally, everything was ready to load. I had soldiers move the dogs to the door. Then they had to lift the dogs high enough that we could grab their harness and lift them the final few feet. We were lucky—not a single dog got loose. Soon everything and everybody was loaded. Gingerly, I awakened Mr. Murphy and helped him down the ladder.

He walked with difficulty, holding his head. "What am I going to write in my report?" he asked again and again. "I have to write something, you know."

"Why, we worked all that out last night, don't you remember?"

"I am not certain that I do."

"Just write that 209 sled dogs driven off course by the weather landed at Prestwick and took off in six hours."

"Yes, yes, that is an excellent solution," he said. I helped him into the office, and then I got out of there as quickly as I could.

I took one last look at the lawn. I saw no remaining evidence of the colonel's grass. And I had a good laugh. "To Paris!" I yelled to the pilot.

A few hours later, we landed at Le Bourget Air Field.

Now we were ready to do something significant for the war effort. Excited, I was hardly able to hold myself back. Once again, the feeling came over me that I was going to win the war single-handedly. Little did I realize how insignificant my effort would be.

Sixteen

PARIS. THEY HOUSED US THE FIRST NIGHT IN OLD, RAT-INFESTED HORSE STABLES
near Le Bourget airfield. The next morning, we divided into two groups
and climbed aboard C-47s. Under Captain Bill Shearer, eight teams went
to Belgium. I also took eight men and half the dogs, and headed for the
front, which was the French-Belgian border. On the flight, we were informed that we would be living in tents at an airstrip. They would house
us in the center of a triangle of runways, five miles from the front. I found
that hard to understand but made no comment.

Later I asked about the safety of living at an air base. "Won't it be a
prime target for an air strike by the Germans?"

"No," I was told. "Because of the large red cross spread on the grass
next to the tents, they don't bomb us."

We were assigned to sleep in a large Red Cross tent. Most of the bunks
were already occupied, so we just lay down beside other sleeping men. Next
day, we ate with soldiers who were both at the front and behind the lines.
The army had taken over an old train and converted the dining car for
cooking. They confiscated an old cow barn for the mess hall.

I particularly remember the meal of the second evening. A few minutes after we lined up, before we got inside the cow barn itself, we heard
a loud commotion from inside. Only later did we learn what had happened
in front of us.

In the darkness, one man accidentally stepped on another man's toes.
The man who got stepped on must have had sore feet, because he screamed,
"Mein Gott!"

Because he yelled in German, somebody grabbed him from behind.
He was taken out of the mess hall for questioning. The Americans soon

discovered that he was a German soldier and had been eating at the airstrip for the past three days. He had no food, was hungry, and so was willing to take drastic risks. It turned out that he had found a dead American soldier, put on his uniform, and walked to the base. Somehow he had managed to get inside. Under questioning, he admitted he had a friend who had lined up with him. Both were arrested and taken prisoner.

➤

After I had been at the base awhile, the colonel in charge of operations came to see me. "You want to demonstrate your team today? We can't take you to the front, because there's too much mud."

It was raining and what had been four feet of snow was rapidly disappearing. I kept thinking of the lives we could have saved if Washington had only said yes as soon as they first learned of the plan. Instead, it had taken them thirty days.

I pushed those thoughts aside, and we demonstrated how the team worked. We showed the officer that we could take two stretchers, one on each end of two sleds. The demonstration impressed him so that he told other officers, and we put on a second demonstration for them.

Two days passed, and no orders came to evacuate the wounded. I was getting nervous. It was now the middle of February 1945. We had to get moving before all the snow disappeared. Our sleds would be of no use in the mud.

It kept raining. That meant warmer temperatures and dissolving snow.

I got in touch with Bill Shearer in Belgium. He had rain and mud, too.

In the end, we didn't save a life. But we did demonstrate what we could have done for the war effort. I comforted myself by saying, "It was a good idea." If the bureaucrats had not been so slow, we could have done important rescue work.

➤

Willie Knudsen, a first lieutenant from my outfit, was a man known for his antics and risk taking. Born in Norway, he was an excellent dog driver who had been around dogs all his life. While we were in Paris, he met a beautiful Parisian woman and fell in love. The situation was complicated, however, by the fact that she was married and had children. Her husband was a newspaper publisher.

Knudsen knew we were leaving soon, which would spell the end of his love affair. He came to me and said, "Colonel Vaughan, sir, I have just heard from my family in Norway. My mother is very sick, and she is not expected to live. Will you let me go to Norway and see her before she dies?"

"Of course," I said, because I believed his story. "Your request comes at a good time, but you can't stay long; you must come back soon."

"Oh, yes sir," he promised.

I gave him a week.

A few days later, I flew home. The men and dogs under Captain Shearer returned by ship, but when they arrived home, Willie was not with them. Whenever anyone asked about him, I covered up. "Lieutenant Knudsen is on a secret mission, and he can't be reached." It was now long past his seven days, and I didn't know what to do. "He may be back tomorrow," I kept telling myself.

I knew I couldn't cover for more than thirty days. At thirty days, AWOL becomes desertion. Willie Knudsen finally did show up—just before the end of the thirty days. The men kidded him constantly, trying to find out what had happened. Finally, once he knew he wouldn't get into trouble, he told us of his "secret mission." Of course, he had stayed in Paris the whole time.

➤

General George C. Patton was someone I knew quite well. Once, when I was home on leave, the general invited Rosamond and me to his house for coffee on a Sunday morning. A number of other guests were also present. The Pattons planned to attend the worship service at St. John's Episcopal Church in Beverly Farms, Massachusetts. Since we were also Episcopalians, General Patton asked if we'd like to join them.

"We'd be delighted," I said.

Patton was big, tough, and brusque. He was immaculately dressed at all times. Although he often wore two guns on his hips, he didn't take his guns to church.

We had hardly been seated when the minister came to the altar. He recognized Patton. He announced that he would not give his prepared service. "We have someone very special in our audience today. From listening to this man, you can get far more than I could offer you." He then introduced General and Mrs. Patton.

"General Patton," he said, "I would appreciate it if you would come to the altar and address us after the first hymn."

"I shall be glad to," the general replied.

As soon as the hymn was over, Patton was greeted by the minister and shown to the pulpit. Instead of launching into a speech, he recognized the minister, greeted the parishioners, and said, "Wars are won or lost by enlisted men on the battlefield, not by officers. In our audience, we have an enlisted man whom I've never met, but he is in uniform. I now ask him if he will come to the pulpit with me."

The startled soldier shuffled out of the pew and went forward, blushing. The general kept the awkward private from saluting him by thrusting out his hand. After they shook hands, the general laid his arm across the private's shoulder. "What is your name?"

He quietly gave his name. General Patton repeated it to the audience, and if I remember correctly, the man's first name was John. "I'm delighted you are here with me, John."

The young man, obviously flustered, wanted to say something, but the words just wouldn't come out.

The general, fully at ease, then turned and addressed the parishioners. "I am glad that John is here with me, and I will now tell you what I think about something." He told a simple story of the people in the war zone and how terrible it was for those on both sides to have battles going on around them. All the while, the private stood beside him. General Patton delivered a message of hope that day. He concluded by encouraging the congregation to pray for the end of the war.

The general then thanked the soldier for being with him and offered a brief prayer of thanks to God. He turned to the minister and said, "And may God bless you." Nodding to the minister, he sat down.

That was the last service General and Mrs. Patton attended at that church. A short time later, the general was killed in a jeep accident in Europe.

➤

After the war, I was visiting a close friend, Neil Ayer, a nephew of General Patton's. He had all kinds of memorabilia about the general. One picture in particular impressed me. It was of Patton standing on a high bank of the Marne River, wearing his dress uniform. He had boasted many times that he was going to "pee all over the Germans." The picture shows the general doing just that—peeing into the Marne River.

I laughed and laughed, especially when I saw that he was giving them a good, long stream of urine. The picture was so typical of him. A man who went all out to win any battle, he was, as they said, tough as nails.

I asked Neil for the picture, and he promised I could have it. Unfortunately, he died before he sent it, so I don't suppose I'll ever get that picture.

Patton was one of my heroes of World War II. I am proud to have known him.

Seventeen

By the spring of 1945, I was considering ways to increase our capabilities and efficiency in handling air crashes. I suggested we parachute doctors and dogs in to crash sites if they couldn't get there any other way.

"Oh, another of Vaughan's harebrained ideas," was the first thing I heard. Far from discouraging me, that reaction may have egged me on. Most of the time people opposed my ideas simply because they were different, and I learned to push until I got them approved or rejected. I talked to my operations officer, Colonel Boyd, about dropping doctors and dogs. He was cool to the animal idea, but I persisted. A few days later, I asked for the use of a plane to do some experimental search and rescue (S&R) maneuvers.

"What do you need the plane for?" the colonel asked.

"I need the plane to drop a dog."

He stared at me. "You're not ready to do that yet, are you?"

"Yes, sir. I am ready. I have a parachute, and I have a dog. Now I need the release of a plane."

"Are you sure it won't kill the dog?"

"Yes, sir, I am sure."

Boyd wasn't convinced. Finally, he said, "I want you to do a practice drop with a fake dog to prove to me that you won't hurt a real one."

I thought it was silly to prove it this way, but I obeyed. I constructed a wooden dog, three feet long and eight inches wide, filled the inside with sand, and covered it with canvas. I had produced the equivalent of a twenty-five-pound dog. To lend it a look of authenticity, I attached a couple of sticks for legs. More as a joke than anything, I made a rope tail and glued fur around the head. I showed it to Colonel Boyd.

He looked it over and said, "I want to observe when you do the practice run."

"Yes, sir. At three o'clock this afternoon, you can walk out of your office, and I'll come down the runway. If the tower informs me that they have no planes landing or taking off, I'll fly over the runway and drop the dog. You can see it for yourself."

"I'll be watching."

We took off a little before three. We got the okay. "Go in low," I instructed the pilot. I had him give full throttle over the operations building so that Boyd could look out his window and see us drop the dog. I took the door off the plane, tied a climbing rope around my waist, and roped myself to the plane. I leaned forward with the dog in my arms, ready to throw it out.

At the proper moment, I pushed the sand dog out. But the parachute didn't deploy. The dog just dangled behind the plane. I immediately understood the reason. I had made the dog twenty-five pounds, but it took at least forty pounds to open the parachute.

I grabbed my sheath knife and cut the line. The dog fell straight to the ground. When it hit the runway, the parachute broke open. The parachute was red.

"Oh, no," I groaned.

I stayed away from the operations office for the next two hours. I waited until after five o'clock, hoping that Colonel Boyd had gone home by then. Unable to delay any longer, I went to the office and checked with his secretary.

"Yes, sir, he's inside. He is waiting for you in his office."

"Thank you," I said with a weak smile.

I rapped on the door and went into his office. Before he could bawl me out, I said, "Colonel, I'm sorry. I know the problem. I didn't make my dog heavy enough. It takes thirty to forty pounds to pop the parachute. You were right, sir. It does pay to do a test, doesn't it? Next time I'll make it." I saluted and turned to leave, hoping he wouldn't call me back.

Colonel Boyd was a fine man with a wonderful sense of humor. The next day, when I got to the base, I read the orders of the day. In the middle of the orders I found an official order: "Vaughan is hereby forbidden to drop mules out of military aircraft." I did indeed have four mules for S&R, but I wasn't going to do mules—they weighed a good thousand pounds.

Eventually, we did drop live dogs. Just before the first drop, Colonel Boyd asked, "Which dog are you going to use?"

"Blackie, sir." Blackie was his favorite dog.

"Why Blackie?"

"Because he bites like hell. If it doesn't succeed, he's the best one to lose." I was determined to have my little joke on the colonel.

I dropped Blackie. It was a success.

➤

The Grenfell mission in St. Anthony, Newfoundland (where I'd served with Dr. Grenfell), had an epidemic of distemper, and it wiped out their entire mission dog team. The mission asked for help, and I jumped at the chance. Within three days, we were flying ten dogs and two sleds to St. Anthony. One by one, the parachute-ready dogs were pushed out of the plane. The whole village was at the target field. Nine of the dogs landed on the field, but the tenth came down in the harbor.

Because I had received two days' notice, I had ordered our crash boat at Stephensville at the southern part of Newfoundland to St. Anthony, in case it was needed. The crash boat arrived at St. Anthony harbor just in time. As the tenth dog missed the field and plopped into the harbor, the alert captain speeded up and caught the dog—less than one minute after it hit the water. All ten dogs were safe and unharmed.

After that, we received a number of letters from the St. Anthony mission, thanking us for donating our dogs. Nine months later, we received a special letter detailing the work the doctors had been able to accomplish because of our dogs.

Subsequently, they asked if we needed the dogs back. We got permission to donate the dogs to them. We would not have been allowed to do it if it had been an American mission. But they were Canadians, and we were able to give the dogs to foreign allies.

➤

The war was winding down by the spring of 1945. What was next for me? I wondered. I didn't look forward to selling Homelite products and returning to the daily routines I felt so far away from. Then came a phone call from my commanding officer, General Kuter, in Washington. He presented exactly the opportunity I needed.

General Kuter told me, "The United Nations is forming an air wing in Montreal, Canada. They are calling it PICAO—Provisional International

Civil Aviation Organization." He explained that they wanted it housed outside of the United States, rather than trying to cram it into the United Nations headquarters in New York. Each member nation had been invited to send aviation representatives.

Then came the good part. He said, "If you like, I will recommend that the new director general take you on as chief of search and rescue." He didn't press me for a decision, but asked me to call him back.

It sounded like an excellent opportunity and just the kind of excitement I wanted. The UN was making decisions that affected the future of all nations, and I could be part of that historic process. Best of all, I could continue in the field in which I was already working.

"General, sir," I said two days later, although I'd known the minute I heard the offer, "I would love the opportunity to get in on the ground floor."

"I thought you would," he said. His recommendation went to the Joint Chiefs of Staff in Washington, D.C. Within three weeks, I left the military service and became a civilian working for PICAO.

The first and primary mission of PICAO—or ICAO, as it became known when the UN accepted it and dropped the Provisional—was (and still is) to write standards for international aviation. This covered everything having to do with the control of aircraft, including such matters as the altitude planes flew, the language pilots used, and standards for radio operation.

Rosamond, Jerry, Jackie, and I moved to Montreal and settled in, and soon the work began. I personally took over search and rescue. Under my coordination, we divided the earth into geographic regions: North Atlantic Division, European Division, South American Division, North African Division, Indian Division, and Pacific Division. PICAO set procedures to coordinate searches for downed planes. We established rescue coordination centers (RCCs) and asked member nations to agree to abide by international rules. Failure to comply meant being isolated and boycotted by members of PICAO. For instance, PICAO members would not sell fuel to nations that did not comply. They also agreed that each member country would control the sale of gasoline within its borders. If nonmember nations wanted their planes to fly into a PICAO country, they had to conform to the new standards. International regulations were to everybody's advantage, and we had little trouble gaining acceptance.

Next we decided we had to organize the flying spaces of airplanes. Now that more and more planes were in the sky, we needed standards so that they wouldn't fly into each other's airspace. We established a standardized system that every country could use. Many countries were already working with each other, but previously there had been no international agreement.

A big aid to search and rescue, weather forecasting, and navigation was the establishment of the Ocean Station Vessels. I was a great proponent of OSV, because it provided places in the middle of the ocean where planes could go to ditch. In the North Atlantic, United States Coast Guard ships went to a particular location and stayed there for ninety days. Then they would rotate with other Coast Guard ships. This OSV setup does not exist today; we don't need it, because planes are safer and can fly longer distances.

Once we got the plan working in the North Atlantic, it was easy to do it in the Indian Ocean, where only one boat was needed. Eventually, we made this plan operational in the other regions. We used vessels from various nations, but most were from the United States. The one drawback was that OSV duty was terribly boring for the crews. For three months, they didn't go anywhere.

Under OSV, exciting rescues took place that saved lives. OSV also made weather forecasting more accurate, and the financial appropriations from the weather bureau kept the service going for years.

➤

The first international Search and Rescue council meeting was held at Montreal, and representatives came from the fifty-six member nations. At the end of the thirty-day meeting they returned to their own countries, asked their governments to accept the preliminary standards, and then reported back to the PICAO council.

Since my title was secretary, S&R Division, I conducted the meetings, assembled the recommendations, and wrote a manual. To the full council in Montreal, I presented the recommendations and the manual for their approval. Once they approved, it became like law—all nations had agreed to abide by the regulations. After we became ICAO, the manual went to the member nations for their approval, mostly a formality. Many nonmember nations saw the value of the ICAO standards and soon joined. Today the standards are accepted worldwide.

Over a four-year period beginning in 1945, I attended all the regional meetings in Egypt, the Philippines, India, Japan, Peru, Argentina, and of course, Canada. I particularly remember the Cairo meeting. The British recommended that we find a way to extend the life of the Egyptian Camel Corps. The corps operated primarily to catch smugglers who traveled across the desert. We listened and observed demonstrations of the work of the camel corps in the desert. We even rode camels and ate bread made from dough that the men had buried in the sand to bake.

As we learned, camels and riders could stay out for only seven days. At the end of that time, they had to return for water and supplies. The British proposed that we help them find a way to stay out for fourteen days. The camel corps, they argued, was much more effective than using planes, because the riders could more easily reach crashes, rescue survivors, and pick up bodies even in light sandstorms when visibility was poor and flying was dangerous. Personnel from the camel corps could also guard downed planes until another plane came for salvage. Otherwise, nomads would go through the plane and take everything.

The United States representative said, "I think we could provide parachutes and kegs for water. We could then drop water and supplies to the patrolling corps on a regular basis."

"Will it work?" someone asked. "Can you do that?"

"And if you do," asked one of the Egyptian leaders, "how much water would it take to extend a patrol to two weeks' duration?"

The Egyptians decided to find out. The next day they answered the question. "Yes, it will work, and this arrangement would indeed enable us to extend the useful life of a camel patrol to fourteen days." They told how many kegs of water they would need per patrol.

The United States representative said, "We will try to donate that many kegs." He called for a practice drop for the members before we concluded our sessions.

Within a few days, kegs and parachutes were brought to Egypt. With great fanfare, we went out to the Cairo military air facility and examined the parachutes and water kegs. Planes dropped several kegs as a test. The first attempt was totally successful. I believe they dropped twelve barrels, and all of them landed without any problems. This simple solution doubled their patrol capabilities, and the Egyptians were delighted. They began training their people for extended journeys.

Nine days after the Cairo meeting ended, a small airplane with nine people force-landed in the Sahara Desert. They reported that no one was hurt, but a sandstorm was preventing air searchers from finding them.

The camel corps went into action. Planes parachuted water to them, enabling them to reach the downed plane. They rescued all nine people.

When I read the report, I knew we had impressed the Egyptians. And I was proud that the United States had taken the initiative to provide the equipment.

> ➤

I had gone to ICAO in 1945 and worked there for exactly four years. I would have stayed longer, but a situation arose that I couldn't ignore. I had been elected president of the Secretariat staff, which made me president of the employees board. A Frenchman was secretary-general, and he was the man with the real power. He did things I considered unethical. I tried to correct them, but with no success. As secretary-general, the Frenchman was supposed to represent all countries. Yet he consistently gave preferential treatment to certain countries, especially those that favored France. Then he promoted a man who was a known embezzler.

I received this information and other facts from the Frenchman's own people. He had a big staff, none of whom liked him. They complained to me, saying the Frenchman needed to be exposed but that they wouldn't do it themselves. They assured me that if I spoke up, they would back me. I knew that I could make the charges stand up, but that it would probably cost me my job. It was a job I liked very much, but I didn't dwell on the matter very long. I knew the right thing to do.

I wrote a letter to the secretary-general himself. It opened by saying, "This is a letter of censure against you." Then I listed examples of his unethical behavior. "I have already sent a copy to every one of the council members, and I have given them full disclosure of your unethical behavior." I concluded the letter with this final sentence: "And I resign."

The ICAO council concurred, to some extent, with my charges. They made some changes but did not oust the man behind the problems. Although that failure saddened me, I had done the right thing, and my conscience was clear.

I went back home to Boston. I thought my life of adventure was over.

Eighteen

IN 1949, IT WAS TIME TO PICK UP WHERE I HAD LEFT OFF AT HOMELITE. I knew they wanted me, and I didn't know what else to do. Maybe it was time to settle down and live like other people.

An interesting new tool—a chain saw—had just come on the market, and I did enjoy introducing a new product. I went out to sell it to lumber camps in New England. Before the war, I had worked among the lumber camps, selling them generators and pumps, so I knew my way around.

Although lumberjacks had heard about the chain saw, I had to demonstrate it to them. Some did buy. In those days, each man owned his own ax and saw. At night he would file the teeth and sharpen the blade to be ready for the next day's work. Lumberjacks loved the new chain saw; but they hated the down time they faced when something went wrong. They didn't want to wait several days or a week for repair work. The anticipated delay was the biggest problem I had selling them chain saws.

Then I had an idea. I was selling saws to six camps and faced competition from other companies that marketed their own chain saws. With my boss's approval, we bought a Ford truck, outfitted it with spare parts and tools, and hired a good mechanic who could talk the language of the woodcutters. We put him out on the road with this truck. He set it up so that every Monday he would be at one particular camp, every Tuesday at another, and so on through the week. On Saturday, the driver returned to Boston, brought in orders, and restocked. By Monday, he was back on the road. It could still take as long as a week for a chain saw to be repaired if it failed the day after the service truck had been there. Even so, no other company offered such good service, and my sales increased.

My world didn't revolve around chain saws, however, because that would have been too confining. I got into polo, skiing, horseback riding, and a number of social activities—anything to keep me busy. The truth is, I was depressed again. The job with Homelite was a letdown after all the international work I had been involved in. I missed the travel, the challenges, and the people.

I let myself drift. Rosamond and I had been happy enough when we returned to Boston, but we were drifting apart as well. My children were growing up, and I didn't pay enough attention to them. I didn't know it then, but I do now. By 1949, Jackie was nearly eight, and Jerry was moving into his teens. He visited his mother often but stayed with us, eventually graduating from Governor Dummer School and then Trinity College. He loved ROTC Air Force Training and went into the service immediately upon graduation. In the Air Force, Jerry had an outstanding service record for twenty-seven years and retired a lieutenant colonel. He and his wife have three sons. (Jackie has done well, too, I must add. She worked for the Harvard Medical School after graduation, married a research doctor, and now has two children, a boy and a girl.)

My work with Homelite lasted two years before my life took an upward turn. In 1951, the Korean War broke out. Still in the reserves, I was called back for TDY—temporary duty. It was the challenge I craved.

My old commanding officer, General Kuter, suggested that I go into psychological warfare because the Air Force needed people who would put their heart and soul into their work. "And you will do that, Vaughan. I know you."

When they offered me the position, I accepted without hesitation for two reasons. First, it sounded exciting. Second, it was a new Air Force activity, so I faced the challenge of figuring out what to do.

We had twelve balloon projects, eleven of which were classified. The first we called the Moby Dick Project, and it had nothing to do with the conflict in Korea. Moby Dick involved high-altitude investigation of the jet stream inside the United States. In those days, no one knew where or how thick the jet stream was. Meteorologists requested that we send our pear-shaped balloons into the jet stream every morning. We did this by sending one out each day from three launching sites, in California, Oregon, and Washington. Each balloon carried a radio transmitter. At five minutes past the hour and thirty-five minutes past the hour, the balloons would each broadcast an identification signal. From hundreds of ground stations, the meteorologists could track their progress. The Moby Dick Project was a great success. We gave the forecasters more information about the upper atmosphere than they had ever had before.

One day we launched a balloon from Alamogordo, New Mexico, to see how far it would go and to track its course. (This had nothing to do with Moby Dick, but was a request from meteorologists for information.) On the chance that one balloon would fail, we launched two of them, forty minutes apart. These balloons carried little signaling equipment because we wanted maximum gas capacity. The higher they were to go, the more gas we put in, but the more difficulty we had controlling them at the time of the launch. The first balloon rose to seventy thousand feet and then lifted above the jet stream. The radio stations tracked rapid movement from west to east. The meteorologists knew that after the balloon had been at seventy thousand feet for a while it would lose some of its lift, come down, and eventually get into the jet stream again and be carried along even faster at an altitude of fifty thousand feet.

We heard nothing from the balloons after twenty-five hours, although we knew both had reached the Atlantic coast. Everyone was excited that they had gone that far. We alerted the meteorological people in Europe, but they gave no indication of having received any identification signal. Actually, no one believed a balloon could reach Europe or Africa anyway.

Fifty-six hours after being launched from Alamogordo, one of the balloons came down in the harbor at Oslo, Norway. The other was found nine months later in North Africa. "Fantastic," our people screamed. No one had believed it was possible. This information vastly aided our understanding of jet streams.

One of our classified projects involved sending animals up. This was long before people became so concerned about animal welfare. Mice were our first subjects. We put them in containers in the payload—a cage under the balloon. We also had it rigged so that at any given time, a razor blade knife, set with a spring in the payload, could cut the cord that held the payload. The payload, attached to a small parachute, would drop from the balloon.

We wanted to get payloads back so that we could study the effects on the mice. To make sure of this, we had to do something that would make people want to return the mice. On each payload, we painted these words: "United States property, reward if returned." Beneath that, we put the amount, sometimes $5 and sometimes $25, depending on how important we considered the payload. Our total budget for recoveries was $500, so we had to use it carefully.

The flights were relatively short. Once we had good results with mice, we sent up various insects and other small animals. They landed all over the desert, and we then paid for their return.

These high-altitude balloons were large. One night, two of our men went to the balloons we were planning to launch the following morning. They inflated one, and on a spur-of-the-moment urge, one of them decided to get into the payload basket and hold on while the other man launched it. Soon he was out of sight, floating low over the desert. Then the balloon started to come down. Unfortunately for him, it came down on high-tension wires. He was left hanging in the air, too high up to cut himself free. When he didn't show up for breakfast, his friend began to worry. At eleven o'clock with no sign of him, his friend finally reported it to me.

I reported to the officer in charge of the base that one of our men was missing. "I was told that he went for a ride on his motorcycle and hasn't come back," is the way I reported it. He understood.

Early in the afternoon, we found our would-be ballooner, still hung up in the high-tension wires. Taking great care, we brought him down by sending him a climbing rope and a harness. He wasn't a climber, but we gave him instructions, and we belayed him down easily enough from his perilous seventy-five-foot perch.

At his disciplinary hearing, he said he just wanted to know what a balloon flight was like and couldn't resist the temptation. "Best ride I ever had," he said, "but the wait for transportation was a bore because I forgot to put C rations in my fatigues."

➤

From the Moby Dick Project, I was reassigned to the Pentagon in March 1952, and again I was under General Kuter. As I was working away at a desk in Washington, my thoughts were focused on the north country.

Before I had been there a month, a message came across my desk that I was to prepare a directive for General George (head of Air Transport Command) to sign. It would then go to the commanding officer of every Air Force base, urging them to send their championship teams in baseball, football, and other sports to any international events that would "bring favorable publicity to the Air Force." I had fun putting the message out. As I did, I thought, wouldn't dog driving qualify as a good sport? Wouldn't it be a great way to gain favorable publicity for the Air Force? I knew about the North American Championship. It would be held in Fairbanks, Alaska. I could enter that race with my team of dogs and represent the Air Force.

After I prepared the directive, I took it to General Kuter to forward.

While I was with him, I said, "Sir, I have completed the mission of preparing the message, but I want to ask you if you can accept my own statement that I am champion of the Pentagon dog drivers."

"Vaughan, what are you after?" He cocked an eye and stared at me. General Kuter knew me well.

"Sir, I am the champion of the Pentagon dog drivers." I could say that without fear of contradiction, for I was the only one.

"And again, Vaughan, what are you after?"

I reminded him of the directive I had written at his request. "Now, sir, I want you to send me to get my dog team in New Hampshire and take the dogs to Alaska. With that team, I will compete in the International World Championship Dog Sled Race in Fairbanks."

The general thought about my idea and finally said, "Yes, fine. Write a request and bring it to me."

"Yes, sir," I said. I then reached into my briefcase and handed him the request.

He shook his head, laughed, and signed his name. I telephoned for my dog team. They were being raced by Keith Bryar, a close friend who lived in New Hampshire. By commercial air and at his own expense, he went to Alaska to help as my dog handler in the competition. I took my twelve dogs with me on what we called "military space available." I paid all expenses for their food and mine as well as the entry fee.

I felt invigorated. I had never been to Alaska before, and just to compete was thrilling. We arrived on a Wednesday. The minute I got off the plane, I was met by a man I still know today, Earl Norris. He was already famous in Alaska because he raced Siberian sled dogs. In those days, the Eskimos and Native Americans dominated dog sledding in Alaska. Earl, who was white, was going to participate in the upcoming race. He knew I was arriving to represent the Air Force because it had been announced in the papers. The article pointed out that I was bringing the first dog team from the lower forty-eight states ever to participate in an Alaskan race.

Earl, then about thirty years old, was short, stocky, and tough. He had been born in Alaska and had driven just about everything from dog sleds to mail trucks to race cars. His wife, Natalie, who was from New York, later became famous in her own right as a dog racer, long before women like Libby Riddles and Susan Butcher came on the scene.

"Norman," Earl asked as soon as I got out of the plane, "would you like me to show you part of the course?"

"Oh, that's great," I said. "I really would like that."

He introduced me to other Alaskans. They helped me harness my team right there beside the plane, and we drove the dogs out of the airport. We hadn't gone far before we turned off the airport highway right onto the Alaskan trail—part of the trail I would be racing over in two days.

As I knew, the three-day race was twenty-three miles on each of the first two days and thirty-five on the last day. On the trail, we met some people. I was a stranger, but they treated me as if I were an old friend.

One woman, who was connected with dog sledding, said to me, "Your sled is too heavy for this race. I'd like to loan you mine."

"That would be very nice," I said, overwhelmed by her generosity.

The next day, using her borrowed sled, I went over the first part of the trail. It felt fine. On the first day of the race, however, a runner on the sled broke before I was half finished. But I had a good team and kept on. Riding on one runner behind a team is no easy task, and I tipped over many times. Each time, I dug myself out, got back on the trail, and went on my way until I fell again.

I was totally exhausted when I finished. To my surprise, I finished tenth out of eighteen entries. When I considered what I had gone through, I was pleased.

For day two, someone gave me another sled, for which I was grateful. Otherwise, I would have had to drop out of the race. The second and third days I did fine and had no trouble. I didn't win the championship, but I did beat every other white man, including Earl Norris. In fact, Earl had trouble with his sled and had to withdraw. I thought it was an accomplishment and was able to say, "I was the fastest white man with a sled team from the lower forty-eight."

The winner was an Eskimo whose last name was Smoke; everybody called him Holy Smoke. The newspaper headline the next day blared, "Holy Smokes the Trail."

➤

After the dog race, it was back to balloons. Psychological warfare and balloons were both under the same command. After we organized the balloon program, General Kuter transferred me to psychological warfare in Washington. Most of the work involved leafleteering. We described our work as that of "sending propaganda in leaflet form over enemy territory in helium-filled balloons."

We had a mobile printing press that we pulled with a trailer, printing thousands of leaflets right in the field. For a year and a half, I worked with different kinds of balloons. Because of their size and shape, we referred to them as pillow balloons. We loaded them with leaflets, perhaps a thousand sheets of paper, and then added helium. The pillow balloons, like all the balloons we used, were open at the bottom. When the balloon reached one thousand feet, the gas would expel from the opening. This helped it drop to a lower altitude. Then it would rip open and dispense its leaflets. The more we helium-filled the balloons and lightened the loads, the farther they would go. Our average target was ten to fifteen miles away to reach enemy soldiers on their way to the front and to educate village people everywhere we could.

In Korea, during the war, we also dropped loosely tied leaflets from low-flying C-47s, the two-engine cargo planes. These flights were made at night from low altitudes. We tied the leaflets with weak twine, and when the packages flew out of the planes into the slipstream, the twine broke, the packages opened, and leaflets filled the air.

On these trips, we took out the door, put it on the floor, and rode on top of it for bullet protection. We received a lot of rifle fire, but the ground soldiers never hit anybody. After we returned from one flight I was on, we counted seventeen bullet holes in our wings and fuselage. None had entered the cabin or cargo space.

We got results that showed we were doing an effective job. The foot soldiers did pick up the papers, but they knew if they were caught carrying such leaflets, they would be killed by their own military police. As we learned from those who surrendered, they usually hid the leaflets inside their shoes.

The purpose of the pillow balloon messages was to influence enemy soldiers to surrender. We printed an American flag on almost every leaflet. We illustrated how they could attach the leaflet to a stick, drop their rifles, and crawl toward the American side. Once captured, they would receive medical attention, clothing, food, and shelter. We promised that if they would surrender, we would treat them as "honorable prisoners of war." (So far as I know, we did just that.) We constantly checked the effectiveness of our leaflet messages by interrogating prisoners as to which ones had been most persuasive.

During that same time, a specially chosen group from our squadron went to France to launch pillow balloons for Radio Free Europe. The people behind the iron curtain in East Germany and other eastern bloc nations were deprived of radio news because the communists jammed the frequencies. We taught the French how to do leafleteering, and they took over our work. Our leaflets to the eastern bloc told the people in their own language that their own government was preventing them from getting the real news by jamming radio signals. We had no positive way of checking how much good the leaflets did. We could not get reactions from civilians we never saw.

➤

Some time later, I was transferred to our headquarters in Tokyo. That's where we wrote, illustrated, and printed the larger, more important leaflets that we dropped. I liked doing that kind of work. In the beginning we had to ask ourselves: What kind of messages are we going to give the communist foot soldiers? Many of them could scarcely read, so we had to keep the messages simple. We decided to rely more on pictures than on printed words.

My staff of three writers and four artists and I functioned like an advertising agency, creating new themes and ideas. Once we agreed on the picture story line, we put the messages on paper in English. Others translated the words into Korean and Chinese. Then the artists went to work.

We used test groups to ascertain the effectiveness of the messages. In the cellar of the U.S. Air Force headquarters in Tokyo, eight North Korean prisoners of war had volunteered to read and respond to our leaflets. Four were officers, four were enlisted men. They had the best of facilities, including a nice backyard where they could exercise. We gave them every amenity possible so that they would enjoy their work and do their best for us. Their single task was to provide reactions to the messages we wrote.

The enlisted men reviewed leaflets in one room, the officers in another. We would tell them the zone at which it was aimed and then ask, "What do you think of this? Does it tell a story?"

I especially recall one new piece of artwork. We had pictured a handsome, smiling soldier, wearing a distinctive UN uniform. He was on one knee and had picked up a little girl's doll. He was putting the arm back on the doll while a little girl standing next to him was crying. This picture was intended to show that UN soldiers were human, liked children, and were willing to help.

I thought it was an excellent message. I hoped that the communist soldiers would reason, "If they treat kids this way, they will treat me the same way. I had better surrender, if I want to stay alive."

When we showed this leaflet to the enlisted men, the first one snorted, letting us know it was awful. Another pretended to expectorate on the floor, which was his way of showing disapproval. The other two nodded in agreement. The officers had the same response. Through the interpreter, we asked, "Why is this so terrible?"

Their answer was, "To hell with little girls. We like little boys. And our girls don't have baby dolls anyway."

The next day we presented revised artwork. The child was now a crying boy. The doll had become a cart, and the soldier was fixing a wheel that had come off.

All the test prisoners smiled their approval. It was a good leaflet.

➤

When soldiers surrendered in the field, we gave them food, a place to bathe, and clean but used clothes to wear. Afterward, they were taken to a special tent, one man at a time, where we could question them about their response to the leaflets. The interpreter would make certain they knew they would not be harmed, no matter what they said. Then he would say, "The Allies want to stop killing your people, and you can help us. Please tell us why you surrendered."

After that, we handed each prisoner a pointer. On the wall, we had posted numbered copies of all the leaflets we had sent out within the past few months. Each man pointed to the one that had impressed him the most. We asked when he had seen it and what effect any of the other leaflets had had on him and his comrades. Through such intense interrogation, we continued to improve our messages. Eventually, we knew which ones worked best and which ones didn't work at all.

➤

The Korean War drew to an end, and by 1955, I was looking toward civilian life again. By the time I left the service, I was almost fifty years old. I wasn't sure what was next, but I had learned that not only did I like adventure—*I had to live that way.* Adventure was everywhere. I had to find it.

Nineteen

"HOW LONG WOULD IT TAKE FOR ME TO LEARN TO TRAIN DOGS GOOD ENOUGH to win the North American Championships?" Keith Bryar asked me shortly after my retirement in 1957.

"I'm not positive, but probably three years. The shortest time, I think, would be two."

Keith lived in New Hampshire and was the minister for a small church. I think he first became interested in dog sledding one Sunday afternoon when I let him drive my team. It was an interesting first lesson. The day before, I had taken the team to an island in Squam Lake and had come upon a fresh deer kill. Before turning back, I treated the dogs to a feast of venison. I forgot to tell Keith, and he started along the same trail I had used the day before. Near the island, Keith tried to take the dogs on a trail that went off to the right. But with vivid memories of the deer nearby, the dogs refused to obey. Keith grew more and more frustrated and began to curse and swear in a way that was unbecoming for a minister.

Despite this unusual introduction to the sport, Keith made it clear that he wanted to learn not just to race but to win. But he knew little about dog racing. "How much money is it going to cost?" he asked.

"A lot of money," I said. "You will have to buy experienced dogs and train them into a team. If the ones you buy don't make the team, you sell them right away and buy replacements. It will be a big undertaking."

"Will you help me? Will you be the trainer?"

"Why not?" I answered, and my helping Keith started just that simply. Teaching him provided a wonderful challenge, and I knew I would love working with dogs, even if they weren't mine.

Without knowing it, Keith Bryar rescued me from depression, and his offer gave me a new focus. I thoroughly enjoyed the new adventure. I worked with him for nothing except food and housing. To support myself, I sold products door-to-door for Niagara, which had introduced a heat-and-massage unit. I spent about half my time selling for Niagara, the other half working with Keith, helping him build a motorcycle and car racing track out in the backcountry woodland of Louden, New Hampshire, where the racing noises wouldn't disturb people.

Keith showed an absolute commitment to learning about dog sledding. Over the next two years, we bought more than two hundred dogs, all of them fine animals. We tried not to own more than thirty-five at one time. If a dog didn't work well with our other dogs, we sold it back. Usually we bought dogs with the proviso that if they didn't work out, we could bring them back. If the former owners wouldn't take them back, we found other buyers. Because Keith wanted to learn as quickly as possible, we had no time to retrain dogs. Any animals that had already developed bad habits, such as chewing harnesses or watching the scenery, were eliminated immediately.

Keith, a man of remarkable commitment and self-discipline, trained hard. The first winter we went to Alaska together we ran the entire race circuit. Every weekend for three months, we raced somewhere. We trained during the week, though never on Friday, the day before a race.

For a beginner, Keith did well the first year. He finished in the money six times and twice finished in second place. That was not enough for Keith, however; he had his eye on first place. The second year, Keith raced in Anchorage's seventy-five-mile Fur Rondy. The first day, he finished second, which carried a cash prize of $300. The second day, however, he lost a dog. The rules were that if a driver lost a dog and couldn't find it before the day was over, he was disqualified. We found it late that night, but the judges interpreted the rules so that he couldn't claim the $300. I argued vehemently, but I got nowhere.

At the big race in Fairbanks, Keith reached his goal. He won first place in the three-day event. It was only his second year of big-time racing. At the banquet that night after his win, Keith sold the sled, the dog team, the harnesses, and everything we had with us except our sleeping bags to "Mudhole" Smith, president of Cordova Airlines. He never drove a dog team again. But he did go back to his small church now that he no longer had a reason to swear.

Keith was a great guy. I had nothing but the highest respect for what he did and the way he lived. Twenty years later, when he was terminally ill with cancer, Keith asked me to come and see him. We had a lovely time together, and when he died, I grieved for a good friend.

➤

After Keith retired from dog racing, I still went regularly to Alaska, most of the time as a handler for others who paid my way. I didn't have any money, because what I earned went to Rosamond to support the family. I would work hard all spring and summer and then, in the middle of winter, I would take off to work as a handler for other New England drivers. We would transport the dogs to Alaska by truck, a five-thousand-mile trip that we did in five days. To do that kind of mileage meant driving night and day, stopping only for food, fuel, and feeding and watering the dogs. We would sleep in the truck, but didn't really get any rest until after we reached Alaska.

The dogs were dropped only twice a day to eat and drink. But they needed exercise, so once during the five-day trip, we would trot all twenty-four dogs at least twenty miles. We did this at five o'clock in the morning, just as dawn crept across the horizon.

On sharp corners, I ran up to the leaders to make sure that they stayed over on the right. At left turns, I went at least one hundred yards beyond the team to flag down any vehicles, for the middle of the team would surely be on the left, even if the leaders stayed on the right. But few vehicles came along that early, and we never had any unhappy incidents.

➤

In the winter of 1959–1960, I opened a store for Niagara products in Lawrence, outside Boston. For the next half dozen years, I operated the heat-and-massage agency. I didn't like the work too much, but it was a way to make a living. And, frankly, I didn't know what else to do. My trips to Alaska, and especially working with dogs, provided needed adventure in my life. Whenever I was away from the business, I felt alive, excited about life again. I yearned for snow work again. I wanted to keep dogs.

Slowly I weaned myself away from the Niagara heat-and-massage business. The snowmobile had become an important recreational vehicle in New

England, and it interested me. In the winter of 1966, I opened a snowmobile dealership.

Besides my trips to Alaska, I found a change of pace in an annual event on Naushon Island, off the New England coast, near Woods Hole, Massachusetts. For thirteen consecutive years, beginning in 1961, I received an invitation to the Forbes's annual deer hunt. David, a distant cousin of Malcolm Forbes, was a friend and the manager of Naushon Island, to which family members would come every summer. Each branch of the family had its own home. David invited me to a special two-day hunt at the beginning of the six-day deer season, the first week in December. Each family member who hunted could have three guests. On the island, without natural predators, the deer overgrazed. He organized the annual hunt as a way to control the deer population.

Each year the same formal invitation arrived, stating that I was to be at the boathouse on Sunday afternoon exactly at half past three with all my equipment. I would then be taken over to the island with the other guests. Guests hunted with the family member who had invited them. No one could shoot more than one deer. If someone came and didn't bag a deer, usually the Forbes host would graciously give up his kill.

All my invitations asked me to be part of the first group that hunted on Monday and Tuesday. Because I was a bow-and-arrow hunter, it gave me the advantage of hunting before the deer were spooked by gunfire. We bowhunters loved this time. When we didn't get a deer on Monday, however, we had to hunt with a gun on Tuesday. By the end of the second day, guests prepared to leave on the late afternoon boat, which in turn met the second group. Two days later, a third group arrived.

On the evening we arrived, David Forbes would give a talk after dinner. For every one of the thirteen years, the talk hardly varied. He welcomed us and laid down the rules that we would observe. They were commonsense ones, such as "You will hunt with one of us. You will wave when you see somebody else [to alert both hunters]. You will hunt only in the area that has been designated for you. Whenever you come upon another man, if you have a double-barreled shotgun, you will crack the barrel so that it can be seen. If you have a pump or an automatic, you must be careful to have the safety on. Of course, never point your gun toward anyone else or carry a loaded gun during transport."

Everyone studiously followed the rules, with one exception. Each year a retired game warden, who wore his uniform the entire time, was invited to the island. Although he didn't bother to attend David's opening talk, he seemed to revel in the invitation, as if it had somehow elevated his station in life. We usually walked to our assigned area, but the game warden hunted from a jeep and went wherever he wished. We always knew where he was from the sound of the engine.

On the first day, we heard a shot and assumed he had bagged his deer. Later we learned that he had carelessly tossed his loaded gun into the jeep. He climbed in, and the gun went off. The one professional in the group had shot himself in the foot.

➤

During that time, I had a third diversion from the business world. For years I had been friends with the polo players at the Myopia Hunt Club in Hamilton, Massachusetts. In 1957, the team captain, Neil Ayer, invited me to become the polo umpire at the club. It seemed like a fun thing to do, and I agreed. Two days later, however, I received a letter from Neil's father, Fred Ayer. He was trying to be diplomatic, but the letter sounded like a warning to me. As well as I can remember, it went something like this:

> I understand you're considering an invitation to become the polo umpire at Myopia. I have played there myself, loved the game, and I was quite pleased to hear of your consideration. But let me remind you that it is a tough job and somebody is always questioning your decisions.
>
> Quite recently in a South American tournament a decision made by the umpire was unpopular to both sides. Members of both teams and a number of the onlookers rushed at the umpire, dragged him off his horse, and killed him. I hope nothing like this happens to you.

Nice letter, I thought. My first reaction was that I had better not accept. But the more I hesitated, the sillier I felt, so I accepted the position. Also, I knew South American polo was different. Those players invested their egos in the games and bet large sums of money. At Myopia, most of the people I would work with were already friends, and they played for the sport. On the other hand, there were a few rough moments.

Once a man charged another in a fit of anger, struck him on the head with his mallet, and knocked him unconscious. The injured man was never the same again. It was terrible, but that was the worst that ever happened.

I had played polo at both Milton Academy and Harvard, but I hadn't been good at it. For one thing, I never had a first-class quarter horse. My mounts were always rough and slow. But I enjoyed the game and learned to love my responsibilities as umpire. For thirteen years, I usually worked one night and one afternoon a week, as well as every Sunday.

Although I wouldn't call my work with the Myopia Club a time of intense excitement, it was challenging, and I kept learning more about the game so that I could do a better job. I liked the players and kept up with many of them through the years, even after I moved to Alaska. I'm proud to have umpired for two world-class players who were rank beginners when they joined the team. Today one carries a nine goal handicap. (Ten is the world's highest.) The other carries an eight. They are Adam and Andrew Snow, my grandnephews. They are invited to play on teams all over the world. Polo officiating was a fun-filled part of my life that enabled me to offset the boredom and depression of ordinary living.

➤

In 1959, after I started umpiring, the Myopia polo team received an invitation to represent the United States at an international competition in Teheran, Iran. The invitation included my going as the team's trainer and coach. I was subsequently invited to be an umpire with an Iranian counterpart.

The Iranians provided us with first-class accommodations. Our hosts informed us that we were invited to a dinner given by the shah of Iran at a lavish restaurant. Donald Little, my nephew and captain of the American team, said casually, "That's great. Is there going to be any real caviar there?"

"Oh, I should think so," the Iranian host player answered. "Do you like caviar?"

"I love caviar. It is my favorite food."

At the restaurant, we waited to be ushered into the reception room for cocktails and hors d'oeuvres. Just then a waiter approached, carrying a mammoth tray loaded with caviar over ice. He set it in the middle of a large table.

"This caviar is a gift from the shah of Iran to the United States polo team," our host said. "It has come from his private stores."

As we learned later, the shah had been told that members of our team liked caviar. He was delighted to give us this gift. Every night in Iran, a large tray of caviar was served to us before dinner.

Amid much pomp and ceremony, the Iranians beat the Americans one to zero in fast-paced polo. Officiating those matches, for which each member of the team was awarded a small silver vase by the princess, was one of the great thrills of my life.

➤

Such moments as those in Iran kept me going. I found just enough adventure to convince me that there had to be more to life than I was experiencing. I didn't know how to find the adventure I craved, yet I knew it was there—somewhere—waiting for me.

For thirteen years I enjoyed small diversions—trips to Alaska, my annual hunting with the Forbes family, and my work with the polo club. By the fourteenth year, I made a drastic change in the direction of my life. I was on the road to adventure once again.

Twenty

WHY NOT DRIVE A SNOWMOBILE FROM THE ARCTIC CIRCLE TO BOSTON? THAT thought came to me while I was sitting in my office at my newly opened snowmobile dealership in Ipswich. Certainly no one had ever done it before. Wasn't that a good enough reason?

I had opened a snowmobile showroom because I liked snowmobiles—better than any other product I had ever sold. Perhaps it was the mystique of adventure I associated with them. Maybe they reminded me of the best parts of my past. Another attraction was that I enjoyed talking about snow and outdoor adventure with people who showed interest in the machines. I also enjoyed the weekly snowmobile ride I led for the members of the Northern Lights Snowmobile Club.

Why not drive a snowmobile from the Arctic Circle to Boston?

I just couldn't let go of the idea. The challenge excited me, and I began to make plans for the trip. One purpose of the trip would be to prove that snowmobiles could run on hard, bare roads, not just on snow and ice. Not only would I have fun, but I could set a world record for distance. And the publicity might do wonders for snowmobile sales.

The more I considered the idea, the more exciting it sounded, and the more convinced I was that I had to do it. I spent a lot of time planning the trip, making sure I covered every contingency. Since I would take a snowmobile I called the Yellow Bird—a Ski-Doo product—I decided to ask the manufacturer, the Bombardier Company, for gas money in exchange for advertising. I phoned my friend Jean Luc Bombardier of the Bombardier Ski-Doo Company and explained my idea.

"Yes, Norman, I like that," he said, "and our company will be delighted to sponsor you." Unfortunately, Jean took his own life a few months later, and the Bombardier Company failed to live up to the agreement. Although I understood, I was disappointed.

To make the trip, I calculated that I would need forty days off work. I planned to drive my truck to Alaska with my snowmobile inside, but I needed another person to ride with me to Alaska and then follow me in the truck back to Boston. When I came up with this idea, I asked my daughter, Jacqueline, to be the driver. She jumped at the chance and said, "Dad, I'd love to be part of this." She asked to bring along her friend Jack Wiley, a fine mechanic, who proved invaluable on the road.

Lechmere Stores agreed to pay for the gasoline. We agreed that I would start just above the Arctic Circle in Alaska, travel across Canada to Montreal, and arrive at their main store in Boston at noon on November 29, 1967, to open their winter sports display. The Boston manager was a little skeptical that I could plan my trip and make it right at noon.

"I'll make it on time," I insisted. "You just be ready for me."

Despite his reservations, he said he would arrange a brief ceremony, and then I would drive my snowmobile another two miles to Boston's convention hall to officially open the Sportsman Show by saying a few words of appreciation to Lechmere for its support.

Next, I contacted the governor of Alaska, who enthusiastically supported my idea. He had only one suggestion: He wanted me to travel every major road in Alaska. Originally, I had calculated that I would drive five thousand miles. The side trips would add seven hundred miles. "Why not?" I said. It would be fun and I would get to see most of Alaska—what a delightful opportunity. The governor asked if I would take back a personal message to the Massachusetts governor. The personal message turned out to be an invitation to the governor and citizens of Massachusetts to visit Alaska. The invitation appeared widely in Massachusetts newspapers.

For weeks before leaving, Jackie and I worked out the details. If I wanted something to drink while driving, I wouldn't stop. Instead, I would stick my arm out and motion "bottoms up," a drinking gesture. Jackie would pull alongside me, Jack would hand me the drink, then their truck would drop back into place. When I finished, she'd pull up and Jack would grab the empty cup from my hand. We agreed on hand signals for food, for gas, and for emergencies.

When I decided to do the snowmobile trip, I focused on attracting the kind of favorable publicity that would help my business. I went to the New

Hampshire department of motor vehicles and asked the director if I could have a new license plate for my Yellow Bird snowmobile.

"Yes, certainly," he said.

"I would like number one."

"Why, I can't give you number one." He laughed at my request. "Don't you know that the governor always orders one, two, and three? In fact, I gave him new plates with those numbers just yesterday."

"That's a great disappointment to me," I said. "I was really counting on number one." He listened as I explained my plan to set a snowmobile distance record.

He loved the idea and asked, "How would you like number four?"

"It's all right, sir, but four isn't going to do a thing for me."

"What do you mean?"

"Think about it. Number four license plate doesn't attract any attention. Number one would be great, because it means the first person to register, and even more, it implies political power behind it."

We talked for a few minutes, and then he said, "Say, I've got an idea. How would you like zero?"

"Yes! That's great. I'd love zero."

He made a telephone call to the prison where they stamped the plates and ordered zero for me. One week later, I had my tags on the Bird and the license in my hand.

My plans finally complete, I was ready to make the journey that would last forty days and forty nights. Just saying those words made it sound like something out of *Arabian Nights*.

➤

The three of us left Boston in mid-October 1967. Eight days later we were in Alaska and ready to start. I loved having my daughter and Jack with me.

I took off the skis and put wheels on the front of the snowmobile. With much fanfare from the local people, we left Circle, the end of the American roadway system, at midday forty days before November 29, 1967. From there it was on to Fairbanks, Anchorage, Soldotna, Kenai, Homer, Seward, and then back to Anchorage; to Palmer, Glennallen, Valdez, and back to Glennallen; to Gakona, Tok Junction, and finally to Border City. In all, I did seven hundred miles in Alaska and didn't have a bit of trouble. We passed through immigration, into Canada, and down the Alaska (Alcan) Highway.

I wasn't traveling in the fast lane, so I had plenty of time to take in the scenery. The best I could do was 35 miles per hour (the minimum, usually to cool the engine, was twenty). I completely wore out a rubber track. In those days, there were lots of unpaved, shale roads, and they were rough on the track. A new one took me the rest of the way, including 4,100 miles across Canada.

➤

I had anticipated that the Canadian police would stop my small, slow-moving machine, and I was right. About ten miles inside Canada, a royal mounted policeman on a motorcycle pulled me over. Being stopped became a daily ritual.

"Where are you going?" he asked in an angry voice.

"To Boston, Massachusetts, sir. And I'm driving this snowmobile all the way."

"Not on this road."

"Sir, I'm in the business of selling snowmobiles, and I really want to set a world record for distance in one of these new machines. If you'll give me a chance, I'll show you that I've gone to a lot of work to make this roadworthy. I've put wheels on in place of skis. I also have a license to be on this road from the director of motor vehicles in New Hampshire."

"You have?"

I showed him the license plate zero on the front. "You see, sir," I said, sounding as respectful as I knew how. "Please read the license for yourself."

"Hmm," he said. He didn't know what to do. Finally he said, "Well, if they made you a special plate, I'll let you go. But I don't want you to ride on this main highway. If you do, you're going to be stopped again and again in this province because we're strictly against snowmobiles on the highway."

"In that case, sir, would you be kind enough to tell me when you are off duty? And also, do any other mounted police come onto this highway except by call?" It was then nearly three in the afternoon.

He laughed, and I knew I had him. "Okay," he said, "you win. I go off at four o'clock. After that, nobody comes out to patrol, but they are available."

"Sir, not with your approval but with your knowledge, I plan to go over to those bushes." I pointed a hundred yards ahead. "I'll pull off the road. I'm tired anyway, so I'll sleep until four o'clock. My daughter, who is driving the truck behind me, will awaken me, and then I'll continue my drive toward Boston."

Again he laughed.

"By the way," I said, "are you a hunter?"

"Sure am."

"You want to see some good antlers?" He did, of course. I showed him a beautiful pair I had on top of the truck, and they fascinated him. We had a friendly chat, and after a few minutes, he slapped me on the shoulder and said, "Well, you'd better go to sleep for a while."

I slept until four o'clock and then started again. Since I had lost a lot of time, I drove as fast as I could. I kept at it through the rest of that day and long into the night. As a matter of fact, I drove all through many nights. We encountered less traffic, and after dark, I could see vehicles coming from a long way off. As they neared, I pulled over onto the shoulder and gave them plenty of room. When no vehicles were coming, I stayed close to the center of the road because it was a smoother ride.

I usually slept during the day and traveled at night. Jackie would drive ahead of me when everything was all right and we had little traffic. She'd buy food for me. Although Jackie and Jack ate in restaurants, I never did. While they were eating and relaxing, I was pushing on down the road.

➤

Getting stopped by the police was sometimes fun. My second encounter occurred on my third day in Canada. I stopped for gas in the late afternoon, and the attendant told me, "They hate snowmobiles in the next town." He warned me to expect the police.

By then, word of my trip preceded me. Often we saw people standing by the road, waving and cheering. I always wore a helmet and drove with my headlights on. Because snowmobiles are tiny, I couldn't stand, but I figured out how to drive with one knee on the seat and remain in an upright position. I wanted the people to be able to see me wave.

"Thanks," I told the attendant, "I think I can handle it." I was so cocky, it didn't occur to me that I couldn't talk my way out of a ticket.

I was barely inside the city limits of the next town when a farmer and his son ran up to me. The boy was carrying a small parcel in his hand. They waved, greeted me, and motioned for me to stop. When I did, they shook my hand.

"You're being nice," I said. "You must have come out just to see me go by."

"That I did." He pointed to a farmhouse one hundred yards off the highway. "I live down there." He explained that he was a hunter and a woodsman.

I thanked him for coming, and then he said, "Do you like wild meat?"

"I certainly do. I love it!"

"All right, son, give it to him," he said to the boy. His son handed me some cooked Dall's sheep wrapped in a paper towel. I thanked him and went on.

After such a nice reception, I began to wonder if the gas station attendant had misled me. As I approached what appeared to be the town's main intersection, at least twenty people were at one corner.

"Glad to see you," I yelled. "Thanks for coming out." The spectators clapped and yelled encouragement. Then I saw the lights of a police vehicle up ahead at the road crossing.

"I'll never get through this unless I run the gauntlet," I said aloud to myself. The light was red, but I figured that if I slowed up, it would change by the time I hit the intersection. That's what happened, and as soon as it turned green, I gunned the engine.

"Thanks for coming out," I called to the policeman, who had raised his hand as a signal to stop. "Nice town!" After a few more blocks, with no policeman in pursuit, I sighed in relief. I was again on the open road.

Soon darkness began to steal across the land. Twenty miles from where I had passed the policeman, I was still congratulating myself. I really put one over on those guys, I thought.

Then I saw two cars ahead. One was stopped in my lane, perpendicular to traffic. As I got closer, I realized it was two police cars, one on either side of the road. They were obviously set up for a roadblock, headlights to headlights; as I approached, they turned on their flashing lights.

When I got up to them, I stopped the snowmobile. "Say, has there been an accident?" Without waiting for an answer, I added, "I'm glad to see you fellows. I was a little lost. I'm not sure where I am. So I'm really glad to see you. Is this the way to——?" and I named the next town.

"Yeah, but you can't go there. You broke the law back there." He nodded toward the town I had just come from. "You ran past the policeman who was trying to flag you down."

"Really? You mean back there in the last town? He wanted to stop me? Is that what he was doing? I waved to him and thanked him for coming out. I thought he was just as curious as the others. So many people were lined along the road, I just thought he was being a nice man and wanted to be on hand to help control the crowd."

"He was there to stop you."

"Why would he want to stop me?"

"You're driving a snowmobile on the highway."

"Yes, I am," I said. "And it's licensed, and I'm having a wonderful time. Canada is one of the most beautiful places I've ever seen. And the people are nice, don't you think?"

I kept the conversation going, telling them about my drive from Alaska to Boston, not allowing them to interject anything negative. Finally, I mentioned my number zero license plate. "See, zero comes even before the governor's number one." I kept the conversation fast and light, but deep inside I was convinced they were going to make me get off the road.

Then he said something about having to arrest me.

"If you arrest me, what good is it going to do? What have you gained? I don't have any money, so I can't pay a fine. Then you're stuck with me. You can take my machine away because I couldn't retrieve it. But that's a pretty hard-nosed approach. Why would you want to do that anyway? I'm doing nothing but driving a licensed vehicle and obeying the rules of the road."

"You didn't stop at the red light back in town."

"I assure you, it turned green just before I reached the intersection. With a policeman there, you don't think I'd run a red light, do you?" Then I launched into a second monologue about how friendly Canadians were. I even held up the small package of meat. "See what a nice farmer gave me?"

I have no idea what all I said but I kept talking. Finally one of the policemen said, "All right," and nodded to indicate I could go on.

"Thank you for being so courteous," I said, rewarding him with a big smile and wave.

➤

Along the way, people often asked questions, and I loved talking to them. A typical question was, "How far can you go in a day?"

"Three hundred sixty-five miles is the most," I said.

That was my longest day, but no one ever asked what my shortest was. My answer would have been, "Sixty-five yards."

One day on the Alcan, I started out, drove sixty-five yards, and threw a chain, which caught in the chain-drive case. We worked on it all day, and just as night was falling, success finally smiled on us. We replaced the chain with a spare we carried.

"Let's stop," I said. "We're all exhausted."

I pushed the machine a little farther until I came to bushes that would hide it from the road. I drove it down into a thicket. With my ax I chopped a few small branches to camouflage it.

We had to drive the truck eighteen miles before we found a place to turn off and sleep. Early the next morning, I expected to find the snowmobile easily enough. But it had snowed during the night, blanketing the land with three inches of powder. Everything looked different. I couldn't recognize anything. We drove back and forth, studying the surroundings. We must have searched for a full hour.

"Can you imagine going home and saying I lost my snowmobile in the bushes?" I laughed. But inside, I was beginning to feel desperate.

Finally, we found the road where we had started the morning before and worked ahead sixty-five yards. There was the snowmobile, nicely covered. We were soon on our way.

➤

A little more than ninety miles from Montreal, Quebec, I spent the night with an old friend, a dog driver named Harry Wheeler, whose family owned the Gray Rocks Inn in St. Jovite. I learned that Montreal, in anticipation of my arrival, was sending a motorcycle policeman to meet and escort me into the city.

The escort turned out to be an older man with retirement in his eyes. He wore his dress uniform, and his chest was loaded with badges and medals. He was actually proud to be escorting an old, crazy guy like me.

Norman Vaughan's father, George Vaughan, pictured here in 1910, was a leather tanner and shoe manufacturer who invented Vaughan's Ivory Shoe Leather and made a fortune. When Norman was twelve, his father moved the family from Salem, Massachusetts, to the more rural environment of Hamilton.

Sports were a large part of Vaughan's life at Milton Academy, which he entered in 1918. He lettered in basketball, track, wrestling, and— his favorite— football.

Dressed as "Vassar Girls," Vaughan and a friend discussed strategy after challenging Maine game wardens and guides to a canoe race down the Rapid River. Vaughan's boat stayed afloat the longest, so he declared victory.

Preparations for the Byrd expedition's dog drivers were made under the tutelage of Arthur T. Walden, who had hauled freight in the Alaska gold rush. Relations between Vaughan and Walden were strained once the expedition got under way. Vaughan's lead dog was Dinny; Walden's was Chinook.

Before leaving with Admiral Byrd's Antarctic expedition in 1928, Vaughan spent a year training sled dogs and preparing equipment in the countryside around Wonalancet, New Hampshire.

Members of the Byrd expedition traveled to and from Antarctica on a tall-masted wooden sailing ship, *The City of New York*, and each voyage was an adventure in itself.

The experience of driving dog teams across the vast, unexplored wilderness of Antarctica made a lasting impression on young Norman Vaughan. He was to revisit some of the same sites sixty-five years later, in 1994.

Expedition members explored the icy blue interior of a pressure ridge in the Bay of Whales, Antarctica. The danger of falling into such a cavern impeded overland travel.

(*Above*) Geologist Larry Gould and five men—Vaughan among them—spent three months exploring the Antarctic continent. As Byrd prepared for his historic flight over the South Pole, they positioned themselves for a possible rescue. Always eager to try something new, Vaughan assisted his dogs with wind power: note the sail on his sled at the far left.

Admiral Byrd welcomed members of the geological party back to the Antarctic base camp after they had traversed more than 1,500 miles of uncharted territory. Left to right: Mike Thorne, Byrd, Larry Gould, Jack O'Brien, Norman Vaughan, and Eddie Goodale.

Accompanied by lead dog Dinny, Vaughan gave many presentations on the Byrd expedition and was greeted as a hero upon his return to the States. He soon discovered, however, that life at home couldn't match the excitement of exploring Antarctica. Outdoor sports, including this wet ride through the New England woods during the spring of 1934, were his solace.

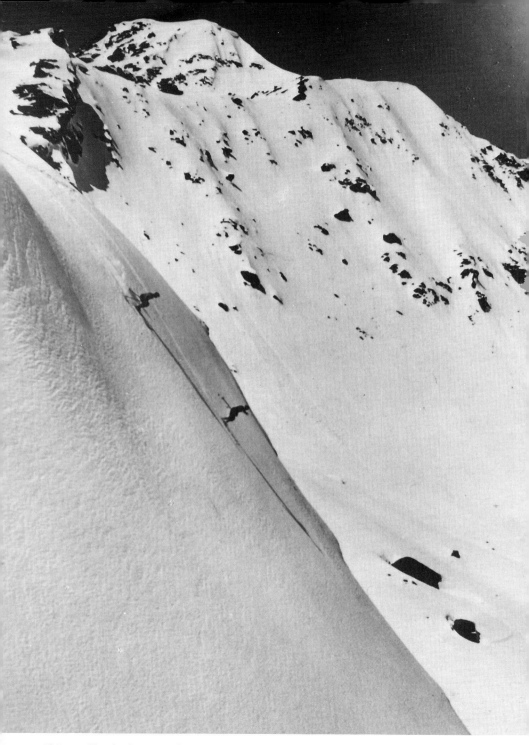

Skiing offered adventure for Vaughan after his return from Antarctica. Here, he takes the plunge down New Hampshire's Mount Washington, some 6,300 feet high. In 1936 he wrote *Ski Fever*, a how-to manual.

Shirtless, Vaughan guided an over-loaded sled across a stream during a winter camping trip with friends near Waterville Valley, New Hampshire.

In 1938, Vaughan met Rosamond Lockwood during a dog sled trip to Franconia, New Hampshire. They were married in Providence, Rhode Island, soon after. Their daughter, Jacqueline, was born in March 1940.

Vaughan volunteered for military service in the U.S. Army Air Corps in February 1942; he was accepted and commissioned a first lieutenant because of his age and Harvard education.

Vaughan trained dog teams in Presque Isle, Maine, where the search-and-rescue unit of the Army Air Corps had its largest station during the war. Nova, one of Vaughan's favorite dogs, led the team.

Vaughan, in sunglasses, inspected men preparing for a mission to find a crashed plane in the mountains of New England during wartime search-and-rescue operations.

Locating crashed planes, rescuing survivors, and transporting victims were some of Vaughan's most vivid memories of his wartime experience.

Vaughan's wartime service included taking his beloved dog teams on war bond drives; this one was in Concord, New Hampshire. His son, Gerard, born in 1935 to his first wife, Iris, perched on the vehicle at right.

Besides dogs, wartime search-and-rescue operations used horses and mules. Vaughan (center) and Captain William Shearer (left), commander of the Presque Isle station, selected mounts at a facility in Front Royal, Virginia. The outfit's C.O. is at right.

Vaughan was promoted to a major in 1942, but, he says, "In this military I.D. photo I look like one of the ten most wanted."

MAJ. N.D. VAUGHAN A.C.

0 9 1 0 8 5

(Below) The *Flying Husky* was assigned to the North Atlantic Division Air Transport Command for use on search-and-rescue missions at sea.

Vaughan dropped a dummy to test his parachute system for dogs. This "dog" crashed, and his superiors were skeptical that such a system would ever work; eventually, it did.

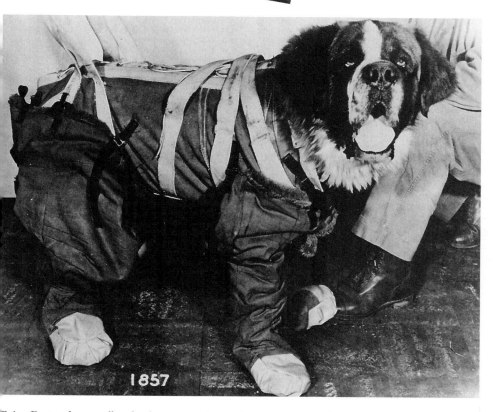

1857

Saint Bernards as well as huskies were dropped from airplanes during rescue operations. The heavier dogs could be used as pack animals.

Both men and dogs participated in training exercises at Presque Isle. "We never lost a dog or had an injury," Vaughan reports.

Dogs and men were flown in transport planes during rescue operations, then dropped by parachute to the rescue site.

On leave from his assignment as chief of search and rescue of the North Atlantic Division of Air Transport Command, Vaughan joined Rosamond, Jackie, and Jerry at their home in Manchester, New Hampshire, in 1945.

In 1945, Vaughan was awarded the Legion of Merit, presented by General A. D. Smith, for his wartime service.

Vaughan camped briefly at Le Bourget airfield in Paris while leading 17 men and 209 dogs to the Battle of the Bulge, where he hoped to transport wounded Americans by dog sled. Delays pushed back his arrival until it was too late to put his plan into effect.

Crash boats were often used in search-and-rescue operations; they also were positioned, in case of emergency, along the three routes President Roosevelt could take to the Yalta Conference in February 1945—in much the same way that Vaughan's sled dog teams supported Byrd during his flight over the South Pole.

SOLDIERS OF THE UN FORCES:
This certificate guarantees good treatment to any enemy soldier desiring to cease fighting. Take this man to your nearest officer and treat him as an honorable prisoner of war.

Douglas MacArthur
DOUGLAS MacARTHUR
General of the Army
Commander-in-Chief

七、 六、 五、 四、 三、 二、 一、

有中國的翻譯員替你要這樣要那樣。

聯軍這過住的好吃的好，還有好的醫藥優待中國的官兵。

成爲人行的副聯軍方高傲步過來不要。

把雙手過頭高舉。

在大路上堂堂正正的過來。

把你的武器毀壞或埋藏起來。

靜候機會秘密地過來。

過新的生活

快來聯軍的後方

在朝鮮的中國官兵們：

7035

During the Korean War, Vaughan wrote and printed leaflets that were dropped behind enemy lines in an attempt to persuade enemy soldiers to surrender. This one reads: "Watch closely for your next chance to escape secretly from your unit. Destroy or bury your weapons. Move out into the open and along the roads. Hold your hands high over your head. Walk—do not run—in a single column toward UN positions. Warm shelter, good food and medical treatment await you at the UN POW camp for Chinese officers and men. Chinese-speaking people are present to interpret your needs."

(Below) Vaughan received this telegram shortly after Admiral Richard E. Byrd died of heart failure on November 11, 1957. Vaughan always considered Byrd a hero; exploring Antarctica under his command was one of the happiest, most exciting experiences of his life.

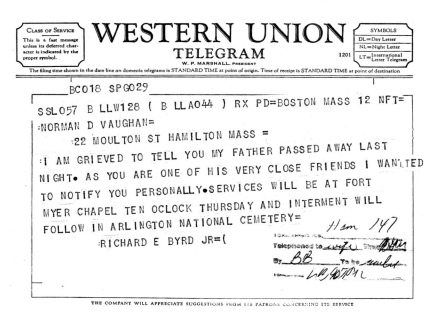

BC018 SPG029
SSL057 B LLW128 (B LLA044) RX PD=BOSTON MASS 12 NFT=
:NORMAN D VAUGHAN=
:22 MOULTON ST HAMILTON MASS =
:I AM GRIEVED TO TELL YOU MY FATHER PASSED AWAY LAST
NIGHT. AS YOU ARE ONE OF HIS VERY CLOSE FRIENDS I WANTED
TO NOTIFY YOU PERSONALLY.SERVICES WILL BE AT FORT
MYER CHAPEL TEN OCLOCK THURSDAY AND INTERMENT WILL
FOLLOW IN ARLINGTON NATIONAL CEMETERY=
:RICHARD E BYRD JR=(

After the Korean War, Vaughan kept busy training dogs, hunting, and umpiring polo matches at the Myopia Hunt Club in Hamilton, which led to a memorable trip to Teheran, where the Myopia team competed against a team from Iran.

On November 29, 1967, Vaughan arrived from the Arctic Circle to open a sportsman show in Boston after traveling 5,700 miles across Canada on a snowmobile. Mechanic Jack Wiley (left) and Jackie (right) followed in a truck.

Vaughan, wearing the same gloves he wore during the Byrd expedition, posed with Polaris, a pedigreed Siberian husky leader.

Vaughan returned to his beloved Antarctica in 1979 as part of a delegation that commemorated the fiftieth anniversary of Byrd's flight over the South Pole. It was a bittersweet experience. Vaughan (with hat in hand) stands next to Laurence Gould (holding book) at McMurdo Sound; immediately behind Gould is Senator Harry F. Byrd, the admiral's nephew. Photo courtesy of U.S. Navy

(Right) The mayor of Nome, Alaska, Leo Rasmussen, greeted Vaughan after his successful completion of the Iditarod in 1978, at age seventy-two.

(Below) Vaughan (far left) drove his dog team past the reviewing stand during Ronald Reagan's inaugural parade on January 20, 1981. Four years earlier, Vaughan and his dogs had crashed Jimmy Carter's inaugural parade. In 1981, after much discussion, he was given a formal invitation.

Pope John Paul II received a mushing lesson from Vaughan and gave the veteran driver a ride during a papal visit to Alaska in 1981.

Vaughan and Carolyn Muegge celebrate at the finish line on Front Street in Nome after the 1987 Iditarod, which they completed in twenty-four days, twenty-three hours, and forty-two minutes.

<small>PHOTO COURTESY OF THE *NOME NUGGET*</small>

Norman and Carolyn were married December 31, 1987, outside the Forks Road-house in Trapper Creek, Alaska, during a light snowfall, in front of reporters, news photographers, and hundreds of invited and uninvited guests. PHOTO BY ROB STAPLETON

Vaughan planned to melt a shaft down to a P-38 buried under an ice sheet in Greenland. The plane was part of the Lost Squadron that went down on July 15, 1942. The first attempts to salvage the planes in 1989 were unsuccessful.
PHOTO BY LOUIS A. SAPIENZA

Carolyn stands next to the gopher hole dug to reach a buried P-38 in Greenland. PHOTO BY LOUIS A. SAPIENZA

Two hundred and fifty-six feet below the surface of an ice sheet, Vaughan found the crushed fuselage of a P-38; it was too mangled to save.

The Pizzagalli Construction Company's silo unloader had dug to within a few feet of a buried P-38 when their gasoline supply ran out and the attempt had to be aborted. But in 1992, the crew returned to Greenland to recover the plane, which is being rebuilt by Roy Shoffner in Kentucky.

Photo by Louis A. Sapienza

Vaughan completed yet another Iditarod in 1990, at age eighty-four. He competed in the 1,151-mile race a total of thirteen times and made his mark as the "oldest and slowest" musher in Alaska, possibly the world.

Photo by Robyn Herling

(Below) At a stop in Skwentna during the 1990 Iditarod, Vaughan checked his dogs' paws; the booties protect the animals' pads from abrasion.

Photo courtesy of People

Fourth-graders at Fort Benning, Georgia, listened as Vaughan told about his experiences in Antarctica.

(Above) The first attempt to climb Mount Vaughan, in 1993, ended in disaster when the DC-6 that carried eight crew and expedition members from Punta Arenas, Chile, to Patriot Hills crashed six miles short of the runway.

(Right) Vaughan, at camp in Patriot Hills, prepared once again to climb his mountain in December 1994.

The successful expedition to reach the summit of Mount Vaughan included (from left in front of Norman and Carolyn) lead mountaineer Vern Tejas, nurse practitioner and mountaineer Dolly Lefever, EMT and mountaineer Ken Zafren, and survival instructor Brian Horner.
PHOTO BY BARB WILLARD

A master dog sledder but a novice mountain climber, Vaughan needed plenty of practice before attempting to climb his mountain. Team members helped him by chopping and kicking out footholds as he approached the summit.
PHOTO BY GORDON WILTSIE

Norman Vaughan reached the top of Mount Vaughan on December 16, 1994, just three days shy of his eighty-ninth birthday. "Dream big," he advised in his summit speech, "and dare to fail." PHOTO BY GORDON WILTSIE

How well the Canadians treated me. I pulled up at the town hall, parked the snowmobile on the sidewalk right in front of the steps, and Jackie and Jack parked the truck right behind me. When I alighted from the Yellow Bird, I stepped out onto a red carpet they had laid down just for me.

A crowd surrounded us, applauding, snapping pictures, and asking questions. I joked and told them about our trip. For a humorous touch, I pulled the antlers out of the truck and set them on the stone steps. The crowd really applauded then. They asked me to pose on the red carpet by the antlers and the snowmobile.

Once we had satisfied the crowd, the policeman walked proudly beside me as we entered the town hall. My escort introduced me to the mayor, who was very gracious. He didn't speak much English, but he knew what I was saying. He invited me to talk to the press. I spoke in broken French, communicating mostly with my hands. The night before, I had learned that I would be expected to give a speech, so I had composed something. The people, amused but polite, listened attentively. I thanked the mayor for the réception, then everyone drank a toast of *le vin d'honneur.* (Since I don't drink, I just put the glass to my lips.) Later, the mayor presented me with a key to the city.

Outside, the escort was ready for us. He took us three miles through the city to the bridge over the St. Lawrence River.

"My dear friend," the policeman said in heavily accented English when we reached the bridge, "unfortunately, this is as far as I can go. It has been my great pleasure to have been your escort today. You are a most welcome guest to our country."

I thanked him profusely and went across the bridge.

I had barely cleared the bridge, heading south toward Boston, when a policeman stopped me.

"What are you doing on the road with this machine?"

I was in a good mood, so I spun a few stories, telling him of the reception by the mayor, showing him the key, and then letting him see the license plate.

Instantly, he became Mr. Courteous. He even saluted me as I drove away.

I didn't get stopped again until I entered Vermont.

In forty days and forty nights, police stopped me forty-one times. It was a great adventure.

➤

When I reached Boston, I drove to the Lechmere Store. The manager stared at his watch and shook his head in disbelief. "You said you'd be here at twelve o'clock. You beat your time by ten minutes! Nice timing!" (He didn't know that I had waited for an hour on a side street.)

Quite a crowd had turned out. Of course, the Lechmere people had widely advertised the event through the local media. One newspaper ad ran a black banner that read: "See Norman Vaughan come in after 5,700 miles from Alaska in a SNOWMOBILE." After I spent twenty minutes at the Lechmere Store greeting and smiling at city officials, a police escort appeared. I drove behind four motorcycles directly to the Sportsman Show, which was at a large convention hall. The policemen led me and my snowmobile right up on the stage. I stopped, got out, and officially opened the show, just as planned.

➤

After the trip, I took the eighteen-horsepower single-cylinder Olympic model snowmobile home to Hamilton, where I had a farm. Later, thieves broke in and stole the engine. But I still have the hood of that snowmobile on which is printed the following words: "The Yellow Bird, 5,700 miles Anchorage to Boston."

Twenty-one

WHILE I WAS STILL UMPIRING POLO, I MET A WOMAN NAMED ALLISON. SHE came to a match, and we chatted afterward. From the first time we met, I liked being around her. She was an intelligent, attractive woman with reddish blonde hair, who was ten years younger than I was. We began to spend time together.

She became my partner in the snowmobile business. She handled all the clothing and accessories while I attended to the machines and their repairs. Since it was a winter business, we rented canoes in the summer for the popular Ipswich River run.

In 1972, seven years after my divorce from Rosamond, Allison and I married. Business went well, but marriage didn't. We soon realized it had been a mistake for both of us. Even as our relationship deteriorated, she still worked with me in the business. We were undeniably better business partners than marriage partners. I didn't love her and never really had. Inwardly, I knew the marriage was doomed, but I held on. Maybe I didn't want to face a third divorce. Maybe I didn't want to face my failure as a husband. No matter how much I tried to hide the truth from myself, I knew the end was coming.

Unfortunately, I was not prepared for the way it did end.

➤

Until the winter of 1971–1972, my snowmobile business in Ipswich made a good profit. By that winter I had a big inventory and offered five different snowmobiles—Bombardier Ski-Doo, Arctic Cat, Yamaha, and two now-defunct brands.

In October 1971, I sponsored an advance model show to open the winter season. On opening night alone, I sold twenty machines. The selling prices ranged from $700 to $2,000. Each buyer put down a $100 deposit, and I guaranteed delivery by December 1.

"This will give me a great start for the winter," I remember telling myself. The machines arrived from the dealers in plenty of time. Everything was right—except for one distressing reality: We had no snow. There had not been one snowfall so far that season. Consequently, I was afraid that some buyers might back out of their agreements. I prepared the vehicles for delivery anyway and then called the buyers.

"Norman, I know I put down a hundred bucks for my machine," my first customer said, "but my wife wants to go to Bermuda. If I don't go with her, I'm in trouble. I can't do both, so it means, well, I don't think I can buy the machine."

I understood and I returned his money, even though the hundred dollars formed a contract to buy.

Over the next three weeks, I heard more excuses and sad stories than I believed possible. Regardless of what they said, the truth was that New Hampshire had received no snow. No snow meant no interest in snowmobiles. Who wants to buy a recreational vehicle they can't use?

By Christmas, we still had no snow. Each day in my showroom, I wondered what to do next. I had $87,000 tied up in machines alone, and a lot of money invested in clothing and spare parts. Because of previously brisk sales, I had borrowed heavily in October. Now I owed the bank principal plus interest.

During the entire 1971–1972 season, we received no snowfall. I managed to survive—barely—thinking surely 1972–1973 would make up for it. But for the second year in a row, we had no snow.

Life was terrible. My business was facing failure, and Allison and I had decided to separate. We both acknowledged that we didn't have enough in common to stay together. Impending bankruptcy put too much pressure on what little relationship we had. The last time I saw her, our tempers flared and it was unpleasant for both of us. Even so, I made a settlement with Allison, giving her the clothing part of the business. She was a good business person and I knew she'd do well.

A few weekends later, I went out of town. Allison was still very upset with me. When I was gone, she called a friendly dealer. "If you'll come down with your trucks," she said, "I'll sell you the whole snowmobile inventory." As I learned later, she accepted a bargain-basement price, far less than the inventory was worth. The dealer came and cleaned out everything, including spare parts and the eight snowmobiles that were in for repairs.

When I returned to the store on Monday morning, I found an empty, dirty building. I was so shocked by the appearance of the showroom that I didn't cry or go on a rampage. I just went numb. The pain and the sense of betrayal were far too deep for me to express any kind of feelings. I walked around the place in a daze. I couldn't believe Allison would do such a thing. I felt worn out and shocked, and I had no idea what to do next. "What can I do? What can I do?" I asked myself again and again. I never did find out the name of the dealer, so I could do nothing to reclaim the things he had bought. Along with everything else, he had taken a vise that had belonged to my father—a memento that I hated to lose.

I didn't want to fight with Allison anymore. I didn't want to see her again. I didn't even want to be around people who knew her. The only solution, it seemed to me, was to leave Boston. But where would I go? Where do I want to live? I had barely asked the question before I knew exactly what I wanted. *I want to live in Alaska.* When friends asked me later, I told them I chose Alaska because I was a dog driver, had been there many times before, and loved everything about the place. That was all true. But in 1973, I didn't list my reasons; I just decided to move and start over. It was a time in my life I want to forget; even now I don't like to think about what happened.

I was then sixty-eight years old. Instead of living in secure retirement, I would start all over again. Frankly, that didn't bother me. In fact, I felt such twinges of excitement that I wondered what was wrong with me. I had nothing in the way of material possessions. I felt free. Alive. I was ready for a new life.

In final preparation, I packed my personal belongings inside a duffel bag. Besides underwear and toilet articles, I included a seaman's wet suit, a few winter clothes, two books, and my backpack. I strapped my snowshoes to the outside of the pack. I wore a pair of vapor-barrier Air Force boots.

I settled as many of my bills as I could by selling everything I owned, keeping enough money for a one-way plane ticket to Anchorage. On the day I left, I put on two pairs of socks and stuck a hundred dollar bill between them. Besides that, I had less than a dollar in change in my pocket. But I was ready.

I had failed in business, and that saddened me. But, because I was raised a New Englander, I don't think I would have ever gone to Alaska if I hadn't hit bottom. In reality, I had been ready to go for a long time, but I hadn't been able to admit it to myself. For the first time in years, I felt enthusiastic about what lay ahead. I faced adventure and new challenges. I was going to be with the best dog drivers in the world.

➤

When I left for Alaska, I owned no dogs—one of the few times in my life I was without canine companions. I figured to get dogs in Alaska. I had no idea where I would get the money, but I knew in my heart it would happen.

My job prospects were not good. Maybe I could become a paid handler for somebody's kennel. In the meantime, all I had was Social Security. I would have to use the small monthly checks as cash, not putting any of it away for contingencies. My first priorities were to find food to eat and a place to stay. That was all I needed to start my new life.

➤

My plane landed in Anchorage. Over the years, I had made friends there, but I decided I would not contact any of them. They would help me, I knew that. But right now I wanted to be on my own, alone. It was a time to put my loss behind me and come to terms with my new lifestyle. I couldn't do that with friends trying to make it easier for me. Consequently, I decided that I wouldn't even try to become a dog handler that year. Maybe later. To do it now would mean ingratiating myself with friends, and I had decided I wouldn't do that.

I thumbed my way from the airport into Anchorage. Thumbing soon became a way of life for me, as I loved meeting delightful, interesting people. Once I got into the city, I had to find a place to stay. I decided I'd start at the bottom and move up. I found the YMCA and told the night manager I wanted a room.

"That will be six dollars," he said.

"I don't have six dollars," I said, "but I assure you I will speak with the manager in the morning and arrange for payment."

He showed me to a room with ten double bunk beds. Except for one upper bunk, all the beds were filled. The room resembled a summer camp. Shoes were strewn across the floor, and clothes hung from the bedposts.

I climbed into the upper bunk as quietly as I could. In the lower bunk lay a very nervous man who kept rolling over and over all night. Every time he rolled over, the noise awakened me. I got little sleep that night. In the morning, I asked, "Did you sleep well?"

"Fine," he said. "I was asleep when you came in, so I'm glad you didn't wake me."

"Yeah," was all I said. I dressed and went downstairs and learned that the day manager, Mr. Graves, would arrive in twenty minutes. I went outside and walked around in the freshly fallen snow. In those twenty minutes, I figured out how to pay for my room.

When Mr. Graves came on duty, I introduced myself. "Your night manager allowed me to sleep in a bunk, even though I didn't have the money to pay for it. First, I want to thank you. Further, I want you to know that I'm prepared to go out and work to pay for my bunk."

"What kind of work will you get?"

Although I had already decided what to do, I said, "I don't know what kind or where, Mr. Graves, but I promise that I'll get money by the end of the week. Now, can you let me have a week's bunk?"

All the while I talked, he had been observing me closely. He was a large, blustery man and seemed like a nice guy. "I'll let you stay a week," he said.

I noticed a new shovel in the corner. "One thing, Mr. Graves, will you lend me your house shovel so I that can go out and shovel sidewalks?" Snow was everywhere in Anchorage.

"How about shoveling our sidewalk here?"

"I'd be happy to do that, but I looked outside just before you came in." I pointed out the window at two men shoveling. "I think they would resent a new man starting now."

Graves went to the window and looked outside. "Well, they're almost finished, so I guess that's a poor start."

"No, sir, it's a good start. One of the shovels will be free, and you can lend me the better one. Then I can go out and earn money to pay for last night's room."

He lent me the new shovel, and I left.

I hadn't had any breakfast yet, and I was hungry. I walked around, getting a feel for that part of the city. I guessed the temperature was about twenty degrees above zero. I stared at places that needed their walks shoveled, trying to make up my mind where to start. I had a sense of the kind of place I needed to try first. Finally I saw exactly what I wanted. In front of a tiny restaurant, I spotted a narrow, curving path about twenty feet long. It was beaten down, but uneven and in need of widening. On either side, the businesses had shoveled their own walks, but no one had cleared the sidewalk belonging to this little restaurant.

Inside, one man worked behind the counter. I made a quick pitch: "Hey, if I shovel your sidewalk, will you give me some eats?" I didn't say good morning or try to give him a hard-luck story. I just wanted to be a tough guy down on his luck.

"Okay—if you do a good job."

I went outside and started shoveling as rapidly as I could. From the corner of my eye, I could see him peering out every few minutes. I had counted on that. After I had done half the job, I went back inside. "I'm progressing well," I said, "but I'd like a cup of coffee before I finish."

Almost immediately I had one steaming cup of coffee in front of me. "Thanks." I couldn't remember when coffee had smelled so delicious; I paused to inhale the aroma.

"Here, have a doughnut," he said, placing a chocolate-covered one in front of me.

For the next twenty minutes, I ate a doughnut, finished two cups of coffee, and enjoyed a rest. As I got off the counter stool to prepare to go back to work, I stared at my hands. Blisters were starting to form. The best way to avoid blisters, I realized, was to wear gloves. I hated to ask for a pair of gloves, but I was desperate, so I called out, "Do you have a spare pair of gloves I can use?"

The man lent me a pair of cotton work gloves, and I went back outside and finished the job as quickly as I could.

Back inside, he gave me all the pancakes, doughnuts, and coffee I wanted. I was hungry and ate a lot. I had laid the gloves on the counter. As I got up, I pushed them toward him.

"Keep the gloves if you want to," he said.

I thanked him and said, "If it snows, I'll come back tomorrow." To my delight, it snowed heavily that afternoon.

After finishing at the restaurant, I started going to places that needed their walks shoveled. Not many people turned me down. At one restaurant, I said, "I'll shovel your walk for three meals." That way I built up credit. I used this technique to take care of my meals until spring. I didn't charge restaurants, but asked only for meals. Over time, I built up enough credit that when I finally got a full-time job, I had eighteen meals owed to me at one place.

Moving on to a nearby residential area, I walked up to a house and knocked at the door. Because the people inside saw my shovel, I had no trouble getting them to open the door. I gave them my pitch: "I'm new in Anchorage, got here yesterday, and I would like to shovel your driveway." I didn't ask to shovel the sidewalks, for they didn't use their sidewalks in the winter. They walked in the streets because sidewalks in Anchorage filled up quickly with the berm from street plows.

I estimated the amount of work and charged $3 or $4. At one place, the owner came out when I finished and said, "I watched you from inside. You worked hard, and you ought to get more than three dollars." He handed me a $5 bill.

By the end of the day, I thought, I'm on my way. I've been here twenty-four hours, started at the bottom, and already I've got money in my pocket and credit for meals for tomorrow.

If I could make it one day, I could survive through the winter. I couldn't remember when I had felt so alive and charged with life, even with puffy, tender hands.

Twenty-two

I SAW NO REAL FUTURE IN SHOVELING SNOW, SO I HAD TO FIND A FULL–TIME job. I decided that my best chance to do that was to join a union, because I learned that practically every job in Alaska revolved around unions. I joined the baker's union. For a short time I worked in a bakery as a cook's helper. Most of the time, I washed dishes, and it was boring work.

I joined every union I learned about, but I soon became discouraged. I was the last person on each list, and that meant I would be the last hired. For the rest of the winter, I picked up a couple of casual jobs, but I could find nothing permanent.

After the winter of 1973, I decided to change my tactics. I started going directly to companies to land a management job. After the fifth or sixth place, I was hired as a temporary camp manager for Mukluk Freighting Lines at Prudhoe Bay, on the north shore, where oil had been discovered. The camp manager had become ill and would be out for five months. The pay was extremely good.

This will be great, I thought. I'll be working on a pipeline that is the largest privately financed project in the world. The pipeline was needed because the time of good weather in northern Alaska is so short for transporting oil by ship. Once completed, crude oil could be pumped every day of the year from Prudhoe Bay, the northernmost point of Alaska, down to ice-free Valdez. From Valdez, the oil would be pumped into huge oil tankers for shipment to the lower forty-eight.

I managed the front desk of a camp with 128 beds. Sixty-eight were what we called "primary" beds—our best accommodations. Everyone who stayed at the camp worked on the pipeline in some capacity. The Mukluk company would send workers, and we'd provide a place for them to sleep and eat. We also took in men from other companies, but they had to pay for their beds. Most of the time, we kept 80 percent of the beds filled. Occasionally, we were at full capacity.

We also had a luxurious mess hall. They had brought in New York chefs at exorbitant salaries and given them the best supplies. It was all-you-can-eat, and the chefs offered fabulous choices, such as lobster or steak every day if the men asked for it.

I liked my work. After five months, however, the permanent person came back, and I no longer had a job. So I returned to Anchorage to the YMCA. Although I didn't like having to leave such a good job, one thing did make me glad to go back to Anchorage. I had learned that under no conditions could I keep a dog team at Prudhoe Bay. I didn't yet have any dogs, but I missed them and wanted them with me.

➤

I started job hunting again, but I had no immediate success. Then one day I got the break I was waiting for. I was thumbing back from Palmer, where I had applied for a job that I didn't get. I was down to my last 25 cents and I was freezing. A rattletrap panel truck stopped for me on my return trip, and I hopped inside. The driver had a long beard and hair down to his shoulders. Immediately I thought, uh oh, a hippie. But when he spoke, I realized he was a highly educated man. He introduced himself as Fred Janvrin, and he seemed like a pleasant fellow, maybe thirty years old.

After I told him a little about myself, he asked about the kind of work I did.

"I'm looking for work. All I've got right now is snow shoveling. I'm living at the YMCA so I have no heavy expenses."

"How old are you?"

"I'm sixty-nine."

"That's against you, isn't it?"

"Yes, but it shouldn't be. People look at a sixty-nine-year-old man as too old to work. Well, I'm not too old to work, and I want a job."

He smiled at that. "Would you take a job as a janitor?"

"Sure would, because they get good pay."

"Would you like to work for the University of Alaska?"

"I'd love that."

"Tomorrow night—if you're interested—show up at the classroom in the garage. You can have an interview." That's when I learned he was in charge of the janitorial staff at the university. Twenty-five men and women worked under him. "I hope I'll see you tomorrow night," he said as he let me out.

"You will!" I yelled as he drove off.

➤

Fred Janvrin had told me to report at ten o'clock, but I got there early. The hour seemed strange, but I soon learned that's when the janitorial staff began its work. I talked with some of the early arrivals; none of them got there more than five minutes early. They wore old work clothes. One of them said that Janvrin was fine, "but wait until you meet the real boss, Bill Krager. He's an SOB."

"But is the job good?"

"It pays good, and I like it here."

"That sounds fine to me," I said.

When Fred Janvrin arrived, he spent a few minutes giving instructions and then sent the crew on its way. He saw me, said hello, and pointed to a room. "I'll see you in there in a few minutes."

I nodded and went into the room. I felt happy just to be there. As I thought about the people I had seen in the other room, I knew I could do as good a job as they could.

Just then a door opened and in walked a man in an expensive suit. Not much older than Janvrin, he was small and wore a scowl on his face. "What are you doing here?"

"I'm waiting for an interview."

"You're not interviewing to become a janitor, are you?"

"Yes, sir."

"Well, you're too old. How old are you anyway?" When I told him, he repeated, "You're too old to do the job."

"I'm pretty strong."

He scowled again and walked out the door. No one had to tell me I had just met Krager.

As I waited, I couldn't stop thinking about Krager's words. They sure sapped my self-confidence. But I sat back and waited anyway. I had missed getting jobs before. If this didn't happen, something would turn up.

Janvrin came in and started the interview. I didn't mention Mr. Krager. After interviewing me for several minutes, he said, "Do you want to come back and try it one night next week?" It was then Friday.

"Yes, I do. I can be back Monday night."

"Good. Try it for one night and see if you can do it, or if it's what you want."

I returned on Monday and got my assignment. The first thing I learned was how to clean a toilet. I had never really cleaned toilets. Even when I lived alone, I had done only a cursory job of it. Now I was going to make my livelihood doing it. Some personal letdown, I thought, chuckling. What would my mother have said? But I took it as a challenge to be the best toilet cleaner at the university.

In the morning, at the end of my eight-hour shift, Janvrin was still around. "Norman, how did you get along?"

"Fine, just fine." I knew he had gotten a report from the man who had taught me. The man had told me I'd done a good job.

"We'll take you on," Fred said, "and pay you for tonight's work."

"Thank you." Again, I chuckled to myself. Imagine my being thankful for a chance to clean toilets. But I was. Now I had a permanent job. It was not a glamorous one, but it was certainly honorable work. To learn the job, I was assigned to help Trent, the head janitor. He was a fine, sociable man, and directly under Janvrin, who was directly under Krager. Step by step, Trent showed me how to clean a bathroom, never giving the impression that he was doing a disgusting job.

Trent also warned me about Krager, who made unannounced inspections. One of the most important places to dust, he told me, was the first place Mr. Krager inspected when he came into a bathroom. "When he thinks we're not looking, he runs his hand along the top of the partition dividing the toilets," Trent said. "If he finds dust, he knows it hasn't been cleaned." Krager didn't know Trent was aware that this was the big test. "So be careful, do a good job, and don't say anything."

"I'll be careful." From then on, all my partition tops were spotless, but I did every part of the job the best I knew how. And I didn't mind doing anything they asked, because I finally had a permanent, secure job. I had pulled myself off the bottom rung. From this lowly beginning, I soon moved up to cleaning classrooms.

By winter, I had bought an older model Ford truck. It didn't run very well, and most nights I had trouble starting it. But I didn't worry. The old

Ford was made so that I could connect an oil immersion heater and a battery plate. No matter how cold it got at night in the parking lot, I could always start the Ford the next morning after work.

One bitterly cold night, I saw a parking place near the door I entered to go to work. I thought it was a good place to park, so I plugged in my car and went in. That happened to be a night when Krager made one of his unannounced inspections. When he saw my car plugged in, he pulled the plug.

In the morning when I went to start the car, I saw that the heater had been disconnected. The battery wouldn't turn the motor over. I replugged it, but it usually took an hour and a half to heat up. In the meantime, I was upset, wondering who would be so mean. I had worked all night and was tired and hungry.

The next night at the janitors' assembly, we were told that, effective immediately, nobody could plug their car into the electrical system at the university garage. We would have to use a separate electrical system at the back of the parking lot. Naturally, this was an order from Krager.

After I heard that announcement, I said to Trent, "This morning when I went to go home, I found someone had unplugged my car."

"I know," he said. "I heard about it. That was Krager's doing. And it upsets me to think that he would do such a stupid, petty thing like that."

"Oh well," I said realizing there was nothing I could do. "I was warned about him before I got the job."

Less than a week after that incident, a strange thing happened. Krager came up to me and said that he was going away for a month. "Do you ever house-sit for anybody?"

As he probably knew, I was still living at the YMCA.

Before I had a chance to answer, he added, "I've got a husky. I've heard that you like huskies, and I'd like you to feed my dog and house-sit for the month I'm away." He didn't offer any money.

I considered it carefully, wondering why he asked me. I hated the guy, but I thought, why not? "All right," I said, "I'll do that."

In meticulous detail, he told me what I could and could not do. I could, for example, use his electrical system to keep the car warm. The following week, I moved into his house, which was not far from the university. Once ensconced in Krager's house, I began to worry about his dog. If something should happen when I wasn't around, he would blame me. I shouldn't have taken on the responsibility, I decided, because who knew what he would do if anything happened to the dog. Fortunately, the dog did fine.

When Krager came back, he thanked me. That was probably difficult for him to do.

➤

I made another career change, taking a job as manager of the university theater. It was a daytime job, and I loved the work. I was in charge of lighting. It was a big job, and sometimes I had to climb high ladders into the rafters, which was scary. After a production, I helped tear down the old sets then build new ones. The University of Alaska put on twelve shows a year, so I had to work closely with the carpenters and electricians.

One time a professional ballet company came to town. I was told that the floors had to be immaculate, so I mopped them carefully. I had become locally famous for swinging two mops at once, so that I didn't have to go over the floors twice. This time I cleaned the stage four times. One time to get the dirt off and then three more times, first with a big mop, followed by two more washings. When I finished, I put up ribbons to keep people off that floor.

The night before the first performance, the theater manager phoned and asked, "Is the stage clean?"

"Yes, it's clean."

"Is it clean enough for dancing?"

"Absolutely."

"How do you know?"

"If you'll come to the theater tomorrow morning at exactly nine o'clock, I'll show you how clean it is."

"Why then? Why can't I see it now?"

"I'd prefer to show it to you in the morning."

"I'll be there tomorrow morning at nine o'clock."

Onstage at five minutes to nine the next morning, a friend brought me freshly fried eggs, bacon, toast, and coffee from the cafeteria. I slid the eggs and bacon onto the stage floor and sat down to eat my breakfast. Just then, the stage manager walked in.

He shook his head and laughed. "Okay, I believe you. The floor *is* clean."

➤

I started to acquire dogs and didn't have to buy any of them. As soon as word got around that I wanted sled dogs, people gave their animals to me. Typically they would say, "I like him, but he's old and getting slow."

"I'll take him off your hands," I always said. "Thanks."

By then I had moved into the basement of a small house on Seventh Avenue. Boarders paid more to live in the better rooms upstairs. I cooked breakfast on a one-burner gasoline camping stove, a SVEA123. My meals were sparse with little variety. Most mornings I had eggs and bread. For a change, I would have just coffee and oatmeal. I was able to keep food refrigerated by putting it on the windowsill.

I kept dogs in the yard and eventually had sixteen. Having that many dogs was like being married to them, because my life had to revolve around their care, but I loved it. They were seldom out of my sight except when I was at work. Occasionally, I would go to dinner with friends, but that was the extent of my social life. I made small, round doghouses out of cast-off wooden reels from the electric company. The dogs could sleep on top of them when it wasn't raining.

I trained the dogs not to bark in the mornings. I would release them one at a time from their chains, and if one barked to go next, I chastised him with a short rubber hose. I didn't hit the dog, but rather struck the top of the dog's house very hard. That was enough. It took surprisingly little to train them to do what I wanted without barking. I kept them there for two years and never had a complaint.

I made a trailer for the dogs out of spare lumber. It was a flatbed with a large box on top. Inside the large box, I inserted sixteen compartments with doors opening to the outside. When it was time to leave for work in the morning, I unsnapped my dogs, and they ran to the trailer, jumped inside, and crawled into their compartments. Once the dogs were all in their boxes, I closed the doors and drove to work. In the summertime, I made certain to park in a shaded area. Before I started work, I let eight of the dogs out of the boxes, tying them to the side of the truck. I left plenty of water, then at noon I returned and put the outside dogs in and the inside dogs out.

Since I ate my supper at the university mess, I knew the chefs well, and they gave me plenty of food for the dogs. I also had a favorite restaurant downtown that would give me buckets of food for the dogs. I had a friend who also owned a dog team, and I often shared extra food with him.

I had to pick carefully through the dogs' food to make sure there were no chicken bones or toothpicks. Sometimes the restaurant threw in a surprise for me, too, usually steak or prime rib that someone hadn't eaten.

After dinner, I took the dogs to Tudor Race Track and drove them for two hours. Some nights I had to be at the university in the evenings, so I couldn't run them until after midnight. Then I would take them to a seldom-traveled road and let them run free for a few miles. Most weekends I took the dogs on overnight trips.

When I moved to Alaska, it was the first day of the rest of my life. Looking back, I now realize how many outstanding things happened to me after 1973. Life was beginning all over again.

Twenty-three

IDITAROD. THE NAME CONJURES UP SO MANY IMAGES IN MY MIND. SINCE 1974, this grueling dog sled race has begun at Anchorage and ended more than a thousand miles away at Nome. No one has completed it in less than ten days. It features twenty-six checkpoints, subzero temperatures, gale winds, and unbelievable physical demands. There are so many problems on the trail that much of the time, survival is the only concern. Of the thirteen times I have entered the Iditarod, at least half the times I encountered difficulties that could have taken my life or permanently disabled me. Once I was lost for six days without food or shelter. But I survived them all. I plan to keep on entering as long as I'm able to mush dogs. Already I have mushed dogs longer than any person I know, and I'm not ready to stop. I can boast that I'm the oldest and the slowest active dog musher in Alaska—maybe in the world.

➤

In 1974, when I was still shoveling snow in Anchorage, I talked with Joe Reddington, Sr., who is known all over Alaska as the Father of the Iditarod. A sled dog man himself, Joe wanted to give Alaskans a chance to run a long-distance race that would allow them to enjoy the challenging beauty of Alaska. The purpose of the race would be to commemorate the old mail route, but it would also serve to keep dog driving from dying out in Alaska. I got involved when I heard they were going to use snowmobiles to mark the trail. Because I'd been in the snowmobile business and loved mushing, I volunteered to help. I borrowed a snowmobile and took a week off from the university.

I was led to believe that I would be in charge of marking the trail, with the assistance of another man. We would break trail for the first leg of the race, a wooded section outside Anchorage. Our first task would be to break through the deep snow and make a trail. Then we had to cut away brush, put up flags, build bridges over brooks, and remedy anything else that made the trail dangerous.

A week before the race itself, on the first Saturday in March, I went to Knik Lake, where I was part of a contingent of five military snowmobiles under the leadership of an Army captain. I had thought I was going to be in charge, but the captain made his position clear. I said nothing to challenge him. I was there to work, not to boss.

As we prepared the trail, snowplows sometimes had to clear the snowdrifts. With my lighter snowmobile, I could mark the trail by staying higher on the snow than the heavier units. Where the brush was thick, we stopped and chopped. As we worked on the first section, other teams cleared other parts of the trail.

The captain knew how to drive a snowmobile, but he didn't know anything about sled dogs. His idea was to have the trail rush down to the bottom of a hill and then turn.

I explained, "That's fine for a snowmobile, but not for dogs. Without a gradual turn, the driver is in trouble." He listened, and I made him understand how easy it would be for sleds to turn over or perhaps hit a tree.

It was exciting to me to have a role in what has become the greatest dog race in the world. How badly I wanted to enter the race that first year. But I lacked trained dogs, a sled, equipment, and money for the entry fee. The first two years of the Iditarod, I was an avid observer. Each time I ate my heart out, longing to participate. I have to do the Iditarod, I told myself. Despite the cost, I have to find a way.

The Iditarod isn't a cheap race. The official mileage of the first Iditarod was 1,049 miles, and they set the entry fee a $1 a mile plus $200, or $1,249. In 1993, the entry fee rose to $1,449. The fee does not include many other expenses, including food for driver and animals, and booties for the dogs. The Iditarod is rough on paws. Early booties were made of mattress ticking, but today they are made of Polarfleece with Velcro fastenings. They last only fifty or sixty miles, so each driver must carry about two thousand booties.

In an article in the *Frontiersman–Iditarod 1987*, the editor made a chart of what it costs to run the Iditarod, including buying sixteen competitive dogs at a price of $30,000. The figures assumed the use of top-bred animals and first-line equipment. The total cost came to $44,169. Of course, it could be done cheaper. I've certainly never had that kind of budget. When I finally entered in 1976, I got sponsors who picked up part of the cost. But it was still not a cheap race.

No question, entering the Iditarod is expensive, but the race is about something more than money. It's about adventure, risk, and the opportunity to be on a trail with a team of dogs for three to four weeks. (I've never made it in less than twenty-one days.)

Doing the Iditarod became the same kind of compulsion that had gripped me when I read about Admiral Byrd's first expedition to Antarctica. I had no idea where I was going to get the money for the race, only that I *was* going to do it. I accumulated dogs from the animal shelter and old dogs that were too slow for other racers. I decided to get a loan for the rest, but the bank wouldn't give me that kind of loan, so I borrowed dogs that didn't make other drivers' first teams. I made up my mind that, somehow, I would enter the 1976 Iditarod.

When I wasn't at work, I was training myself and my dogs. It's such a strenuous event that nobody attempts the Iditarod without thorough training. I drove every day I could and swam whenever possible.

Most nights after dinner, I went out with a lamp attached to my helmet and drove my team on a designated racecourse that stretched around Anchorage. In those days, the course was about fifty miles long, but in recent years it has been shortened by encroaching land developments. The dogs and I averaged about twenty miles. If we got started by seven o'clock and ran until eleven, it would be midnight before I got home, fed my dogs, and settled them in for the night. Occasionally we went thirty miles, but not often. After about four hours on the course, I was ready for bed.

Word soon got out to the university workers that crazy old Norman Vaughan was going to enter the Iditarod. It amazed me how many people questioned me about it. The Iditarod was still new then, and it was a frequent subject of conversation. People would pass me in the hallways and ask, "How's your training going?" or "When does the Iditarod start?" Some said they envied me for trying the race. A few were skeptical, of course, reminding me that I was over seventy years old.

"As long as I can walk, I can drive a sled," I told them.

One of the instructors at the university, Con Bunder, built me a sled in his workshop, which saved me a lot of money. He also collected donations from other workers, keeping it a secret from me. When the sled was ready, he displayed it in the dining room for everyone to see. A beautiful piece of work, it remained on display for three weeks.

The next day, Con called out to me as I was walking along, "Hey, Norman, how about a cup of coffee with me this afternoon? I'd like to tell you about your sled."

"Sure, I'd love that," I said, relishing an opportunity to talk about dogs and racing equipment.

"Meet me at five o'clock," he said. "I'm busy until then. I'll wait for you at the back door of the cafeteria."

"I'll meet you there," I said, thinking it was a little late. Five o'clock was when people started flocking to the cafeteria for supper, but I agreed to go anyway.

At five, Con was waiting for me at the kitchen door. As we walked into the dining room, I saw that it was already filled with people. I wondered why so many were there so early.

Just then, someone held up a sign, *Norm to Nome.* ("Norm to Nome" became my personal slogan; I even keep a bumper sticker on the rear of my truck with those words on it.) Everyone started to applaud and yell, "Norman! Norman!"

I stared in amazement.

After everyone calmed down, Con said, "Norman, all of us know about your wanting to drive your dogs in the Iditarod. And we want you to know that we're all behind you."

I started to thank him, but he held up his hand. "To prove to you that we're your friends, Norman, and that we're with you, we have been collecting money on your behalf." He handed me an envelope. "Here, open it."

I tore open the envelope. It was a bank draft for $2,350!

I opened my mouth to thank them, but no words came out. Tears flooded my eyes. I had never been so touched by such an act of generosity.

The money had not come from students or wealthy individuals. It was from donations by the university's working people—janitors, carpenters, and mechanics. They were people with the romance of Alaska in their souls.

I'm not sure even today how I got through the presentation. It was a blurred mix of shock and joy. I felt honored and cared about. When I finally managed to say a few words of appreciation, I didn't speak eloquently, but I believe they understood how grateful I was for their generosity. Even today, it remains a special moment in my life.

I spent the money for clothing, more harnesses, and food for the race. And in the 1976 Iditarod, I drove that beautiful handmade sled.

➤

The preparation for the '76 Iditarod was unbelievable. It was impossible to carry three weeks of food for dogs and driver, so we had to send it ahead to be cached at checkpoints along the trail. As we raced, we picked up food at each check station.

At each checkpoint, a checker had the drivers sign in. That proved they had made it that far. The food bags were usually lined up alphabetically so that drivers could easily locate their own bags, which was especially important at night.

The Iditarod is a well-run race that gives special attention to the welfare of the dogs. In one race we had eighteen veterinarians—and not a single doctor for us humans. If dogs become sick, racers can cut them from the team without penalty at the next check station, as long as they cross the finish line with at least five dogs pulling the sled.

➤

Everything started smoothly in my first Iditarod. On the afternoon of the fifth day, when I had covered about three hundred miles, I had to cross a river of water and broken ice. In doing so, water went over the top of both bunny boots. As soon as I crossed the river, I took off my boots and poured out the water. I didn't stop to put on dry socks because I felt I had to push on. That was a serious mistake. I told myself it wasn't far to the next stop. It turned out to be ten miles, which was two hours of travel.

During those two hours, the temperature dropped rapidly. I lost feeling in my feet; both froze before I reached the next checkpoint at Fairwell Lake. It was dark so I decided to push on to the airstrip that was our overnight camp. There was a barrackslike building where we all slept. The other drivers were either eating supper or in their sleeping bags when I arrived.

I didn't want to admit to myself that I had frozen my feet. I walked into the barracks unsteadily. I felt all right except for the lack of feeling in my legs. I was afraid to move very much, so I asked a friend, "Would you feed my dogs? I don't have any feeling in my legs."

"I'd be glad to," he said.

While he was outside, I tried to take my boots off. It sounds easy enough, but it was a difficult task because I had no feeling in my feet. Someone helped me. Then I tried to take off my socks.

"Here, let me help," said a man bunked near me. After he took them off, he stared at my feet and whistled. "They're frozen."

"Yeah, I know," I said.

I felt embarrassed about having frozen feet. Just before the race, we had all listened to a lecture by Dr. William J. Mills, Jr., the world's leading expert on cold-weather injuries.

Through the kindness of other mushers, I soon had a tub of water and a thermometer. I put my feet in water that was 103 degrees. Dr. Mills had said the temperature should be 103 degrees, no more, no less, because that produced good circulation without burning the feet.

The returning circulation was very painful, but it was good to know that it was coming back. When my feet finally thawed, they ached terribly. I tried to sleep, but I kept waking up with tingling pains. In the morning, my feet really hurt, and they were covered with swollen water blisters.

I went to the checker. "It looks like I've frozen my feet. All I have to do is get the water drained from these blisters, and I can go on."

"I'm not sure that's a good idea," he said. He wanted me to get medical attention. While we talked about my feet, a pilot friend came by. He was flying to Anchorage and back the same day. He said he'd give me a ride both ways.

"Perfect," I said. I jumped on board and went to see Dr. Mills.

"These look bad to me," Dr. Mills said. And then he added the words I didn't want to hear. "I think you'd better go to the hospital."

"Can't you just drain the water?"

He shook his head. "You definitely can't get the blisters drained and still go on with the race."

Although I pleaded my case and assured him that I would be fine, Dr. Mills insisted that I drop out. He was right, of course.

With a heavy heart, I finally agreed. I arranged for someone to drive my dogs back to Anchorage and I checked into the veterans hospital, where

I spent nine days getting over the effects of frostbite. The blisters healed fine, leaving no scars, but subsequently, calcium deposits formed in my right ankle and became increasingly painful.

"When the pain gets too bad," Dr. Mills said, "you'll have to have the calcium scraped from the bone."

As I followed the progress of the race, I felt bad that I wasn't still in it. I was disappointed in myself and depressed about withdrawing from the race. "Wait until next time," I kept telling myself. "I'll make it next time."

Twenty-four

I THREW DOWN THE NEWSPAPER IN DISGUST. "THIS IS TERRIBLE. JUST UNBE-lievable." Until I spotted the article about the upcoming presidential parade, I had been enjoying my breakfast at the university cafeteria.

Jimmy Carter had been elected president in November 1976, and as usual, the inaugural parade would take place on January 20. But *Alaska was not sending a representative or a float to the inaugural parade.* Apparently, it was a simple lack of interest. "What a terrible thing," I said to those sitting nearby. "Here we have a great state. Someone should be in that parade."

"Yeah, maybe," one of my friends said.

"Too bad," said another.

"I think I'll have to take my dog team and represent Alaska," I said.

"Sure, Norman, you do that," one of them said.

"You going to call Jimmy Carter first and tell him? Or are you just going to surprise him?"

I ignored their jokes. It *was* a wild idea. But why not? I didn't ponder my decision more than a few seconds. I knew right then that I was going to drive to Washington, D.C., to represent Alaska.

After I received permission from the university to use some vacation days, I called my friend Tom Dowd. He was fifty or so, and an outdoor enthusiast. "Tom, do you want to go on a wild ride?" I asked.

"Where are we going?"

"First, I want to know if you're ready to go on a wild trip. Do you like the idea?"

"Sure, why not. What is it?"

"Take off with me and drive night and day, straight through to Washington, D.C. I want to drive my team in the inaugural parade."

The silence was eventually broken by his laughter. But he said, "Sure. What truck are you going to use?"

"I'm going to use my old truck." It was a beat-up 1953 Ford pickup. "I'll take nine dogs." At that time I had twenty-five dogs. Over the next two days, I arranged for friends to keep the other sixteen while I was gone.

University employees began to bet on whether or not I'd make it. The general feeling was that I wouldn't even reach Washington in my old truck. Others felt that even if I did manage to reach Washington, I wouldn't get into the parade.

"You think they just let anybody march in an event like that?" one of them asked me. "Why, man, the U.S. Army runs that parade. They plan those things months in advance down to the last detail. Every float has a consecutive number. No way are you going to get in."

"I'll get there, and I'll march down Constitution Avenue with representatives from the other states," I said. I had no idea how I would do it, but I never doubted that I would represent Alaska.

Tom and I left Anchorage early on the morning of January 12. We had seven days to drive five thousand miles. Both of us took sleeping bags and little else beyond the winter clothes we were wearing. We put the nine dogs inside their crates in the back of the truck. The night before, I had greased everything and filled the tank. My plan was to drive without stopping except to refuel and drop the dogs for a few minutes twice a day.

The drive through Canada was bitterly cold. Even with the heater on and my sleeping bag wrapped around me, I was never really warm until after we left Canada. We also had one problem with the truck but still managed to reach Washington the afternoon of January 18. Knowing that I had to work fast to get into that parade on the twentieth, I immediately headed for the office of Senator Ted Stevens. I assumed that since he represented the people of Alaska, and I was one of his constituents, he would be delighted to help me get into the parade. After all, wasn't I going to represent the whole state?

We parked the truck, and I left Tom with the dogs. I headed for the senator's office, got lost a couple of times, but finally found it. Unfortunately, the senator wasn't in. That was a disappointment, but I insisted, "I must see him immediately."

"I'm sorry," the receptionist said, "but I'm not sure he'll be back this afternoon. Perhaps you could talk to someone else about—"

"No," I said. "I've got to see Senator Stevens. Nobody can do what I need him to do."

"If you would just tell me what you need—"

"I have to talk to the senator and it must be today." Then I sat down. "I'll wait."

A few minutes later, two members of the staff came out and introduced themselves. One of them said, "I know you want to see him, but he's terribly busy. Even if he does come back this afternoon, I don't know if he can see you."

"I really need to see him."

"Can't we help you?"

"You can always help, but I don't think you can make the decision."

"What decision?"

"It's complicated."

"If you tell me, maybe I can help." He kept pushing for information, always pleasant, never allowing his smile to disappear. I could see he wouldn't give up and that I would never get to see the senator without going through him.

"Okay, I'm from Alaska," I said, "and I have arrived to participate in the inaugural parade."

"What?" After he got past the shock, he said, "I didn't think Alaska was going to send anybody."

"I'm here with my dog team, and I'm going to drive them in the parade to represent Alaska. Think about it. How could Alaska be represented any more graphically than by a man driving a dog team?" I knew I had his interest, and after I told him all the trouble I had gone to just to reach Washington, I added, "Wouldn't it be a shame if Alaska wasn't represented?"

"I'll do what I can for you," he said.

He left me, and I sat in a reception office and waited a good half hour. Senator Stevens did come in, and I got in to see him. Trying to be diplomatic, he said, as if I didn't know, "All of these things are done in advance. *Months* in advance."

"Yes, sir, but Alaska failed to do anything. Consequently, I took it on myself to come down and represent Alaska."

"I think it's too late—"

"Not if you intervene," I insisted.

He tried to dissuade me, but I wouldn't give up. Finally he said,

"They're having a meeting this afternoon with all the participants in the parade, explaining where they should be, what their numbers are, how to conduct themselves, what to do if their vehicles fail, how to pull out of the parade—those kinds of things. I don't see how it's possible to get you into the parade."

"I don't either, sir, but I've got to get in." Then I had one of my strange ideas. "Say, why not give me a half number? You know, something like twenty-four and a half." He just stared at me, but I pressed on. "I want to do something for my state, and I know you want to help me. I want spectators to know that Alaska is proud of itself."

"I don't know what I can do, but I'll tell you what. I'll put my staff assistant on this." If I remember correctly, her name was Julie. The senator called her in and told her why I had come. "Get this man into the parade." With those words, he laughed and winked.

"The inaugural parade?" Julie asked. "Sir, the parade is all set. At this date, there can be no changes."

"I didn't ask that. Can you get him in?"

"Sir, I don't know. But I'll try."

"Try."

She escorted me into her office and started making phone calls. No matter what she tried to do, she got nowhere. Everyone with authority had gone for the day, or she couldn't reach the person she needed. "Let's start first thing in the morning," she said.

That would give us twenty-four hours.

"I'll be back in the morning," I said. I didn't feel discouraged. Somehow she was going to pry those doors open for me.

Tom and I went over to Bolling Air Force Base to get a room. I was retired military, of course, but I didn't have my credentials. "Look, you've got to take care of me," I pleaded. "You can't put me out on the streets. I don't have any money to pay for a motel, and I've got all these dogs besides. I've got to have a place to stay tonight. Tomorrow I'm going to be working with Senator Stevens's people all day." I talked us into a room.

The next morning Julie was ready for me. She had already made a few phone calls. Then she took me from office to office all over the city. We talked to just about anyone who had anything to do with running the parade. Without exception, they all said, "No. Impossible. It can't be done."

Those words didn't faze Julie. "You can't turn this guy down. We don't have a representative from Alaska. If we had two or three floats, we could say he's too late to get in. But this man has driven more than five thousand miles just to represent Alaska. Can't you find a way?"

Julie persisted. Somebody owed her a favor. She strong-armed another person. The doors began to open. She took my advice about a half number. I became number 57½.

Late on the afternoon of January 19, the day before the parade, I returned to Bolling Air Force Base. By then I had received a letter of introduction to a high-ranking official at the base. I went to see him and explained what I was doing.

"Do you have everything you need?"

"Everything but one, and you can supply that." I didn't know if he had asked out of courtesy or sincerity, but since I had the advantage, I kept it. "I need a jeep."

"No problem—"

"And a driver for the jeep and a long piece of cable."

"You've got them," he said.

I explained to him that the way to hold dogs back and prevent them from rushing ahead is to have a motorized vehicle, an intelligent driver, and a cable.

He gave me everything I asked for.

➤

The parade started at noon on January 20. I got to the starting area about six in the morning. Officials were demanding credentials. All the others had numbers on their windshields, but I had not received any number for display.

When the officer asked for my credentials, I said, "My credentials are my dog team." I pointed to them. "I'm representing Alaska."

"But where's your sticker with the number on it?"

"I didn't get one, but I'm in the parade."

"But you don't have a number."

"I'm number fifty-seven and a half. I just got permission yesterday," I said. Again I referred to my dogs and the military vehicle behind me. "These are my credentials."

The poor man didn't know what to do, but I kept insisting. Others were behind me waiting, so he finally let me in. Once the parade started, I rode on the runners behind the sled with the cable running between my legs to the jeep. The jeep held us back. The dogs could run as hard as they wanted, but they could only move as fast as the jeep would allow.

Representatives with odd numbers lined up on the right of Constitution Avenue; even numbers started from the left. Then they fed into a single line. When I got in after number 57, I messed up the order. But I didn't slow down the parade. I heard the first announcer say, "Now comes fifty-seven and a half. It's a dog team from Alaska."

The parade went smoothly. People applauded, cheered us on, and I loved every minute of it. After the parade was over, we returned to Bolling Air Force Base, spent the night, and started back to Alaska early the next morning.

It had been a wonderful adventure. I felt good about the whole thing, no matter how crazy it sounded to everyone else.

I was already looking forward to the next inaugural parade.

Twenty-five

In 1977, I DECIDED TO ENTER THE IDITAROD AGAIN. THIS TIME I WOULD FINISH the race. I knew I would have made it in 1976 if I hadn't been stupid about my feet; I wouldn't let that happen again.

I paid my entry fee of $1,249. This time I started the race with twelve dogs, but two of them couldn't make it, and I had to drop them about 150 miles into the race.

Apart from the loss of two dogs, I was doing well. About two hundred miles into the race, I entered Ptarmigan Valley. From the previous year, I knew that the trail went down the middle of the valley and then through some woods. When I started into the valley, it was seven o'clock at night. I was in last place, but two teams were only a few miles ahead of me. I decided to push on, hoping I could catch them before I had to stop for the night. The trail was rough and covered with six-inch sastrugi. This happens when the wind sculpts the snow into what look like tiny waves. When the runners of the sled hit the sastrugi, they break right through the tops of the waves, leaving marks. Everything indicated that the previous teams had crossed this area.

I hurried on. Darkness descended at just about the time snow began to cover the trail, making it impossible to tell if the other sleds had been there. My lead dog began to wander in her search for the trail. Then, without any warning, she turned around and came straight back to the sled. I was pointing in the right direction, but she was pulling with the other dogs, and they were attempting to pull me backward. This was a "no-no" in musher language.

I got off the sled and led her around to the front. I spoke to her and tried to start her again. As soon as I walked away, she turned and followed behind me. No matter what I did, I couldn't get her to go forward. Finally, I made her lie down, and I backed away from her. As she started to get up, I'd say, "Down." She obeyed.

Once I had control, I had her get up, and then I yelled, "Hike!" To my relief, she obeyed. But now it was too late; she had completely lost the trail. Although it was dark, I could see that we were between two mountain ridges. I knew the course ran between them, but where was the trail? The valley stretched five miles from side to side, so there was no way of knowing. There were no trail markers. I decided to do the only sensible thing and stop for the night. Although it meant spending the night without shelter, I wasn't worried. Surely we could find the trail in the morning. I fed the dogs and then ate and went to sleep. I was carrying only enough food for one day, and I ate all except a chocolate bar. I didn't carry a tent, believing that lying in my sleeping bag in the lee of the sled would be enough.

At daybreak, I decided to try to pick up the trail at one of the five passes that I could see. I went up the first one until I was staring at an ice wall and knew I'd made the wrong choice. I had spent all day in that first valley. The second day, I chose the next pass—same end. The rides back down to the valley floor were indescribable. It was icy and my brakes couldn't stop the loaded sled. At sudden stops, we piled into rocks or clumps of willows and aspens. Sometimes I was dumped from the sled and the dogs dragged me alongside. By the end of the descent, I was worn out. We slept in the valley and were warm enough, but the dogs had nothing to eat or drink except snow. I ate my chocolate bar.

The next day, I decided we would try the third pass. Several hours later I hit another dead end. I was surprised that nobody had come to search for us. I kept expecting to hear planes or see snowmobiles.

The fourth day, I started up the valley toward the next pass, but I ran into alder bushes that had been weighted down by snow. As we went through the bushes, they snapped back at us, frightening the dogs. Terrified, they began to scramble. They tried to turn around, but we had to keep going forward. Pulling the sled was just awful. We were in there four hours before I could get us out. Four slow, torturous hours that sapped our strength.

By then it was late afternoon of the fourth day. The dogs and I were ravenous. We stopped and bedded down. I woke up in the morning and said, "This is serious. I can't go back over those alders." I decided to feed the dogs the only thing I had—the harnesses of the two dogs I had dropped. Dogs will eat harnesses when they're hungry enough, so I cut them up and divided the pieces among them.

During the next night, however, they started to eat the other harnesses. In the morning, I realized I had only five harnesses left for ten dogs. The next night I put the remaining harnesses under my sleeping bag.

About noon of the fifth day, I began to feel quite chilled. No wind had come up, and for a moment I couldn't understand what was happening. Then I knew: *hypothermia*. This was the first stage. My only chance of survival was to get into my sleeping bag. I did, and by five o'clock, with dusk approaching, I realized that the chill was gone. Still, I continued to lie there. I couldn't sleep, but I rested and saved my strength. The dogs were tired and hungry and stayed curled up. I'm not going to give up, I vowed to myself. Somehow I'm going to survive this. I don't know how strongly I believed my words, but I couldn't allow myself to think about giving up.

On the sixth day, I decided that if help didn't arrive by the next day, I would kill the smallest dog and use her to feed the others. As distasteful as it sounds, I would drink the dog's blood to sustain myself.

But at late dusk on the sixth day, I saw something moving. Far in the distance, I could barely make out an intermittent glow. The image wasn't clear, and I wondered if I was imagining someone coming to rescue me. I now knew I was in a serious predicament. Straining to see, I finally made out the headlights of snowmobiles. They weren't coming in my direction, but they were searching between the two ranges. I got out of my bag and waited. I saw them turn. Apparently they found my trail. Not more than fifteen minutes later, the first snowmobile pulled up. A man hopped out and yelled, "Are you all right? We've brought you something to eat." It was my friends Gene Lenard and Frank Harvey.

"I appreciate the offer," I said, "but all I want right now is coffee. Drink is what I need. If you give me food, I'll only vomit. Will you spend the night or go back? How far is it?"

"Thirty-five miles."

They gave me coffee, and I've never enjoyed it as much as I did then. The dogs were whimpering, but my rescuers didn't have anything for them. They would have to wait until we reached camp. They would make it, but it saddened me that they had been without food for so long and would have to run another thirty-five miles.

They tied my sled to the back of Gene's snowmobile. I stood on the runners, balancing the sled to keep it from tipping over. On the down-grades I had to stop it from plowing into the snowmobile. My dogs were tied to Frank's snowmobile, but they kept getting unhitched.

Frank's snowmobile caught up with us at a hunter's tent in the middle of the Ptarmigan Valley. He had started with ten dogs, but now he had only eight on line. Two had gotten off without his knowing it. I should have put the dogs in front of me so I could watch. Instead, we went on as we were, and I worried about the dogs the whole way back.

Another worry demanded my attention. I had to stay upright and not tip over. If I flipped, my driver wouldn't even know it. We hit many icy areas where we skidded wildly. By sheer force of will, I managed to con-centrate and lean in the proper direction so that I didn't tip over. We finally reached camp, and wearily I got off the back of the sled. Right behind us was the second snowmobile.

To my dismay, I counted only five dogs with him. He had lost half of them. Frank was not a dog man, so he didn't realize that the dogs needed to be checked constantly. He had gone too fast for the poor dogs. Five dogs lost! My heart sank. I knew they had to be suffering. I couldn't do anything in the dark and the cold. I decided to spend the night and search for them in the morning. Though I was very upset, I couldn't do any-thing. After all, these men had just saved my life. Besides, I was too worn out to express my feelings.

A woman in the guides' camp where I was taken gave me all the soup I wanted. She kept it hot by leaving it on the edge of the stove. Before she left me, she said, "If you want more, it's there and warm. I've also left some bread."

I thanked her, but all I wanted was sleep. As tired as I was, though, I had trouble sleeping, thinking of my dogs out in the cold.

Shortly before dawn, I got up and ate a slice of bread and a little more soup. I felt stronger. Later that morning, I was able to eat a good breakfast. Gene and Frank came in to eat, too.

Gene, the head snowmobile driver, asked, "What are you going to do?"

"We've got to find my five dogs," I said firmly.

"I can't help you there. I've got to drive to headquarters and tell them you're found. Frank can stay, though."

"All right," I said, "go on ahead and tell them you brought me in and that I'm all right. I'm staying here because I've got to find those five missing dogs."

After Gene left, Frank took me back out on the trail. We stopped at the hunter's tent again. The door flaps had been badly ripped, and we found one of the dogs inside. He had knocked all the cans off the shelf. Because the food was frozen, it wouldn't come out. Being thwarted biting through one can didn't deter the dog from trying another, and then another. All the cans had been bitten into and paper labels were everywhere. It looked like a wolverine had crashed the supplies.

"I'd better clean this up," I said. I did the best I could. Afterward, I held the dog in my arms on the sled behind the snowmobile, and we started to search for the other four missing dogs. We didn't find any others that day, and I was heartbroken. We went back to camp. The next day we returned to the tent, hoping the others had come, too. None had. Then we went farther down the trail and found two more dogs. They were both sick, weak, and worn out—but alive. On the third day we found one more. That left only one dog out there alone.

Altogether, Frank and I searched for five days. On the fifth day, I was ready to give up when we found the last dog. He lay on the side of the trail, whimpering. He had gotten so hungry, he attacked a porcupine. The quills stuck out all over his face and mouth. It had to have been a horrible experience, because the dog couldn't help himself afterward. I opened his mouth and forced water down. There is no easy way to take quills out of a dog, and especially on a trail with no tools. Because we couldn't do anything for him out there, I held his limp body in my arms and soothed him as I rode the sled. He passed out, and I was afraid he would die before I could do anything for him.

When we arrived at camp, the woman gave me a pair of scissors. I cut the quill tips, which released the gas in each one. Then I could pull them out more freely. The agony that dog suffered was unbelievable. I pulled out 102 quills, which I carefully counted. Fifteen days later, the vet found two more inside his throat. It was a slow process, but eventually, the dog started to recover.

Finally, we were ready to go home. I had not completed the race, but I was alive. So were my dogs. I will always be grateful to Gene and Frank.

"Next year," I said to my friends.

In 1978, I entered the Iditarod for the third time. This time I did it! I completed the race. It was a slow time—twenty-one days, twenty hours, and sixteen minutes—but I did finish.

➤

Although I've called myself the oldest and slowest, I've never officially finished last in the Iditarod. They give a red lantern to the last person to reach Nome (the idea being that, because you're last, you need a lantern to find your way home). I've been in thirteen Iditarods and completed six, but I never finished last. What usually happens is that the next-to-last racer wants the red lantern and asks me to pass him. I've always given the red lantern to anyone who asked for it. After all, I've had my share in other races.

Fifty-four racers finished the 1984 Iditarod, and I was one of them. When we were 115 miles from Nome and it looked as if we would all finish, I asked the three other slow mushers, Scott, Ralph, and Norm, "Do any of you want the red lantern?"

That year some company had put up a one-time $500 prize to the person who came in last. The four of us discussed this dubious honor and agreed that Scott should get the red lantern. He had worked so hard. We planned our strategy accordingly.

The next morning, I dressed and started first. It was before dawn, with only the moon for light. I was on the trail maybe an hour before the others. I was sure the trail would leave the river and turn left, as it did the year before, but it didn't leave the river. That confused me, but then I thought, they've got a new trail here and nobody told me. I followed the trail markers for ten miles. By then dawn was long past, and the sun was shining.

I saw markers and defecation, so I was sure I was on the trail. Yet a voice inside my head kept trying to get my attention. Something wasn't right, it said. Then in a flash it came to me. *I wasn't seeing sled tracks.* When I looked carefully and saw pieces of bark, all doubt evaporated. I was on a woodcutters' trail, not the Iditarod trail. When I had started to follow the markers in the dark, I hadn't been able to tell color. I was stunned to realize that I would have to mush ten miles back just to rejoin the right trail. I would be twenty miles behind the other tail-enders.

Meanwhile, the other three men traveled past me on the right trail. At noon, they stopped at an emergency shelter to eat. They saw a trapper there and asked, "Do you know Norman Vaughan? Did you see him go through this morning?"

He shook his head. "No, I didn't see him. And I know him. He sure hasn't passed by here."

They stared at each other, and all three men came to the same conclusion. One man finally said it. "Vaughan has hidden somewhere. He's going to come in last and get the $500."

By now I was closing on them. I knew they would stop somewhere to camp, so I decided to keep on going until I caught up with them.

I pulled in about an hour after they stopped for the night. I won't try to describe the language they used in their greeting, but it was loud and very colorful. Exhausted, I wanted only food and rest. It hadn't even occurred to me that they would think I was cheating.

Tired of their comments, I said, "I got on the wrong trail. Just that simple."

"Oh, sure you did."

"Just listen." Once I explained, they all acknowledged that they had seen the woodcutters' markers, but it had been light then, and they hadn't lost their way. I think they apologized, but I was too tired to care.

The next morning, we all went into Nome. Scott won his red lantern.

Twenty-six

By early 1978, my work at the university theater was coming to an end, but I didn't know it. In fact, I had never been so busy. I enjoyed the work, and my coworkers even elected me president of the staff association.

Alaska is heavily unionized, but workers at the university were not in a union. We believed we were not always treated fairly, and we knew we had no bargaining power, so joining a union became a constant topic of conversation—and often of argument. A movement began to join the Teamsters' Union. Although a popular idea, some employees strongly opposed it. When they elected me president of the staff association, I made it clear that I wanted what was best for the workers. Knowing that Krager was on the other side, I committed us to joining the union, which we eventually did. The polarization increased.

I found myself in a difficult position, but for many of us, joining the union was simply our way of demanding fair treatment from Krager. I started to release statements in the university paper to the workers, under my own name, criticizing Krager. Over a period of months, the articles grew bolder. One article began, "Krager must go." Though it was a forceful statement, I didn't feel angry. I simply believed that the man didn't know how to work with people and that as long as he stayed at the university, nothing would get better for the employees.

Many congratulated me for having the courage to speak up and use my own name. But I also had my share of opposition. After that article, some people wouldn't even say hello. It saddened me, but I didn't back down. Regardless of the opposition, I did what I believed was right. Fortunately, I had more followers than detractors, and I was reelected. That mandate convinced me I was doing the right thing for the staff.

Then Krager took action. In the spring of 1978, when it was time for contract renewals, he sent me a letter. By then I had been at the university four and half years. He stated that because of my age, seventy-two, I would not be offered a contract. Although he didn't say it, it was clear that I was going to be fired. So I made the only reasonable move: I stopped work, accepted a termination bonus of a few hundred dollars, and retired.

Then it dawned on me what a mistake Krager had made. The law said he couldn't terminate me because of my age. "Why, that's age discrimination!" I shouted. "That's against the law." I went to the Department of Labor and complained that my civil rights had been violated. I brought along my high efficiency reports, but Krager's letter was my strongest piece of ammunition.

It took a long time, but eventually the case went to court and I won. I received a whole year's back pay, about $18,000 plus benefits. After the court's verdict, I went back to work at the university—but only for a month. I just wanted to prove that Krager was wrong. Eventually Krager was fired, but it wasn't because of me. As I understand it, the university had received so many complaints about the way he treated people, he was finally terminated. Fred Janvrin succeeded him.

One of the major reasons I quit after one month is because I received an invitation to go to the South Pole. The year 1979 was the fiftieth anniversary of Admiral Byrd's historic flight over the South Pole. The truth is, the idea of a celebration started with me. Despite that, I had to fight for an invitation.

Two years earlier, I had written to my two senators, the United States Air Force, and the National Science Foundation. I proposed a half-century celebration of Byrd's flight and insisted that it should take place at the South Pole. Naturally, I didn't say, "And I want you to invite me," but I implied it by volunteering to organize a group to go. I added that I looked to the Air Force to take us because they regularly transported scientists and supplies to the Antarctic.

I sent a copy of the letter to my son, Jerry, who was then a lieutenant colonel in the Air Force. His responsibility was to assign Air Force transports to emergency jobs around the world. For example, he was the one who assigned Air Force personnel to pick up the 915 suicides in Jonestown, Guyana.

Jerry passed the letter to the general of his base. "My father is hoping to go back to the South Pole to celebrate the fiftieth anniversary of the 1929 flight." Without directly saying it, he implied, that he would love to go, too.

The following week, Jerry attended a party where the general was present. He said, "Jerry, that was a great letter you sent me the other day— the one written by your father. I fully believe we need to honor that event. If it does come about, I would like to see you go."

In 1977, two years before the anniversary, Jerry began to set up the air schedule for the event. By 1978, the idea had taken such hold that going to the Antarctic to celebrate Admiral Byrd's flight had drawn congressional interest.

One day in 1978, an irritated Jerry phoned. "Dad, I just got the list of people going to the Pole. I'm sorry, but your name is not on the list."

"What do you mean, not on the list?" I stormed back. "It was my idea."

"Sorry, but I've just gotten the official list." He read the names of the dignitaries. Larry Gould was the only name on the list from the original expedition.

I couldn't believe it at first, thinking there had to be a mistake. It had been my idea. I felt rejected and hurt. Then I felt angry. If anyone had a right to make the trip, it was me. In 1979, only six of us who wintered those fourteen months on the ice were still alive. My lifelong friend, Eddie Goodale, was in a nursing home with Alzheimer's disease. Naturally, he couldn't go. Three others were physically unable to make the trip. My good friend, mentor, and the second-in-command of the historic expedition, Larry Gould, was rightfully on the list. I decided I would fight this until they added my name.

I thanked Jerry for telling me and asked him to send me a copy of the list, which he did. Then I went to work. I had a year to add my name. First, I contacted my senators, one of whom wrote back and said, "The whole party should not go if you don't go." His letter encouraged me, but it was not enough.

When I called the National Science Foundation, the person I spoke to said, "We understand, but Larry Gould can represent you and all the other members of the expedition at this celebration."

"Nobody can represent me!" I said, anger filling my voice. "I am myself, and I stand on my own feet. *And I want on that list.*"

"I'm sorry, sir, but there's nothing—"

"Sorry is not enough." I wondered how many times I'd heard a bureaucrat say, "I'm sorry." But it wasn't going to stop me. The more the doors slammed in my face, the more forcefully I pursued the matter. For months, I lived between anger and frustration, but it never occurred to me to give up. I knew that if I kept pounding, someone would finally open the right door.

For the next six months, I phoned or wrote to everyone I knew who might have any authority or influence. Larry Gould announced that he wouldn't accept his invitation unless I was invited. Shortly after that, I received a formal invitation from Congress.

➤

When I boarded the military plane in California, my greatest hope was fulfilled. My son, Jerry, was commander of the aircraft. He flew Larry and me from a tiny base on the California coast, across the Pacific, and on to the Antarctic. We didn't travel with the members of Congress, who arrived at Christchurch, New Zealand, directly from Washington a day later. Although others were on the plane going to Antarctica, Larry and I were the only Byrd Expedition members connected with the fifty-year celebration. I was especially pleased that Larry and Jerry could spend time getting to know each other. Larry Gould was a powerful influence in my life. I had long revered him—and still do. In fact, when my son was born, I had named him Gerard *Gould* Vaughan.

➤

After we landed, someone escorted Larry and me to the visitors' quarters. We were getting the VIP treatment. A worker carried my bag to a room with a window and two beds, both of them made up with Army blankets, sheets, and a pillow.

"Are all the rooms like this?"

"Yes, sir, they are."

Fifty years had made for a lot of changes. I hadn't thought much about what Antarctica would look like in 1979. I had naively brought my sleeping bag. I was dismayed to think how the rough-and-tough life of Antarctica in 1928 was now reduced to sheets and pillowcases. Maybe I was just disappointed. Maybe I was so caught up in reliving 1928–1930 that I didn't want to admit that the modern world had touched even Antarctica. I was so upset that I wouldn't sleep in the bed. I threw my sleeping bag on the floor between the beds. It felt good to feel a touch of the old Antarctica.

I did, however, use the bathroom and shower.

The first few hours at McMurdo Sound were a strange time for me. I felt resentment toward the other people who were now there. I kept remembering the day we had landed on the ice—just one shipload of forty-two men, facing fourteen months in a barren land. Our settlement at Little America had long ago floated out to sea on a piece of ice that broke off and became an iceberg. All around me were signs of the new Antarctica. People seemed to be everywhere. I kept thinking they had no right to be there. After all, we came first and charted this unknown land. Now thousands had come. And they had brought along many of the comforts of modern civilization. It wasn't logical thinking, but it was the way I felt.

A terrible sadness came over me. As I sat on the bed, the names of those men I had lived with fifty years earlier flashed through my mind. Freddie Crockett . . . my nemesis Arthur Walden . . . Jack O'Brien . . . Mike Thorne . . . the admiral himself. Now they were gone. Only Larry Gould, Eddie Goodale, three other men, and I were still alive. For a few minutes, I wished I had not returned. After a little quiet time with my memories, I began to feel better. Of course, Antarctica had changed. But in my memories, I hadn't allowed it to happen.

"The past is past," I said to myself. "It's now 1979." But the sadness lingered, so powerful were those images. Larry called me for dinner, and I tried to forget that he was eighty-four years old. We were introduced to several people who were working in Antarctica. Larry amazed me as he spoke glowingly of them and their wonderful accomplishments. There was a mechanical shovel, and a nuclear plant—although the United States and other nations had agreed not to use it.

Eventually, I became so absorbed in their achievements that the pain and sadness drained from me.

➤

On November 28, the day before the anniversary, we were given a tour of what was left of Sir Robert Falcon Scott's base. In 1911, after reaching the South Pole, Scott and his men died only eleven miles from One Ton Depot, where they had a cache of food and supplies. Had they reached their supplies at One Ton Depot, they could have made it all the way back to their base camp. Just standing on that historic spot brought back memories of our own time on the ice. A nostalgic wave swept over me, but this time I brushed it aside. Yes, I remembered things vividly, but now I was ready to leave the past behind.

The following morning, I prepared to leave for the South Pole. Larry Gould didn't feel well, however, and thought he should stay at McMurdo Sound. I was disappointed. I had wanted so much to share that moment with him.

We boarded a large ski-equipped aircraft that was to take us 850 miles into the interior. By then, the senators and dignitaries had arrived. Among them was Senator Harry Byrd from Virginia, a nephew of Admiral Richard Byrd. In 1929, Larry and I had trudged south with our dogs, turning back just 273 miles short of the Pole. I smiled to myself as I realized that fifty years later, I would finally reach the South Pole.

We landed, deplaned, and walked toward a dome-shaped, underground building. The sign outside read:

Geographic South Pole
Average Mean Temperature Minus 56° F
Altitude 9,181 feet
Ice thickness over 9,000 feet

➤

Commander Breyer, grandnephew of Admiral Byrd and the host for the day, stood next to me when I read the sign. I smiled. Fifty years earlier I had wanted to reach this very spot. Now I had an idea how to mark this special occasion. "Take my watch," I said as I removed it from my wrist. Commander Breyer looked at me strangely. I said, "Now time me."

I dropped into a sprinter's crouch. He smiled in understanding and called, "On your mark! Get set! Go!"

I circled the Pole. "Stop!" I yelled. "How long did it take me?"

"Seven and a half seconds."

"I now declare myself the fastest man in the world." He laughed.

Word got out about my historic run. It has now become common-place for visitors to "run around the world." I'm sure that by now my record has been broken.

➤

The anniversary ceremony was quite simple and, to me, unimpressive. It lasted only minutes. Maybe I expected something more—a little more praise and commendation for Byrd. Nobody got excited, nobody said any-thing special. The stilted words didn't seem to give the admiral his due for everything he had accomplished.

Since I was the only one there from the first expedition, they turned to me to say something. I was brief. I complimented Admiral Byrd for leading our expedition, and four more, without a loss of life. I said that Byrd never asked anyone to do anything he wouldn't do himself. I told them that Byrd had been my hero, and a man I deeply loved.

Before we left the South Pole, I borrowed four buckets, filled them with snow, and melted the contents. I put the water into bottles and brought them back with me. I still have them, and I like to look at them and think that I brought a piece of the South Pole back to Alaska with me.

➤

After we were airborne on our way back to the base at McMurdo Sound, the pilot asked me, "Have you ever seen Mount Vaughan?" He referred to the mountain Admiral Byrd had named after me. Actually, he had named three mountains for the Three Musketeers, as they called us: Freddie Crockett, Eddie Goodale, and me.

"Yes and no," I said. "In 1929, when I was with the dog teams, I saw all the mountains. But specifically to know that I was looking at Mount Vaughan, the answer is negative."

"How would you like to see it today?"

"I'd love to see it," I said. "I can't think of anything that would make a more memorable ending to this trip than to actually look down on Mount Vaughan."

"Then you'll see it today."

He had to navigate only a little out of the way. We saw the mountain range. But just before we got to Mount Vaughan, clouds moved in, ob-scuring our view. I didn't get to see the mountain after all. Naturally, I was disappointed, but I thanked the pilot for trying.

Larry Gould was feeling all right when we got back to McMurdo Sound. I told him everything that had happened. He chuckled at my story about running around the Pole. "You still haven't changed," he said.

That evening we gathered around the statue of Richard E. Byrd that is erected at McMurdo Sound. It was a good group, with lots of talk, and Larry and I filled it with amusing stories about Byrd and about the expedition. Then Larry gave a good, long speech. They asked me to talk, but following Larry Gould is tough, so I made my remarks brief. Emotionally, though, the celebration at McMurdo Sound was the highlight of the trip.

As I flew home, I thought, Admiral Byrd would have appreciated our celebration of his work. Yes, he would have liked it very much. I was glad that I had persisted in getting an invitation.

Twenty-seven

IN NOVEMBER 1980, RONALD REAGAN WAS ELECTED PRESIDENT. HIS INAU-
gural parade was due to be held on January 20, 1981. By then the Iditarod
had become an international event, and this time the Iditarod committee
had been asked to select three people to represent Alaska in the inaugural
parade. I was not one of those chosen.

I didn't like their decision, and I raised hell about it. "I went on my
own for the last inauguration. You wouldn't even have thought of sending
dog sled teams if I hadn't done it first. I'm ready to go, and I feel that I
should be invited to go a second time."

"You didn't win the Iditarod," one of the committee members said.
"We want to send our fastest people, not the slowest ones."

"What difference does it make that I didn't win the Iditarod? When
no one in Alaska had any interest in the last inaugural parade, I went on
my own and got Alaska represented. I came up with the idea of using dog
sleds, didn't I? Now you want to go with my idea and ignore me. Do you
want me to crash the parade again?"

They reconsidered their decision. As a result, I became a member of
the trio from Alaska. I joined Joe Reddington, Sr., and a delightful fellow
named Herbie Nyukpuk, an Eskimo from Shishmaref.

The Iditarod committee paid for my transportation and gave me a per
diem, which I appreciated. They didn't provide housing, so I would stay
with the Wheelwrights, old friends in Washington.

Four days before the parade, we flew commercially on Federal Express
with our dogs. Each of us had decided to take nine dogs. The people at
Federal Express treated us as if we were royalty. Even though it was a cargo

plane with only basket lunches, they made us feel as if they couldn't do enough for us.

We landed at the Federal Express terminal many miles from Washington, D.C., where a truck awaited us. They transported us and the dogs to a farm about sixty miles from the capital where our dogs would stay until we left. The first night we put our dogs in the farmer's field, not far from the house. The farmer and his wife could hear the dogs from the house, but because of a grove of trees, they couldn't see them. Only later did we realize this was a serious mistake.

At the farm, we lined up the dogs and staked them on picket lines. Curious neighbors for miles around started coming by. They had heard about the dogs, and most had never seen real huskies before. One of the visitors was a young fellow about seventeen, with his arm in a sling. He was friendly and talkative. He spent a few minutes with Joe, then with Herbie and me, all the time asking questions. Later, I particularly remembered that he asked each of us, "Which one is your leader?" It didn't seem unusual at the time.

My leader, Joee (named after Joe Reddington's son), was at the end of my line. Joe had named his leader Feets, and he and his dogs occupied the middle of the section. Herbie's leader, Candy, was on the end of his line.

After most of the visitors had gone, we fed and watered the dogs, and they settled down. We assumed everything was all right. Subsequently, Joe, Herbie, and I went to dinner. When we left, the young man with his arm in a sling was still around. About that time, several of his friends showed up. Because he now knew so much, he became the man of the hour. He took pride in pointing out the three leaders. He had accumulated a wide variety of knowledge, including the approximate value of the animals, and freely shared this information. The other boys asked many questions, and then they left. The young man went home, too.

We checked on the dogs after dinner. They had bedded down for the night. I went to the Wheelwrights'; Joe and Herbie stayed with other friends.

Long after the farmer had gone to bed, a thunderous commotion in the yard awakened him and his wife. The dogs barked and wouldn't stop. The farmer went to the window and saw three people in a pickup truck stopped outside the fence that enclosed the dogs. He yelled at them through the window and then raced out of the house toward them. Before he could reach the dogs, the truck had driven away.

Just one look told the farmer the reason for the noise. Three dogs were missing. Just outside the fence was a farm wagon loaded with dog food. It was obvious that the people who took the dogs had also stolen a large case of canned food and a bag of dry food.

The farmer and his wife didn't know what to do next, so they called us at the Wheelwrights'. I talked to them and then called the others. We had to figure out what to do about our missing dogs. By then, we had learned that the thieves had taken the three leaders.

We called Al Crane, the man assigned to see that we got everything we needed for the parade. He came over to the Wheelwrights', and we talked until daybreak, trying to figure out what to do. Al Crane had a good idea. "If we keep the theft to ourselves and don't tell anybody, we're not going to find the dogs. We can't try to chase them tonight because it's too late. We've got to tell the police these dogs are stolen."

The more we discussed his idea, the more it seemed like the right thing to do. The parade was three days away. We decided to call the police and notify the news media that the three leaders had been stolen.

The news people loved having a human-interest story to make the inaugural event more exciting. The next day, it seemed as if every time we turned on the radio or TV, we heard about the theft.

Officials at the Canadian border started checking for the dogs. The press carried pictures of the dogs. Dozens of media people wanted interviews. Meanwhile, we had to figure out how to do the parade without our leaders if we didn't get them back, although we hoped it wouldn't come to that.

Joe Reddington felt the loss most keenly. Feets was a valuable dog to him and had been his key leader for several years. Finally, he phoned his wife. "Send another lead dog," he said. Although Joe could afford to do that, Herb and I didn't have the money to send for another dog. If the dogs were not returned, Herb and I would each have to do with the eight we still had, walking in front of our teams if necessary.

On January 19, the morning before the parade, a widow was in her kitchen cooking breakfast. She glanced at the TV and saw a picture of Joee, who was distinctive with his white fur and vivid blue eyes. When she saw this picture, the woman gasped, "My goodness! That dog is in my basement."

Two nights earlier, her son had told her about three dogs he wanted to keep down there. "One of my friends is going away for a few days," he said. "He doesn't have anyplace to keep his dogs, so I said we'd keep them for him." After the boy promised to feed them and clean up after them, his mother agreed. She had seen the three dogs briefly when her son took them into the basement.

Now she knew that the dogs in her basement were the three stolen dogs. She also realized that her son was involved in the theft. It was, no doubt, a tough moment for her.

But she called the police. "I think the three missing dogs are in my basement."

The police, believing they were breaking up a ring that stole prize dogs, assumed they would encounter resistance. They pounded on the door, their guns drawn, and yelled, "Police! Open up!" The woman threw open the door, stared at the police with guns drawn, and screamed. Hysterical, her arms flailed and her screams grew louder.

After the police calmed her, she took them downstairs and showed them the stolen dogs. They phoned us, and then brought the dogs to us. We examined them carefully. They didn't seem to have been harmed or mistreated, so we put them back on their chains alongside our other dogs.

We later learned that the thieves had intended to ask us to pay $2,000 for the return of each dog. We had never received a ransom note, probably because they were too scared once the theft made the headlines. Even though the police urged us to press charges, we couldn't feel right about it because all three boys were minors.

➤

The next morning, the parade was delayed an hour. As the world later learned, Reagan was at Andrews Air Force Base. The year before, the Iranians had taken hostages from the American embassy in Teheran. President Carter had negotiated their release, and this was the moment the Iranians chose to release them. They were on their way home. Everybody accepted the delay with a wonderful spirit of patriotism, and I didn't hear a grumble.

Then the parade began. As we approached Constitution Avenue and prepared to filter into the parade line, on the other side of the street was a float that included sixty black horses, all tightly assembled. The dogs, thinking they were moose, started to bark and tried to charge them. For a few minutes I feared complications. But we kept calling to them and using our brakes to slow them, and they finally settled down.

Soon after the horses started their march, the street became spotted with manure. We followed immediately behind and over the deposits. Our brakes, lined with automobile tire tread for friction, became filled with manure and lost much of their holding power. The sleds were difficult to control. We rode the brakes constantly until we reached the White House. By then, the dogs had become accustomed to the horses, and we passed the president and his guests on the reviewing stand under full control.

Before the parade began, I had tied pink ribbons around the necks of the three leaders. As we passed spectators, I could hear them yelling, "Yeah, those are the ones. The dogs that are wearing pink ribbons!"

Others called out encouraging and apologetic words, such as, "Sorry it happened here." "Glad you got them back." "Thanks for coming today." It was heartwarming.

➤

"The pope is coming to Anchorage." The first time I heard the news in the fall of 1981, I didn't think much about it. Why should I? I wasn't Roman Catholic. For weeks, every newscast and newspaper carried something about the impending visit of Pope John Paul II.

Then I had an idea. What better way for the pope to get a real sense of Alaska than to give him a ride with my sled dogs? The more I pondered the idea, the more I liked it. First, it would be a memorable experience for him, maybe even the high point of his trip. Second, I'd have a great time doing it. Third, the ride would promote the Iditarod.

Next I had to consider the arguments of those who would try to talk me out of it. One big problem, of course, was security. I'd have to figure out a way to give him a ride in an open sled behind a team of dogs and still protect him from sniper bullets. I bought three sheets of Plexiglas and had them mounted on the sides and in front. When he sat on the sled, only half of his head would be above the glass.

I contacted the committee in charge of his reception. As I had expected, they initially thought it was a crazy idea, but I persisted and they listened. Finally, they concluded that it might be a good idea after all.

"You understand, we couldn't do this without getting the concurrence of the Secret Service," a member said.

We learned that there was only one Secret Service agent in Anchorage. I went to see the agent. He said, "No, it wouldn't be safe," but I kept talking.

I had thought this idea through quite thoroughly. The pope was scheduled to celebrate mass. When he came out of the cathedral, my dogs and I would be waiting. We would help him into the sled, drive two blocks, and then push on to Delaney Park, where people could line up behind ropes. I would drive him to a specially made altar, where he could bless the people, perhaps even have a short service. Then he could be on his way.

Part of my plan included having dog drivers run alongside the team, one for every two dogs. They would each hold a leash to a pair of dogs. There was no chance that my dog team could run away with the pope, and I proved that to everyone's satisfaction.

After I fully explained what I had in mind, the Secret Service agent gave in. "Okay. It sounds acceptable to me," he said, "as long as the pope is protected."

Once I had the verbal permission of the Secret Service, to my surprise, everyone agreed that it was an excellent idea. The committee gave me permission to go ahead. I went over the course several times, trying to anticipate everything that could possibly go wrong.

Then one voice dissented. He was a dog driver. He was also a Catholic. When he heard about the plan, he insisted, "Shouldn't a Catholic drive the pope instead of a Protestant?" Many—perhaps most—of those on the welcoming committee were Catholics. Naturally, they thought he had a good point. The archbishop, however, said that since the sled ride had been my idea, I ought to have the right to do it.

The arguments got quite heated. Finally, the committee decided that they would choose the driver by the toss of a coin. I didn't like that solution and opposed it. This had been my idea; I had taken it through the steps and even had it approved by the Secret Service. Didn't that give me the right to drive the pope in my sled? And I argued that the pope was not just for Catholics, but an international delegate of good will for all people.

The Catholic contingent wouldn't give in. I couldn't see how such a thing could happen. There wouldn't even have been an argument about a driver if I hadn't come up with the idea. When I realized that tossing a coin was the only way to settle it, I sighed and said, with deep reluctance, "All right."

God was good to me on that toss: I won two out of three. After I won, I invited the Catholic dog driver who lost to be one of the handlers beside the dog team. He accepted.

Everything was all set. Then, just three days before the pope's arrival, I got a call from the archbishop. "We have an interruption in our plans."

"What kind of interruption?"

"Washington doesn't like the setup. They got the report from their Secret Service agent, but they don't agree." Apparently someone in Washington had said to the archbishop, "We can't let the pope run that kind of risk with only one agent. What kind of an excuse could we give the world if we protect the pope with *one* security man?"

I was prepared to hear him say they had canceled the sled ride, but it wasn't that drastic. "Washington is sending out an additional ninety-nine agents to take care of the pope."

Once the ninety-nine agents arrived, they still didn't want the pope to take a dog sled ride. I argued that it was safe, but they remained unconvinced. After a heated debate, the agents delegated me to give the pope a ride on my sled—but only in the Anchorage airport, surrounded by wire. It was a terrible demotion, but it was that or nothing. The great trip I had planned had been whittled down to a symbolic ride.

Using the same route I had outlined, Pope John Paul II traveled in a small car completely covered with bulletproof glass. Once he reached the airport, I was to drive him to his plane, a ridiculously short trip. When the pope appeared, I was standing at the back of the dog sled. I had the dog team harnessed and a professional dog driver standing beside each pair of dogs.

After I was introduced, I had an idea.

"Your holiness," I said, "would you like to drive the dog team and let me do the riding?"

He smiled quizzically and looked at the archbishop before answering. The archbishop said, "If Vaughan says its safe, it's all right with me."

"What must I do?" his holiness asked.

"It's very simple," I said. "You stand on the runners and hold these handlebars, and I'll do the rest. You just ride along to the plane."

He stood on the runners, held the handlebars, and looked at me as if to ask, "What now?"

"Your holiness, there's one thing I feel that I should tell you before we start," I said. "Two of my dogs have terrible names. If I shout at them because they're not working properly, it might offend you. In that case, I'll be very glad to take them out of the team."

He waited for the translation and then asked, "What are their names?"

"One is Satan and the other is Devil."

He thought a few seconds, and then he smiled. "No. Don't take them out. Just as long as I am doing the driving."

At the plane, the pope stepped away from the sled and extended his hand. "A good ride," he said. We shook hands and said good-bye. As the crowd applauded, he mounted the steps to the plane. He paused and blessed me, the crowd, and the dogs before entering the plane. It was certainly the first time the pope had ever blessed Satan or the Devil.

Twenty-eight

In 1981, I entered the Iditarod again. I had a splendid start and no trouble, although, typically, I was far behind the leaders. On the seventh day, I traveled at about the same speed as three other drivers, one of whom was a woman, Barbara Moore. We all arrived at Rough Ridge checkpoint at about the same time. When I pulled in, it was about eight o'clock at night, and the temperature was between twenty-five and thirty degrees below zero. At the checkpoint, we found a small group of students with two supervisors who had come out on the trail to learn about survival. They had brought food and tents to the Rough Ridge checkpoint.

Our first task, as always, was to care for the dogs. Just as we got ready to feed and water them, Barbara said, "I'm just too cold to take care of my dogs right now."

I knew those words were serious, for I remembered my own experience in 1976. I didn't want to frighten her, so I turned to one of the men and said, "Let's feed her team." Then I asked the other one, "Will you take her inside the tent?"

"Yeah, good idea," he said. Two of us started to take care of the dogs. But I paused to watch her hobble toward the tent. She was limping badly, as if she had no feeling in her legs. I called after her, "Lie close to the stove." If her problem was only being cold, the stove would be enough. I was already sure it was more serious than that, however.

We fed the dogs and went inside. Barbara lay on a thick bed of spruce boughs in the well-heated tent, but she was not any better. After we questioned her, we realized that one foot was colder than the other. She admitted that she had been extremely cold all day. When I examined her bunny boot, I found a small hole. Bunny boots were the warmest things mushers could wear then, but that small hole defeated the boot's purpose. When she put weight on the foot, it squeezed the warm air out and sucked the cold air in. The foot had not yet frozen, but it was a very serious problem.

"I'll show you an old Eskimo trick," I said. "The first thing to do is to take your stocking off." We helped her. Then I opened my shirt and pressed the sole of her bare foot against my stomach. I kept it in one spot as long as my stomach could stand the cold. Then I moved her foot a few inches. When the cold was too much, I moved it again. Slowly, circulation started to return to her foot.

All the while I worked with her, she lay on her back. I knelt quite near the stove to keep myself warm. Someone gave me food and hot coffee to keep me warm. I must have drunk seven or eight cups. Finally, we thawed out Barbara's foot, got her inside her sleeping bag, and made her comfortable on the spruce boughs.

When it was time for me to go to bed, there wasn't any room in the heated tent. Earlier, the radio operator had invited me into his tent. I sighed to myself, thinking about going from warm to cold. Outside it was cold and windy, or I would have slept in my sleeping bag right on the snow beside my sled. When I crept into his tent, I realized that the radio operator had lain down right next to the door. I carefully stepped over the sleeping man and had just gotten comfortable inside my bag when it hit me: I had not taken a leak since the coffee. But now I had to go. *Now.*

Ever since I froze my feet, I'd had a bad foot. When I tried to get my boot on in the cramped tent, I couldn't bend my bad ankle to slip it into the shoe. What should I do? I wondered. I couldn't go outside. But it was getting urgent. Then I thought, this is a waterproof boot. I've walked through slush in this boot. So I did the only sensible thing I could think of: I peed in the boot. Then I pushed my boot into the corner of the tent where I wouldn't knock it over in my sleep. I crawled back inside my sleeping bag and went to sleep.

During the night, however, the rest of the coffee worked its way through, so I had to use the boot again. When I finished the second time, I had just about filled it.

Early the next morning, I woke up and looked at my boot. The urine had frozen solid. When I headed for breakfast, I put on woolen socks and one shoe. I carried the other shoe. Walking a short distance on the snow in one stocking foot is not a problem as long as you shake off the snow. I saw the remnants of a fire and stirred it. Finding a nice pole, I turned the boot upside down and stuck it on the pole. The pole had a forked end, so it held my boot nicely.

I saw that Barbara was now getting along, eating toast and drinking coffee. She shared some of it with me. She had figured out a way to patch up the hole in her boot and said she felt well enough to continue.

Just then one of the men came into the tent and said, "I just saw the funniest thing. Outside, somebody is trying to cook his boot. He's got it hanging upside down over the fire."

"It's mine," I said, too embarrassed to explain. "I got it wet."

When I went out to see my boot, it was empty but still wet. I had no choice but to put it on. Fortunately, it gave me no trouble.

For a couple of years afterward, my friends referred to me as "Piss 'n Boots."

➤

Over the months, the pain in my right ankle increased. After I had frozen my foot in the 1976 Iditarod, Dr. Mills, the Anchorage surgeon, had warned me that it would get worse. He told me that when the pain got too bad, I would have to have the calcium scraped from the bones. By the summer of 1981, I limped badly. Every step brought real pain, so I gave in. "I have to have it done," I told myself.

In September, I went to Boston to have the operation. I lay in bed for several days with my ankle and foot in a cast. They inserted two steel rods through my tibia. When they released me, I hobbled around on crutches. I was in bad shape for a while that summer.

➤

Unknown to me, two men from Atlanta, Pat Epps and Richard Taylor, took a vacation to Greenland in 1981 in their own plane. Epps owned an FBO (Fixed Base Operation). Taylor was a leading architect, who specialized in solar and wind energy.

The two men stopped at Sondrestrom Fjord in Greenland. While they were there, they heard about the Lost Squadron of 1942 and the planes that were still buried in the snow. They decided to search the area by plane, but saw nothing. They hired a Norwegian with a ski-equipped aircraft to take them out on a more thorough search. Still finding nothing, they returned to Atlanta. They happened to tell an Associated Press reporter that they had searched for the Lost Squadron. A few days later, a short piece about the search appeared in a Boston newspaper.

Crocker Snow, my superior officer in World War II, read the article and mailed it to me with a note: "These men are looking for your planes."

I was excited because I had always wanted somebody to show an interest in those planes. I wrote back to Crocker, explaining how we could get the planes out. He sent my letter on to Pat Epps. Pat phoned Crocker and then called me.

During the conversation, Epps asked me the crucial question, "Do you know where they are?"

"Yes, but not specifically," I said cautiously. "After all these years, they are under at least forty feet of snow. Maybe even eighty."

I explained that I believed I could locate them from a photograph I had if I returned to Greenland. As I talked, I could tell he was getting excited. Finally he asked, "How old are you?"

I was seventy-five, and I told him so.

"Aren't you too old to go back?"

"Emphatically no!" I said. "In fact, if you want those planes, we'd better go back right now. *And we'd better do it together.*"

"We don't have the money to go back now," he said, "but I think you'd better come down to Atlanta, and let's talk."

When I flew to Atlanta in October, I had been on crutches for three months. My doctors had told me to use them for at least six more weeks, but I didn't want Pat and Richard to see me on crutches. No matter what I said, they'd think, we don't want to take this old guy along. Why, he can't even walk. The romance and excitement of returning to Greenland so captivated me that I would have done anything to get the chance to return. I wasn't going to let anything like crutches or discomfort stop me. So I left my crutches on the plane.

After I had gotten to know the two men, Richard casually asked, "Do you have a limp?"

"Oh, I limp once in a while."

"I had never noticed it before," he said. "But today I saw you limping and wondered if you had hurt yourself."

"The truth is," I said, "I had a little operation a couple of months ago. But when I came to Atlanta, I left the crutches on the plane so that you wouldn't see them."

We laughed about it and then I asked, "Did you notice that every time we went anywhere, I always walked behind you?"

"Now that you mention it, yeah, I did notice that."

"Reason number one is that I wanted to be polite. Reason number two, I didn't want you to see my limp. And you didn't."

By then they had long decided I wasn't too old to make the trip, so we could laugh about the ankle. Little did I know that before long I would have to have a complete knee replacement on the same leg.

➤

In late October, we flew to Greenland. It was late in the season, but we hoped to get in a couple of good days of searching. The trip was successful in that we laid the groundwork for the ensuing years. But we did not find the airplanes.

We made several trips to Greenland to locate the planes. (Since 1981, I returned to Greenland twelve times.) One time a storm hit us with hurricane-force winds; the windchill factor made the temperature around two hundred degrees below zero. Once the storm abated, we started packing up to go home. Richard was devastated over the lack of results. We had worked so hard and still had not found the planes. He and Pat were grousing, but I was whistling as I loaded the plane.

"Shut up, Norman!" Richard barked.

Stunned, it took me a second to realize what he meant.

"Shut up! We've failed!' The despair was evident on his face.

"No, we didn't fail. We went as far as we could go. We haven't failed until we quit." I was not ready to admit defeat, and I wasn't going to let Richard give up, either.

To his credit, he was ready to go back the following year.

➤

By exhausting the talents of two leading subsurface radar firms, and through the help of an Icelandic glaciology team with subsurface radar equipment that they assembled themselves, we eventually found all eight airplanes. I had estimated they were about forty feet under the snow. With such a snow covering, we assumed the planes would be undamaged. We further assumed that once we found the planes, we could tune them up, refuel them, and fly them out. It sounded possible at the time.

Still, it was going to be tough selling anyone on the idea of putting down money to go after planes stuck in the Greenland ice sheet like flies entombed in amber. Pat Epps ran an ad in *Trade-a-Plane:* "For sale. Lockheed P-38F Lightning. 50 hours total time. $259,000." The one show of interest that ad attracted wasn't nearly enough.

The next year Pat Epps found Remo and Angela Pizzagalli of Pizzagalli Construction. As general contractors specializing in sewage treatment plants, they had experience in digging holes. So a partnership was formed. They would provide their own equipment and dig for their own P-38 while the Greenland Expedition Society used a hot water gopher to melt down to another buried P-38.

Pizzagalli's plan was to use a modified silo unloader to cut a sixteen-foot shaft down to the plane by cutting and scooping up ice. Such equipment wouldn't fit into the DC-3 we were flying to the site, however, so through Epps's connections we leased from the Air Force two C-130s on skis.

Work began with two holes a hundred yards apart: GES and the gopher on one end, and Pizzagalli's silo unloader on the other. The gopher made steady progress, but after eighty feet the hole filled up with water from melting show. We pumped thousands of gallons of water out of the shaft. The silo unloader, meanwhile, made slower progress. On June 6, the gopher hit something 256 feet down. Gordon Scott, who was in charge of the excavation, went down the shaft on a winch and, through the ice, saw the yellow tip of a prop. It looked promising. Then, with a steam hose to melt the ice and a pick to chip it away, he worked feverishly to begin freeing the P-38 from its prison of ice. It was crushed but salvageable.

I knew the other P-38 would be intact. I just knew it. But now wet weather was interfering with the silo unloader. The Pizzagalli crew worked valiantly to beat the odds, and their system was good, but as we began to run out of time, the gopher was moved over to their hole. One morning, when the Pizzagallis were within sixty feet of the second P-38, the hole filled completely with water; several days later, just as suddenly and unexpectedly, all the water drained out. Work resumed, at the frenzied pace of twenty-four hours a day, until our gasoline supply was exhausted. We had to stop. I felt terribly sorry for the Pizzagalli crew.

The summer of 1992—summer is the only time we could work in Greenland—we were able to melt ice all the way down to the second P-38. The man who financed the expedition, Roy Shoffner, like me, had faith that the plane would be intact, and he took a $600,000 gamble. The P-38, when we got down to it, was in good shape. We took it apart and sent it to Kentucky for reassembly in Roy's hangar. Shoffner is still restoring it. At the time of this writing, the plane is three-quarters rebuilt. He is doing a thorough job, replacing every rivet. I'm sure the plane will fly again. The aviation world owes Roy, reconstruction engineer Bob Cardin, Pat Epps, and GES a tremendous debt.

Twenty-nine

I LIKE TO THINK OF 1985 AS ONE OF MY BEST YEARS. I STARTED SPENDING summers in Atlanta to be with Pat Epps and Richard Taylor in preparation for the Greenland expeditions. But there's a better reason why I remember that year.

Early in the summer of 1985, I was carving a roasted pig at a hangar party in Atlanta. We had gathered to celebrate the twentieth year of Epps Air Service. A lot of fascinating people had come, and I was having a wonderful time. At one point, three women walked up to the table. We started talking, and I found them interesting and attractive. All three looked as if they were in their early forties.

As we continued to talk, I particularly enjoyed Carolyn Muegge, who had started a business in Atlanta called Executive Expeditions.

After a while, I said that I was getting ready to return to Alaska in the fall. I told Carolyn, "I need a dog handler for the winter. Can you come?"

Even though she thought it was a once-in-a-lifetime opportunity, she wasn't sure whether she could take off work for an extended period of time. She couldn't give me an answer. In two weeks, she was going to Salem, Massachusetts. It just so happened that I planned to be there at the same time. We agreed to meet for lunch and she would give me an answer then.

By the time we met in Salem, Carolyn had come up with a plan. She had recruited two friends, Jim Buford and Mildred Neville, to come to Alaska and help with the training. "We could take turns," she said. "That way three of us could be part of the experience, and no one would have to be gone for the whole time."

I thought it was a bad idea, but I didn't want to say that, so I just listened.

Carolyn excitedly explained her plan. "The first one could come up for three weeks, maybe as long as four, and then go back to Atlanta. After their return, the second could go, and then the third. How does that sound?"

After we talked a little more, I thought, this sounds like one of Vaughan's crazy ideas, so I said, "Yes, sure, why not?"

The first arrival was Jim, who had white-water paddled with Carolyn. After he had been there a few days, he phoned Carolyn to say that he was having one of the best times of his life.

"I made a mistake," Carolyn said after listening to his glowing report, "I should have gone first, but I chose to go last. You're having too good a time."

"Too late now," he laughed. "I'm having fun, and I wish I could stay."

He stayed for three weeks, and then Carolyn finally arrived two weeks before the Iditarod, which started the first week of March 1986. It was her first time driving a dog sled, and she loved it. She didn't do a lot of dog sled driving, but she did get experience packing food caches for the checkpoints and learning about all the last-minute preparations. Carolyn is quite athletic, and she caught on to the sport easily, so I invited her to ride the second sled on the first day of the Iditarod. Because of the high emotional pitch of the dogs at the beginning of the race, the rules state that each driver must take another person—a handler—on the trail for eighteen miles until they reach the second checkpoint at Knik. Then the handler leaves and the driver is on his own.

Carolyn never complained about the ride, but later she did say that she was so scared, she white-knuckled the sled all the way. It turned out that she had hit a tree head-on during her ride and was knocked off the sled. I didn't notice until I heard people shouting along the trail. I looked back and saw her running to catch up. She had been too embarrassed to complain about being hurt.

At the end of the first day, she got off, and I went on alone into the night with a headlight Velcroed to my hat. Carolyn remained behind and cried as my sled disappeared into the night. She vowed then and there that she herself would run the Iditarod.

➤

Each year, a few members of the Iditarod committee complained because I consistently finished the race about ten days after the winner. The top racers were coming in by the eleventh day, and most of the others reached Nome after fourteen to sixteen days. I usually took twenty-two days. The most common complaint I heard was, "Vaughan is keeping the officials at the check stations too long."

That wasn't true. As soon as I learned that the winner had finished, I phoned the race people in Nome and told them, "Don't keep checkers out for me; I will phone every night."

Nevertheless, the Iditarod committee passed Rule #51 in 1987, unofficially known as the "Vaughan Rule." It said, in effect, that those who were more than five days later than the first team to reach Unalakleet (a check station on the west coast of Alaska) were automatically withdrawn.

The new rule made me angry. First, withdrawal implied wrongdoing, even though it was not a disqualification. Second, I knew the ruling was aimed directly at me.

In 1987, when the rule went into effect, Carolyn had entered the Iditarod with her own team. We traveled the trail together. She and I, and a Native American named Tony Birch, were held up for four days by a storm before we reached Unalakleet. The snow was too deep for us to move at a pace faster than a crawl. It took the dogs two and a half hours to go three-quarters of a mile, and the next checkpoint was twenty miles away. We were out of dog food, and we couldn't expect the dogs to keep going with no food. At the end of the four days, a passing snowmobile opened the trail for us. Naturally, we didn't make Unalakleet before the time limit. At the next checkpoint the checker said that he heard on his radio that Norman Vaughan was more than five days late at Unalakleet and "He is withdrawn." I was still on the trail, but no Iditarod officials contacted me. Although they certainly must have known about the storm, they asked no questions, made no concessions. Instead, they simply withdrew me.

When I heard the news I was angry and Carolyn was devastated. I said, "I do not wish to *withdraw* from the race. I *will* continue." Both Carolyn and I kept pushing our teams toward Nome.

After the last official finisher passed under the huge burl-adorned arch on Front Street in Nome, the race officials had the arch towed away, and race headquarters closed its office. Carolyn and I phoned the next village whenever we passed a checkpoint. Each village sent messages ahead to the next village. They had mobilized to keep track of us all the way to Nome.

The remaining miles seemed endless, but we were thrilled to finish the race just the same. We arrived in Nome on the twenty-fourth day. When we reached Front Street, you might have thought we had won the race. A large crowd had assembled, and they clapped and whistled. A fire engine blew its siren and followed us with flashing lights as we approached the hastily replaced arch. What a glorious moment when Carolyn and I finished the Iditarod with our two teams.

Because she was withdrawn, the committee refused to give Carolyn a belt buckle, which made me angry. The belt buckle is given for completing the arduous trip to Nome, regardless of the time it takes. When the race started in 1974, they gave a belt buckle every year. Nowadays they give one only the first time a person completes the Iditarod.

➤

After the race, Carolyn went back to Atlanta to carry on her business. Two months later, I flew to Atlanta to meet with Epps and Taylor, for I am vice-president of the Greenland Expedition Society. From there, I accompanied them to Greenland. I saw Carolyn during my brief stop in Atlanta and again when we returned from Greenland.

Reluctantly, I admitted to myself that I loved this woman. I had not expected to marry again, but I had not expected to meet Carolyn, either. Obviously she cared for me, too, but I hesitated to talk marriage. She had one divorce behind her, and I had gone through three marriages. We talked quite a bit about our relationship. She reminded me that not only was my record for marriage not good, but that I was thirty-seven years older. She had never imagined marrying someone who was eighty years old. The one serious hesitation on her part was that if we married, she would have to give up her business and move to Alaska, which meant that she would be thousands of miles from her only son. She understood that Alaska was the only place I wanted to live. She loved Alaska as well and wanted to come, but her decision was a hard one to make.

I pointed out that when a younger woman marries an older man, too often the comment is, "She married him for his money." But in this case, she didn't have to worry. "No one will ever say that about you, because I don't have any money! If you marry me, it will be because you love me."

After much discussion, we decided to get married in Alaska, in a rustic setting at Forks Roadhouse in Trapper Creek, on December 31, 1987. A few months earlier we had bought a one-room log cabin nearby. Carolyn and I arrived by dog team. We expected a dozen or so people to come to our wedding. To our surprise, two hundred guests shared the joyous event with us.

It had snowed heavily for several days before the wedding, and the snowplows had not yet cleared all the roads. Dog teams and snowmobiles transported guests from the nearest road, some five miles from the Road-house. One man hitchhiked for eight hours to get there. A couple skied in. A helicopter brought in a group of four. An AP reporter and a writer from *Alaska Magazine* showed up. And the local television station sent a film crew.

As we were rehearsing inside the Roadhouse, John Tracy, a local TV anchor, asked if we would mind getting married outside, where, he said, the lighting was better. We agreed. In a light snowfall in twenty-degree temperature, we were married by a dear friend who had been commissioned for the day to perform the ceremony.

➢

In a 1992 *Outside* magazine interview, Carolyn spoke of her first trip to Alaska: "In three weeks up there, I fell in love with Alaska, the Iditarod, and Norman."

Later in that same article, she said of me, "He never quits wondering. He's like a preschooler exploring his playground."

In a 1991 interview, Carolyn said, "I'm always amazed at how much Norman wants to learn. He has such curiosity and zest for life." A 1993 *People* magazine article quoted her as saying, "Norman is a dreamer. *Can't* is not in his vocabulary."

I think Carolyn understands me well.

Thirty

"I HAVE NAMED A MOUNTAIN FOR EACH OF YOU THREE MUSKETEERS," ADMIral Richard Byrd had told me in the early 1930s. He had named three Antarctic mountains after Eddie Goodale, Freddie Crockett, and me.

"That's great," I said, feeling honored. "I've got to go down there and climb it."

"I suppose you will, Norman," he said, then laughed. "I suppose you will."

Years went by, and I had no opportunity or money to live out my dream of climbing Mount Vaughan, 10,302 feet. Over the years, I thought about climbing it, but I could never work out a plan to fulfill the dream. Until the eighties, except for scientists, no one could reach the interior of Antarctica.

In the seventies and eighties, as growing numbers of people came to Alaska to climb Mount McKinley, I thought more about my unrealized dream. In March 1991, Will Steger came to Anchorage as one of ABC's *Wide World of Sports* announcers for the Iditarod sled dog race. He had received a lot of notice for his Trans-Antarctic Expedition, in which he and five other men crossed Antarctica by dog sled. I had to see him.

After the Iditarod race, Carolyn and I arranged to have breakfast with Will. We discussed Antarctica from the beginning of the meal to the end. Looking at his maps, we discussed logistics, especially handling dogs, necessary provisions, and the huge cost of transportation. I came to realize that if we went, we would have to charter two planes, and make multiple flights to carry all the dogs, supplies, and personnel.

As the three of us talked, Carolyn and I kept eyeing each other. Fueled by Will's enthusiasm, we could see the excitement in each other's faces.

"Do it," Will said more than once.

He told us about his educational program that had reached millions of children all over the world. He sent daily reports to his organization. It, in turn, put the news on the computer network for thousands of schools. If we went, we could help educate others, too; it would be more than just the selfish pursuit of climbing the mountain. I began to see Mount Vaughan as a real possibility instead of just some futuristic dream. My age didn't concern me. I moved slower than younger men, of course, but that wouldn't stop me from climbing to the top of the mountain. After all, the distance across the Ross Ice Shelf was only half that of the Iditarod.

Will told us of an upcoming Antarctic conference in July 1991 at Hamline University in Minnesota. We decided to go. Will and his team would be there, along with scientific experts on the Antarctic. We'd be able to meet Ann Bancroft, who had been a member of Will's North Pole expedition team and who was now preparing to lead her own American women's expedition to the Antarctic. Her plan was for five women to ski across the continent via the South Pole.

"The conference would be a great place for us to access everybody," Carolyn said.

"It will also help us make a final decision on whether we can do it," I added.

For weeks after our meeting with Will, Carolyn and I talked with Antarctic buffs and attended meetings on subjects even remotely related to Antarctica. The more we learned, the easier it would be to make our decision.

At the Hamline conference, Carolyn and I spent time with Will and his team. We discussed problems and ideas. We were able to see the clothing and gear they had used. We talked with Ann Bancroft about the equipment she and her team were going to use. (In the Antarctic austral summer of 1992–1993, Ann led a successful expedition.)

During the conference, Will received a telephone call from a man at *National Geographic* magazine. They had learned about a new annex to the Antarctic treaty that all nations had agreed to, that would prohibit dogs in Antarctica. "We called," the man said to Will, "because you were the last person to have driven dogs in the Antarctic and we'd like to know how you feel about this."

"But I won't be the last. Norman Vaughan is going to be the last one to drive dogs," Will said. "And he's right here with me."

This news stunned us. The annex was due to take effect on April 1, 1994. "Yes, I will take dogs and go to Antarctica before the deadline," I said. So far as I can remember, that was the first time I actually said I would go. Until then, my remarks had been tentative; I had veiled them with "maybes" and "ifs."

"If we're going to do it," I said to Carolyn afterward, "we have to start now." The austral summer of 1993–1994 would have to be our target date, ideally between November and January. We would need to be out of Antarctica no later than the end of January 1994, when the days began to shorten and the weather deteriorated.

"Do you realize what that would mean?" Carolyn asked. "We would only have two years to pull this off."

Will had said it took three years to fully prepare for an expedition.

"We'll need to make our decision soon," I said.

We had assumed that it would take three years to pull off an expedition because of the need to raise funds and get permission from the National Science Foundation (NSF) to take the dogs. But now we would have to cut it short if we were going to travel across Antarctica by dog sled before the deadline. My dream included using dogs, just as we had done on the 1928–1930 Byrd expedition. I even wanted to retrace our original route.

"The most difficult part is getting a permit from the NSF to take dogs across Antarctica," Will had warned us. Although he had applied more than two years in advance, he had received his permit only one month before he left. We were to learn that Will was right. Obtaining a permit became one of the biggest hurdles we had to jump. The United States was proceeding as if the treaty annex had already been signed.

➤

The morning after the conference, as we drove back to the Oshkosh Air Show, our heads were swimming with information, enthusiasm, and our first tentative plans.

When Carolyn and I stopped for breakfast, our conversation still brimmed with ideas, but we had not yet committed to the expedition. We sat across the table from each other and looked directly into one another's eyes. Carolyn said, "Are we going to do it?" We squeezed each other's hands across the table and both nodded.

"Norman, do you know what this means?" Our eyes glistened.

I took a deep breath and, still holding her hands, said, "Yes."

We had committed ourselves and there was no turning back. Our expedition had begun. *We were going to Antarctica.*

In the months ahead, we faced some hard realities. We didn't lose our enthusiasm, but we had daunting decisions to make and difficult problems to overcome.

At one point, Carolyn said, "This is scary. I've never been there." Then she smiled and said, "But I'm ready to go."

I had never doubted it.

My dream had become Carolyn's as well. Going to the Antarctic became our full-time occupation, with no time for a real job.

➤

"How do we finance it?" Since we faced a cost of just over $1 million, the financing question was the first problem we had to solve. Byrd had obtained money through corporate sponsorship and from wealthy friends. I didn't really know how to go about this; we contacted many large companies and got virtually no response. It seemed obvious to me that, even though no one said so, my age frightened them.

In one case, the advertising manager turned us down because he was afraid to risk a very expensive promotion "if you have to cancel the trip at the last minute." He made no direct reference to my age, but we all knew what he meant.

Then I remembered the Kohler Company of Wisconsin, which had provided the first Byrd expedition with lighting plants. We contacted the company and eventually met the president, Herbert V. Kohler, Jr., the godson of Admiral Byrd.

He greeted me as if I were a long-lost friend. "You know, Norman, there's only one thing in my life that I wanted to do and couldn't. That was to go to Antarctica." When Kohler was sixteen, Admiral Byrd had asked him to go on one of his Antarctic expeditions as a dog handler. "I wanted to do it, but my father said no."

"Now, Mr. Kohler, this is your chance. You can join us at the mountain." I explained what I intended to do. As we talked, his excitement increased.

"We will support you," he promised.

A bad hip kept Herb from climbing, but he was still enthusiastic about Antarctica. Byrd had also named a mountain after Herb's father. I wished I could take him to Antarctica not only to show him Mount Vaughan, but to climb Kohler Mountain together.

We didn't ask for a specific amount of money. But we left excited, assured that we could count on Kohler's financial support.

Another supporter of Byrd's expeditions, Collins Avionics, rallied behind us, giving us $89,000 of state-of-the art radio equipment so that we could stay in touch with base camp and the rest of the world.

This was extremely important because, like Will Steger, we had set up an educational program. We would issue daily reports to the States that would be sent by computer from the Center for Global and Environmental Education at Hamline University to classrooms and schools all over the world. Later, when Prodigy became one of our major sponsors, we were able to reach not only schools but the general public as well.

Everything took time. Getting sponsors and raising money were the two most difficult parts of the preparation. We needed one person to concentrate on fund raising, and we were happy to find Jennifer Johnston. A real go-getter, she wouldn't hesitate to call on potential donors. She also helped with publicity, which got a boost when David Roberts wrote an article about us that appeared in the September 1992 issue of *Outside*.

Carolyn and I had to personally visit corporate offices, and in doing so we lost precious time needed for preparation. We needed to devote more attention to recruiting team members and selecting dogs; we needed to decide what gear and clothing to take; we needed to get it, test it, and then start training the entire team. All members would have to learn to work with dogs. Carolyn and I had to learn to climb.

In the meantime, as Will had predicted, we faced all kinds of problems getting a permit to take twenty dogs to Antarctica. We encountered delay after delay and countless bureaucratic runarounds. Despite Will's warning, it still frustrated us. But we continued our preparations as if we already had permission.

We also faced the problem of how to ship enough food for the dogs to make the 550-mile trip across the Ross Ice Barrier. We were urged to send food and equipment a year in advance by boat.

Adventure Network International (ANI) was the only commercial venture that went into the Antarctic interior. In the summer of 1992, we met with Ann Kershaw, the new manager of the company. Together, we planned our strategy and tried to work out costs. It was turning out to be even more expensive than we had figured.

We decided to ship the dog food and two snowmobiles for the National Geographic Society on a chartered Russian cruiser that was scheduled to go to the Ross Ice Barrier, near Little America. This excited us because it would save us exorbitant flying costs. Just one year's supply of dog food, donated by Eagle Pet Products, weighed more than a ton.

The National Geographic Society had agreed to send two cinematographers, who would follow our dog team expedition on snowmobiles. We realized that it would save them a great deal of money to move their snowmobiles down to Antarctica by boat instead of by air at the same time as the dog food. They didn't yet have snowmobiles. Although we hadn't yet signed any contract with the Society, Carolyn and I gambled our own money and bought two snowmobiles for National Geographic so that they could be shipped by boat.

We bought the snowmobiles in Anchorage (the Society later paid for them), and one of our sponsors, Federal Express, air freighted them to Sydney, but they still had to go another three thousand miles to Perth. FedEx made miracles happen. The equipment and dog food arrived *one day* before the boat left.

Everything was going well. Then came the first bad news.

The cruiser arrived in Antarctica, but it didn't travel eastward toward Little America. Instead it went to Marble Point, near McMurdo Sound and more than 450 miles from Little America. Knowing the cost of fuel, we couldn't retrieve our goods. It would have been a 900-mile round trip from Little America and more than 2,000 miles from ANI's camp at Patriot Hills. It might as well have been 10,000 miles.

To add another calamity, a New Zealand inspector on the ship announced that the Antarctic treaty prohibited raw chicken from entering the Antarctic, because it could pass on Newcastle's disease (a distemper) to the penguins. Our bags of dry food listed chicken by-products as one of the ingredients. The inspector didn't seem to know or care that the chicken had been thoroughly cooked at high temperatures at the Eagle Pet company plant. Besides, all the scientific bases at Antarctica served chicken in their dining rooms!

"You can't land the dog food," he told the skipper. "It contains chicken by-products, which are forbidden."

"What shall I do with it?" the skipper asked.

"Take it north of sixty degrees south latitude and dump it overboard."

The captain couldn't unload the dog food. He did, however, unload the two snowmobiles, along with the ANI cache of fuel.

That was bad enough, but then we received a bill for $21,000 for moving the freight; I was enraged and refused to pay.

Representatives from ANI and the company that had chartered the boat had been aboard to oversee our shipment. When we asked why we had not been contacted, ANI said, "Radio reception wasn't good, and nobody could be reached. They had to make a decision because it was time for the ship to move on."

The fiasco was heart-breaking, but the Eagle Pet people graciously donated another supply of dog food. And FedEx agreed to transport it again.

➤

The National Science Foundation, which coordinates American scientific programs in the Antarctic, had to approve our applications for taking dogs to Antarctica. They kept putting up roadblocks. Finally, we appealed to our senators, Ted Stevens and Frank Murkowski. They helped us reach the State Department, which declared our expedition of historical and scientific value to the United States and helped us get our permit.

It still took *one year and nine months* before NSF, under heavy pressure, signed our applications. The approval came only two months before we were to leave, which put us in a frenzy to finalize everything.

But we did it.

➤

The other team members were all climbers. There was Vern Tejas, an Alaskan and an accomplished mountaineer. Among his many achievements, he was the first person to solo climb Mount McKinley in the winter. He was also the first Alaskan Seven Summiteer, meaning he had climbed the highest mountain on each of the seven continents.

Other team members were Brian Horner, a cold weather survival specialist; Dolly Lefever, a nurse practitioner, skier, and climber; and Ken Zafren, an emergency room physician. We arranged for an Antarctic base camp, Camp deGanahl, for our radio operators, George and Betty Menard. Larry Grout, our dog handler, and Jerry Vanek, our veterinarian, would go ahead with the dogs to Punta Arenas, Chile. They would handle customs, entry permits, and quarantine for the dogs.

We had two sessions together training the team at our home in Trapper Creek. We worked with the dogs, tested systems, and practiced traveling while roped together and doing crevasse rescue and self-arrest. We tested tents and stoves, and calculated how much food we would need. We also built team spirit, in the hopes that we would be compatible in the Antarctic. Everybody got along well during training.

To keep costs down, we finally decided not to use ANI for transportation, but to charter a DC-6 and a DC-3 from Allcair Air Transport. Bruce Allcorn, the owner, became our pilot. On the first trip, he would carry dogs, gear, and three team members to a base at Patriot Hills in Antarctica.

We were still having financial problems. We had promises for $350,000 that we badly needed, but the money just didn't come in. We were getting close to our departure date. Carolyn and I made daily phone calls. When National Geographic paid, Bruce was able to secure the things he needed.

When we arrived at Punta Arenas, we still didn't have all the money, but I believed it would come in. We had made plans A, B, C, D, E, and F, depending on how much money we raised.

Other delays hit us. Bruce had to set up base camp and transport the dogs, but the weather was so bad he couldn't fly for most of the next two weeks. Our second plane, a DC-3 on skis, had to be inspected by Chilean authorities, and they had to come from Santiago, four hundred miles away. That meant more waiting.

Now we had to refigure. Lack of money meant giving up plan A—starting at Little America and repeating the route I took in 1929. Now we would have to go directly from Patriot Hills to Mount Vaughan, another two hundred miles to travel. We had enough food and supplies to do that.

The money trickled in, but not fast enough. During our eleventh hour, while trying to find more money and revising plans further, Herb Kohler came through with an additional $150,000. He had called his friends to help him.

We finally had enough money—barely—but the weather was still bad. Bruce had not been able to fly, and he was still having problems getting certification of his DC-3.

In the meantime, we spent hours and hours every day refiguring our food, gear, weight, loads, and distance. We constantly crunched numbers. Because we had less time and money to accomplish our goal, we packed everything again and again. We were down to plan C. We went to sleep with nothing but numbers in our minds. We dreamed of numbers. We totally revamped the whole program, finally reducing it to a workable plan.

On Thanksgiving 1993, all our promised money still had not arrived. But believing the remaining $100,000 would come in, we were ready for Bruce to take off for Patriot Hills. The veterinarian, Jerry Vanek, was on board. George Menard, our radio operator, planned to set up a radio camp immediately for weather reporting, and Larry Grout would handle the dogs. Bruce, his crew of five, and our three members left Chile in the four-engine DC-6 for Camp deGanahl, 1,750 miles away.

The plane flew back over the field where we stood. Bruce signaled with the lights three times, letting us know that all was well on board.

Carolyn and I stood holding each other in amazement. "It's really happening," Carolyn said with glistening eyes. "It's finally begun."

With great joy and a sense of relief we returned to Punta Arenas. *We've done it. We've done it,* I kept thinking. Sixty-five years after my first trip to the frozen continent, I would soon be there again. As I thought back to the days when we first talked with Will Steger, I realized how naive I had been. If it hadn't been for our dreams and the faithful support of the many people behind us, that plane would not have flown from Chile to Antarctica that day.

"Unbelievable," someone said in a hushed tone.

It expressed my feelings precisely.

$$\succ$$

"The plane crashed at half past four this morning!"
Those words greeted me the next morning.

None of us wanted to believe the report. Once it sank in, I asked, "Was anyone hurt?"

"Everyone is alive," said the first report.

Thank God for that, I said silently.

"I want to go back to bed and have you wake me and tell me it's only a dream," Carolyn said.

As we waited for details, we fought denial. Then other thoughts floated through our minds. What had happened? Was anybody hurt? Were the dogs all right?

Oh, my God, the expedition is over, I kept thinking. *All this, and now it's over.*

We eventually learned that only one person was injured—our vet, Jerry Vanek, had a broken leg. Assuming that it was only a minor injury, we were relieved.

The news got worse.

At Patriot Hills, a patch of blue ice is used for wheeled aircraft landings. It's not a landing strip, only undulating "cuspid" ice that looks like frozen swells of an ocean. In the Antarctic, the weather changes rapidly. By the time the DC-6 arrived at Patriot Hills, the weather was awful, visibility limited. The plane had flown into the ground six miles short of the runway. The crash ripped off the landing gear and three props. One sliced through the fuselage right where Jerry Vanek was sitting. The impact ripped Jerry's seat out of its bolts, and he hit the floor on his back, still seatbelted. Dog crates were smashed as they were thrown forward in the cabin.

Gasoline gushed everywhere. One engine was on fire, and they feared the plane would burst into flames. Fortunately, the fire didn't spread. Larry Grout hurriedly got all the dogs off the plane and tethered them, then had to let them loose when another fuel line broke. Everyone got out except Jerry, who was in unbearable pain. The others finally were able to lift him out onto a dog sled.

As the weather continued to deteriorate, George Menard tended to Jerry. Within forty-five minutes, an ANI medic and the camp manager arrived by snow machine, and they helped George get Jerry back to camp.

The loose dogs followed behind the snow machine, but they had been traumatized like everyone else. Four of them ran off. Five times over the next thirty hours, Larry went out looking for the missing dogs. But he never found them. They had run downwind, and it wouldn't have been natural for them to turn and run back, particularly in such an unfamiliar place. (Later, searchers from the ANI camp found paw prints twenty-five miles away, near a crevasse field, but they never found the dogs.)

We needed to get Jerry back to Punta Arenas, where he could receive proper medical attention. ANI quickly provided a C-130 to bring Jerry and the remaining dogs back. Although I very much wanted to go on the plane, I decided to stay in Punta Arenas to make decisions about the expedition if necessary. The plane landed safely at Patriot Hills with our doctor, Ken Zafren, and Brian Horner, who was also an EMT. They loaded Jerry and the dogs. After one hour and thirty-five minutes, they were airborne and heading back.

Jerry had almost an eight-hour flight from Patriot Hills to Punta Arenas. By the time he arrived, it had been thirty-six hours since the accident.

Carolyn and I accompanied him from the airport to the hospital. That's when we learned the seriousness of his injuries. He had multiple head and facial injuries, a broken arm, and a very badly broken tibia. He was in excruciating pain and couldn't remember anything about the accident. After a week, when he was stable, he was moved by air-evac jet to the States for surgery. On board, a doctor and nurse cared for him.

Barbara, his fiancée, had flown down so that she could return on the jet with Jerry. Nine months later, I became a commissioner of marriage for the day and married Jerry and Barbara on the shore of a beautiful lake with Mount McKinley in the background. (Jerry has continued to improve and is now okay.)

➤

It was a sad, traumatic time for us, the lowest point of the last two years. Now I had to decide on the future of the expedition. Should we go on or give up? Despite the tragedy, I was determined to go on.

We were so close. None of us wanted to stop now, but we had no money and very little time. Our only hope was to leave without the dogs and fly with ANI right to Mount Vaughan for the climb.

ANI said it had five seats for a flight on January 2, 1994. It would cost us $25,000 each. The National Geographic team would take two seats. I would take the third. Vern Tejas, our lead mountaineer, and Brian Horner, survival expert and medic, would take the last two seats. Ken would go home. Dolly would climb Mount Vinson and then go to Australia to climb the last of her seven summits. (She would be the first American woman to become a Seven Summiteer.) Carolyn agreed to stay behind in Punta Arenas and relay information. This was a sickening decision, both because I needed Carolyn and because she had slavishly worked to make the expedition possible.

>

I felt tremendous pressure trying to figure this all out. Relations grew testy among members because we were all waiting in Punta Arenas instead of being on the ice. We were like wild animals in a cage.

Carolyn and I went to ANI to discuss the matter. To salvage the expedition, we had to raise $90,000—long distance—in two weeks. By scrounging, begging, and borrowing, we came up with the money. Ken, Vern, and Brian had gone back to the States. The two-man National Geographic crew had gone to Washington, D.C., but their guide, Michael Funke, was still with us. Then ANI told us they had another seat available on the flight to Patriot Hills. That meant Carolyn could at least go to the ANI base camp there and relay communications back to Alaska for the educational program. Even if she couldn't climb Mount Vaughan, at least she would be in Antarctica. I called Vern and Brian two weeks after they returned to the States.

"January second the plane leaves," I said. "We're going to be on it."

We didn't leave on January 2. Bad weather at Patriot Hills prevented our departure until January 5, 1994.

No sooner had we landed at Patriot Hills than the weather turned bad again. We sat in our tents and waited. Camp would close down on January 25, when the last plane would come in to take everyone out. It was leave with the plane or stay on the ice for months, which would have been impossible.

During our wait, we met a group of people who had been to the South Pole. They were stuck at Patriot Hills with us. In the group was the famous entrepreneur Charles J. Givens of Orlando, Florida. Like the others at Patriot Hills, he had become caught up in our saga. He offered many encouraging words.

The weather didn't let up, and by January 20, 1994, our sixteenth day, our time had run out. Even if the weather suddenly cleared (and it didn't), we wouldn't have enough time to reach Mount Vaughan, climb, and be back by January 25.

Our window of opportunity had closed. I called our team together. Givens and the others stood nearby and listened. Carolyn went to our tent because she didn't want to hear what she knew I was going to say.

"It's over." Those were some of the hardest words I've ever had to say. "We're going to cancel our effort to climb Mount Vaughan *this year.* We're going to go home, but we will come back next year."

As I said those words, I meant them. I wouldn't give up. We'd make it next year. I didn't know how, but I knew we would.

"May I say something?" Charles Givens asked. When I nodded, he said, "I've been living here throughout these sixteen days trying to get back to the States myself. I know what you people have been going through. Your courage and determination have impressed me. I'm a believer in dreams. I want Norman's dream to come true, so I offer $100,000 for you to come back next year."

I don't know if I laughed or cried, but a wave of joy came over me.

Charles Givens had just opened the door, and I knew that I would not let it close again.

Thirty-one

CAROLYN KEPT A JOURNAL DURING THE 1994 EXPEDITION TO CLIMB MOUNT
Vaughan. This is the story in her words.

➤

The final stage of our expedition began Wednesday, November 16,
1994, at 4:45 P.M.

After we locked our front door behind us, Norman stopped and kissed
me. "Finally," he said. The sense of relief in his voice matched my own.
As we walked away, I don't remember the rest of what he said, but his
voice sounded excited, merriment twinkled in his eyes, and his stride was
brisk.

This time we were really going to climb Mount Vaughan. After three
and a half years, we were ready to complete our long, arduous journey.
Most people would still have been mourning the defeat of a dream. For
Norman, it had been only a dream deferred.

Despite his frustration and disappointment, he never spoke of giving
up. Even before we left the Antarctic ten months earlier, we had begun to
make plans for our return. The word *can't* is simply not in his vocabulary.

Half an hour later, we arrived at the Anchorage airport. Once we
reached the waiting area, I let myself think about how I felt. Excitement
hadn't touched me yet. Right then, I could think of only one word: relief.
No more funds to raise. No more faxes. No more last-minute calls beginning with, "I know you're busy, but could you—?" No more refiguring
weights, prices, dates, and schedules. We were finally on our way.

Until then, I hadn't allowed myself strong feelings, but now emotions came to the surface. I felt remorse and regret, but more than anything else, I felt anger. We had overcome seemingly impossible obstacles, only to have the opportunity to take the dogs snatched from us. A wave of bitterness swept over me. The plane crash was the one thing that had been totally out of our control.

At the end of 1994, taking dogs was out of the question. A new wave of anger came as I remembered the fiasco with the wasted dog food and the two snowmobiles. I felt particularly bitter toward one sponsor that had used us for its own purpose and caused us a critical loss of time in raising money. I thought especially of the plane crash that had robbed us of a wonderful opportunity. I struggled to push all that behind me—I kept saying to myself, "Don't cry over spilled milk"—but the feelings surfaced anyway. I knew I had to put those feelings away—and I would. Once we reached Antarctica, I would be ready to face whatever lay ahead of us. But for a few minutes, I wanted to scream out at all the injustices we had faced.

I turned then and looked at Norman. Our eyes met and he beamed. Just that simple look from him made me feel better. I took his hand.

At the airport we talked with a number of friends who had come to see us off. In the hour before boarding, they plied us with hugs and best wishes. One of them asked, "Aren't you excited?"

"No," I said truthfully. "I've been too busy to think about enjoying this. That'll come once we get on the ice."

"Do you feel okay about this trip?" someone else asked. The question contained a veiled reference to the previous failure.

"Both Norman and I feel confident," I said. "We've refused to let the previous trip deter us. We've been in training for the mountain climbing. The good news is that Norman's actually in better shape than he was a year ago."

All the work was finally behind us. We were ready to get on with climbing the mountain.

➤

We had packed and repacked many times, trying to keep our luggage weight under fifty pounds each. Each extra pound would cost an additional $30. Money was even tighter than during the previous trip, and we couldn't afford to pay for much extra weight. That meant we couldn't take extra clothes. What we wore down would be what we wore back.

We allowed ourselves two extra pairs of socks, an extra set of underwear, and an extra set of long johns. The rest of our gear included a hat, gloves, face mask, sunglasses, goggles, climbing boots, crampons, ski poles, climbing gear, ice ax, repair kit, medical kit, cup and bowl, toiletries, Thermos, water bottle, and sleeping pad and bag. I carried a small package that I kept hidden from Norman. Each of our loads weighed sixty-six pounds. We also had the additional weight of our Omni subnotebook computer, our fifteen-pound Collins satellite telephone in a briefcase, a Trimble Global Positioning System, a telephone solar panel, and two motorcycle batteries. Besides that, we had to bring pole replacements for our tents that we had cached at Patriot Hills last year along with our snowshoes, some food, and some climbing gear. Our climbing ropes were at Patriot Hills, too, but everything else—our food, stoves, cooking equipment—went separately as part of our "group gear."

The logistics of this trip were much easier than last year, when we had traveled with twenty dogs and thirteen people. This time, including the pilots, plane engineers, the National Geographic team, and two supernumeraries and their guide, we would have a total of fourteen people but no dogs. Norman, Vern Tejas, and I flew together. At Punta Arenas, we would join our fourth team member, Gordon Wiltsie, who was our official photographer, guide, and also the representative of Adventure Network International. We knew of Gordon's good reputation and were glad to have him along.

We flew two days to get to Punta Arenas and then waited five days until November 27, when the weather cleared enough for us to fly to Antarctica.

As soon as we left for Patriot Hills on ANI's C-130, excitement kicked in. The air was filled with anticipation. I remembered how different it had been the year before when sadness filled out hearts, and we had come back without accomplishing our goal. This year it would be different.

Once we landed at ANI's base camp on the ice at Patriot Hills, we set up our tents. Again we waited. At times, it seemed as if going to the Antarctic was nothing but a waiting game. ANI had only two Twin Otter planes, and we had to wait until they picked up and flew climbers to Mount Vinson and the South Pole. Then we waited for the right weather. The winds would whip up, die down, and then start again, all within a matter of hours. In my diary, I wrote, "Nature is very humbling and we are at her command."

Norman and I weren't upset over the delay. Our plan from the beginning had been to reach the summit on December 19, which would be Norman's eighty-ninth birthday. We weren't in any rush.

Finally, on December 1, we got word that we could leave. Our plane took off with us and the National Geographic crew. A second Twin Otter would follow in a couple of days with food, other supplies, a guide for the National Geographic photographers and the supernumeraries.

Mount Vaughan is 750 miles from Patriot Hills, where the Ross Ice Shelf emanates from the Transantarctic Mountains. The Twin Otters couldn't fly the entire distance on a single tank of gas, so we stopped at the Thiel Mountains to refuel. We had only been back in the air for a few minutes when the pilot, Bryan, spotted a fog bank gathering ahead. He cut back on the engines and began flying lower and lower. The fog got so bad, he finally had to land at a level spot about 9,300 feet above sea level.

As soon as Bryan shut off the plane's engine, he turned around and looked at us. "Welcome to Nowhere Land."

We clambered out of the plane and began to set up camp. A quietness filled the air, and I saw nothing but white in any direction. Apparently, this land saw little wind, because the ground was smooth, with little sastrugi. An eerie feeling came over me. I thought, We're out here on this spot where no one has ever been before, and probably no one will ever be again. This must be the sort of feeling Norman had when he and the rest of the Byrd Expedition's geological party gazed on land no humans had seen before.

Daylight continued twenty-four hours a day, but as we set up our tents, I felt the penetrating cold from being over nine thousand feet high. Gordon prepared food, and we all huddled together in the cook tent to eat and wait for the fog to lift. Finally, weary after the strain of travel, we decided to go to sleep. None of us knew how long we would be there; a few hours at most, we assumed.

We had to reverse our days and nights. We went to bed that "night" at five in the morning. After sleeping for several hours, we woke up, ate breakfast, read, and watched the weather.

"We can fly again. The fog has lifted," Bryan said just before midnight. We had only a ninety-minute flight to reach Mount Vaughan, and we were eager to get moving. We loaded everything into the plane and took off. We felt great anticipation as we drew nearer and began to recognize some of the mountains that we had seen in aerial photographs.

Vern, sitting in the back of the plane with the best view, kept saying, "We're getting closer. We're getting closer. Here it comes, here it comes!" He pointed.

Finally Mount Vaughan came into view. We whooped, hollered, and screamed when we saw it for the first time.

Bryan flew around the mountain twice for us, which enabled Gordon and the National Geographic people to take photographs. From the plane, we could see the route we would climb. We had planned to climb the back side because aerial photographs suggested it would be an easier route. However, when we saw the back side, we could tell that the route was a lot steeper than we had anticipated. We felt quite excited and anxious, realizing that the challenge was much greater than we had expected.

"It's a beautiful mountain," Vern said, "and certainly not a walkup."

I felt a little intimidated, but managed a laugh. I had never actually climbed a mountain, although we had practiced climbing techniques back in Alaska.

"We've got a great challenge!" Vern yelled, with exuberance.

I couldn't read Norman's thoughts, but I knew it was one of the most important moments in his life. He was staring at *his* mountain, as if he wanted to imprint every feature on his brain.

"We're here," I said unnecessarily, and hugged him.

➤

We arrived at three-thirty in the morning on December 3. As soon as we landed, the two photographers hopped out and set up their cameras. They shot us coming out of the plane. Gordon also took photographs for *Life* magazine. As soon as we were all out of the plane, I grabbed Vern's hat.

"Kneel," I said. No one knew what I was up to.

Vern knelt.

"For luck," I said, and then Norman and I kissed Vern's bald head.

I paused to survey the mountain in front of us and watched as a serac, a giant pinnacle of snow, pulled away from a glacier and sank into the slope below. Tears came to my eyes. I had no words for the inexpressible beauty around me.

In my diary, I wrote:

> *What an emotional moment as we stepped out. The mountain stands looming over us with the sun dancing off the face. Seracs cascade down. The route is about 40 degrees and the first fifth is a knife-edge, not the easy 30-degree slope we thought we were going to have from the photos. Everyone is thrilled, including the climbers, who see quite a challenge ahead of us.*

➤

On landing, the pilot had traced a big circle in the snow with the plane's skis. Bryan reminded us to stay within that circle so that we would be safe from crevasses.

"Time to set up camp," Norman said.

Gordon and Vern walked outside the circle, probing for crevasses and setting up wands for a boundary. Norman had named our base Camp deGanahl, after Joe deGanahl, who had been a dog driver and navigator on the first Byrd expedition.

We got busy pitching tents and setting up camp. As we worked, I kept staring at the sky and the landscape. The weather was absolutely beautiful. A thin, wispy cloud encircled the summit, hiding the final challenge from us. In a few days, we would be up there in that cloud. The rest of the sky was clear, and I couldn't detect the slightest movement of air. I was content at that point just to stare and revel in the splendor around me.

Once we had camp set up, we waited two days for the other plane to arrive with the rest of our supplies. Waiting provided a chance for us to explore and to practice our techniques. Wearing crampons, we walked roped together, then practiced self-arrest as we slid down the slopes.

Vern saw signs of high winds atop the mountain peaks, so we built snow walls around our tents; however, for four days we had beautiful weather. We joked about being in Hawaii or Florida. "I expect pink flamingos to fly overhead at any moment," one guide said, laughing.

We would have to set up at least two more camps on the mountain before we summited. I kept staring upward, trying to imagine what it would look like at various levels. I was still overwhelmed.

On December 4, Vern and Gordon went ahead to lay out the first part of the route. They were particularly eager to know the challenges of the knife-edge, the first part of our ascent. We also needed information about the slope of the route and the conditions of the snow.

After they returned, they told us that the knife-edge wouldn't be as bad as we had anticipated. "The snow on the first part is good, but it gets soft halfway up," Gordon said.

"There are no good camping spots until we're thirteen hundred feet up," Vern added.

Over dinner, we planned our strategy. Before we turned in, Norman read a particularly prophetic passage from Dr. Robert Schuller about climbing mountains.

> *Faith is daring to fail. Great goals are never reached until you decide to dare to fail. I will not be afraid of failure, for God has promised that He will be my help. He will not allow me to stumble or fall. God will plant my feet firmly one step at a time. And with each upward step, I shall climb without a fall.*

Norman then officially named Camp deGanahl, calling camps one and two Goodale and Crockett.

➤

On December 7, we took our first steps on Mount Vaughan and headed up the knife ridge as a practice run. We wanted to know how Norman would do with his footing and what kind of pace he could sustain. His artificial right knee and a fused right ankle made it hard for him to balance; he also had trouble feeling his feet, which had been frozen during an Iditarod race. We climbed about five hundred feet.

As I watched Norman walking along, almost eighty-nine years young, my heart beat with pride. He never complained about physical limitations or asked for extra consideration. He would be slow, but we all had known that. Norman did exceptionally well and didn't falter once. We took it easy and constantly checked his Polar pulse monitor. We had to keep slowing him down. He was so excited that he wanted to run up the mountain.

As we climbed, we gained a wider view. The scenery changed constantly as the sun cast different lightings. Far from an all-white world, the

Antarctic displays a myriad of hues—blue sky, brown plateaus, and mountains of pink granite. I saw nunataks—the tops of buried mountains—and the enormous Amundsen Glacier. Antarctica's small glaciers were the size of Alaska's large ones.

At one point, I heard an odd but familiar noise. I turned to see a small avalanche tumbling down the face of Mount Vaughan.

That night, Norman gathered us together and read thoughts from his diary, explaining why the trip meant so much to him and about his strong desire to reach the summit on his birthday. As he finished, he broke down and cried.

The rest of us were close to tears, too.

➤

On December 9, we began the actual ascent. In the Antarctic summer, there is no night or day, but when the mountain blocked the sun's rays and we were cast into cold shadow, it seemed like night. We climbed during the "day," when the sun shone on our side of the mountain and it was warm enough to manipulate the carabiners, ropes, crampons, and other gear. To reach our first camp, we had to negotiate a steep ridge. It looked like the most difficult part of the climb. We realized that if we fell, we'd slide a long way. We had clear instructions on this. We were to yell, "Falling!" Our guide would intentionally fall in the *opposite* direction, as a counterbalance. That was the only way a fall could be stopped.

Norman was feeling good, and we climbed strong that first day. We frequently checked his pulse, making sure he didn't exceed his target rate.

Vern and Gordon kept kicking in steps, asking, "Is this okay? Does this need to be wider? Should we step here?" It touched me to see their concern for Norman's feet. It was difficult walking on that knifelike ridge. We couldn't walk on either side but had to ascend the spine itself. It took us longer than we had anticipated, six hours, to climb the thirteen hundred feet and reach Camp Goodale.

We took only one lunch break that day. We called it lunch, but ate only candy bars. That wasn't wise. Norman needed more food and more rest, but we didn't yet realize it.

We made the second day, December 10, a rest day, because the climb had been arduous. Norman stayed in the tent the whole day, resting and sleeping.

On December 11, the weather was so bad that we stayed at Camp Goodale a second day. On December 12, we began our climb to Camp Crockett, our next camp, which Gordon and Vern and the crew at deGanahl had set up in a near whiteout. The weather continued to deteriorate, and the winds increased. Even though the climb was only three hours long and the grade of the slope not nearly so steep as the previous day, Norman looked tired at the end of the day. We didn't stop for lunch, but took a few breaks for rest and water. When we got to Crockett, Norman was experiencing mild snow blindness. I put drops in his eyes and made him stay in the tent.

It was very windy with horizontal spindrift, and we had whiteout conditions. We stayed put. Either Gordon or Vern brought food to us. While Norman slept, I read, worked at my computer, and wrote in my diary.

We relayed messages to Camp deGanahl, which then relayed them to Betty Menard at Patriot Hills. She passed them to the ANI offices at Punta Arenas. From there, they went by e-mail to Rhonda Greider in Los Angeles, who disseminated them to the various people on our list back in the States, including Prodigy and Babbie Jacobs, our Alaska connection. This was our daily routine.

➤

We waited three days at Camp Crockett. The day before we left, Gordon and Vern climbed close to the summit, marking a trail for Norman by chopping and kicking in footsteps.

"It's much steeper than we had expected," Gordon said when they returned.

The final push to the summit was going to be fourteen hundred feet. That was too much to do in a day, so we would have to set up another camp. Because the slope was so steep, the only possible site was behind a serac that had been created when a block of icy snow pulled partly away from the mountain. We set up Camp Gould (named after Larry Gould) six hundred feet above Crockett and eight hundred below the summit.

We came to realize that Norman had not taken sufficient breaks the first day. He hadn't eaten enough, and the ordeal had sapped his energy.

His body hadn't had time to recuperate for the climb up to Crockett. Now, quite unlike himself, Norman was having to force himself to eat.

We faced another unexpected difficulty. We had relied on Norman's pulse monitor to let us know when he should rest. Now, when we needed it most, the monitor failed. We had to stop often and do a manual pulse count, which wasn't easy.

➤

On our way up to Camp Gould, we went slower and took more water, food, and rest breaks. We reached Camp Gould in about five hours. Vern and Gordon had set up a tent before we had left Crockett, for which I was thankful. As soon as we got there, Norman was able to go straight into the tent.

For the first time, we felt the severity of the cold. In the crevasse created by the serac, it was about minus twenty degrees. We were now in shadows, with no rays from the sun to warm us. Lower on the mountain, our green tents had absorbed the rays that beamed down twenty-four hours a day, keeping the interior about forty degrees above zero.

At Camp Gould, only Vern, Norman, and I spent the night behind the serac. Gordon had gone back down to Camp Crockett to spend the night with the National Geographic crew and Alejo, their excellent Chilean guide.

Because Norman was still tired the next morning, we decided to stay another day. He felt stronger than after the first day, but we worried that the steepness of the impending slope would greatly tax him.

We received reports of bad weather from a National Science Foundation pilot who had flown over our camp. They were having a total whiteout at McMurdo Sound, and we could see clouds forming in the distance. Gordon urged us to continue. "If the bad weather rolls in and we haven't gone on," he said, "we'll have to abort the expedition and return to base camp."

"Can you go on?" I asked Norman. We were running out of time—and food. The pilot and crew at base camp had been eating more food than we anticipated. We couldn't afford to get stuck on the mountain and face the threat of short food rations.

As the weather continued to worsen, we considered our choices. We could try for the summit, even though Norman still felt tired. Or we could stay where we were and risk aborting the climb because of the weather. The crew at base camp was getting restless and the National Geographic photographers wanted to get a clear shot of the summit. I knew what Norman's response would be, and I felt angry. "Norman shouldn't be pushed," I said. "This is his climb, his moment of glory, and he is being pushed too much." Even though we were going very slowly, I was concerned about overtaxing his body.

Norman decided to go for the summit. In doing that, Vern was adamant that we should take a tent along. "We may have to bivouac up there," he said.

We began to push for the summit late in the afternoon of December 16. Gordon and Vern had found another serac that we could camp behind if Norman got too tired and couldn't make the summit. But as we pushed on, we stopped often for water and food. We didn't let Norman carry his pack. We didn't even let him carry Zippy, the stuffed dog tribute to the sled dogs of the original polar explorers. By then, we had learned from our mistakes.

Vern and Gordon had to chop and kick every footstep. We climbed a forty-degree slope most of the way. The weather looked ominous on the horizon. Clouds rolled toward us. Six and a half hours later, we were close to the summit.

Vern pointed and yelled, "Fifty feet."

We stopped to let Norman lead. I followed directly behind him. Gordon and the National Geographic crew stood near the summit to take pictures as we approached.

Norman paused and shouted back to me, "Only two more steps to go!"

As we took the last upward steps, I kept thinking, "I can't believe it. It just doesn't seem real."

As Norman took the last step, Gordon yelled, "You did it, Norman, you did it!"

I led everyone in an old football cheer that I knew Norman would remember from his days on the gridiron:

> *You gotta get down, chick-a-boom, chick-a-boom, chick-a-boom.*
> *You gotta get up, chick-a-boom, chick-a-boom, chick-a-boom.*
> *To the right, chick-a-boom, chick-a-boom, chick-a-boom.*
> *To the left, chick-a-boom, chick-a-boom, chick-a-boom.*

We repeated the cheer three times, and each time we shouted louder. At the end, we were screaming as loudly as we could. Then everybody cheered and clapped.

Despite the fierce wind, we made Vern kneel so that we could kiss his bald head again. Norman had icicles hanging from his beard, and I had a very cold nose. Vern screamed as I bussed his bald head.

➤

From the summit, we could see hundreds of miles all around us. We pointed to the route we would have taken with the dogs.

"Look, Carolyn!" Norman pointed out Vaughan Glacier.

After years of staring at pictures, we were finally seeing it with our own eyes. We could also see Mount Crockett. Norman pointed out Scott and Amundsen glaciers and Mount Betty. We could see out over the Ross Ice Shelf; in the opposite direction, we identified the Polar Plateau.

I could picture the six dog teams crossing below, with six young men— Norman among them—skiing alongside as they passed before this magnificent mountain range for the first time. In my mind's eye it was 1929.

Then it was time for Norman to read his summit speech:

> *By climbing this mountain for my eighty-ninth birthday, I dared to fail and met success. I have fulfilled a sixty-five-year-old dream. I am grateful to the people who have put me here. I never could have gotten here without Carolyn, my wife, especially, who I am proud to say is standing beside me, celebrating this moment. To my sponsors, to the Mount Vaughan Antarctic team here and at home, to all the volunteers and supporters, to friends worldwide, and most important, to my family. I am now ready for my next challenge.*
>
> *A message I wish to bring everyone is to dream big and "dare to fail." This climb has been in tribute to Admiral Richard E. Byrd, Dr. Laurence McKinley Gould, and to my good friends, Edward E. Goodale and Freddie Crockett, who drove dogs with me here in the Antarctic. Standing here on top of Mount Vaughan, we can see Mount Goodale to the north and Mount Crockett to the south. We saw for the first time all these mountains and glaciers in 1929.*

This climb is also in tribute to the tenacious spirit of the Antarctic sled dogs who never gave up. They have been my inspiration.

Our dogs couldn't come this year. But Zippy is here to pay tribute to the end of the era of the sled dog in the Antarctic as set forth in the new protocol of the Antarctic treaty. Zippy also commemorates the four dogs who wandered off after the crash of the DC-6 last year. They are Stricker, Magoo, Pudge, and Pandy.

I will miss the dogs of the Antarctic. Good-bye to you wonderful huskies. May your memory live forever in our hearts. You always did what was asked of you no matter how tough it was and often sacrificed your lives for man's quest at the bottom of the world. I salute you, and I toast a new era of worldwide scientific cooperation for the next fifty years here in the Antarctic. May it always stay pristine and become the world's greatest park!

➤

After that, everybody wanted to take photographs of us on the summit. Meanwhile, Vern started setting up the tent so that we could spend the night there.

From my backpack, I pulled out the eighty-nine colored sparklers with streamers that I had secretly carried from Anchorage. Because it was extremely cold, I hurriedly stuck them in the ground. I wanted to celebrate and then get inside the tent.

After I placed all eighty-nine in the snow and paused to admire them blowing in the wind, we called Norman over. I tried to light them, but the wind blew too hard and our hands were too cold. Instead, we enjoyed the streamers waving in the wind as we sang "Happy Birthday."

"Norman, the whole mountain is your birthday cake," I said. "The snow is the frosting, and it's topped with eighty-nine sparklers for candles."

The pleasure I saw reflected in his face made it a special moment for me.

➤

"I don't feel very well," Norman said a few minutes after his birthday party. "I think I'm going to throw up."

His knees began to buckle, and he looked ready to faint. "Help! Help!" I yelled as I grabbed him. Gordon heard me and came running. He grabbed Norman's other side. "Please, God," I prayed silently, "don't let him faint. Don't let him collapse." All the while, the National Geographic men were filming.

After a few seconds, Norman indicated he could walk with our help. We got Norman into the tent and inside his sleeping bag. We put six chemical heat pads under his armpits, in his groin area, and around his kidneys. Then we zipped him up inside the sleeping bag. His hands were extremely cold, and he couldn't move his fingers. When I examined him, I saw that he had the beginning of frostbite on one finger, and the rest were frostnipped.

During the celebration, Norman had stood on the summit, talking with people, enjoying the view, hardly aware that he was growing colder. Finally, the combination of exhaustion, excitement, and cold overcame him.

Gordon, Vern, and I didn't say much, but we knew he was on the edge of hypothermia. Fear clutched at me, but I wouldn't give in. *He's going to be all right. He's got to make it through this.*

We monitored his pulse and watched as he slowly warmed. I fed him warm fluids and gave him sugar to eat.

After a few hours he said, "I've stopped shivering."

Even though I was confident Norman would be all right, I didn't sleep all night. Every time he stirred, I became instantly alert. And then I checked his pulse.

During the night, Norman awakened, looked at me, and said, "I can't imagine being in a better place in the whole world than right here, right now."

➤

To my relief, he felt much better the next morning. We wanted to try again to light the "candles" on Norman's "birthday cake" and take photographs, but the fierce wind made that impossible. Because it was so bitterly cold, we managed to take only two pictures.

Common sense told us that we had to leave the summit as quickly as possible. If we didn't, Norman would again be threatened with hypothermia and perhaps collapse on the way down.

Within minutes, we had everything packed and started the descent. I took the lead, with Norman directly behind me, followed by Gordon and Vern. I was scared as I thought about walking down and staring at the vastness below. Each step made me think of stepping off a window ledge. One wrong step could plunge me down the forty-degree, ten thousand-foot slope.

As soon as we got off the summit, the wind stopped. I began to enjoy myself, and it felt quite comfortable coming down. It took us five hours to descend to Camp Crockett, where we took a thirty-minute break. It was slow going, and Norman was tired. We decided we could speed up the descent if we lowered him in the sled that Alejo had brought up. We packed him into the sled and I took the lead and dragged it, while the others stayed behind to hold it back if it plunged forward.

At first, we were as slow as if Norman were walking, but we improved. I was also carrying a heavy pack, and my hips were aching. I didn't say anything because I didn't want to wimp out on the team.

At Camp Goodale, we decided it was too risky to lower Norman on the knife-edge, so we let him walk. As usual, he never complained, but I could see the tiredness in his face, and his pace was excruciatingly slow.

It took us twelve long hours to make it all the way back to Camp deGanahl. All of us were exhausted by the time we arrived at base camp.

Bryan and Randy, the plane's engineer, had cooked a celebration dinner of steak with bearnaise sauce, mashed potatoes, and chocolate pie. After dinner, Norman got a well-deserved ten hours of sleep.

The next morning, we prepared to leave. After the plane was loaded and the engines revved, I took Norman's hand, and we walked away from the others. We stood by ourselves and stared silently up at Mount Vaughan, trying to indelibly imprint the vision of that mountain in our minds. This was the last time we would see the mountain and our trail.

Norman pointed to the route, and our eyes followed it upward.

With our arms around each other, the tears fell. We could have stayed and cried all day.

We did it, I kept thinking. *We did it*.

When I heard Bryan calling us, I said, "It's time to go."

"Yes," Norman said softly, but he continued to stare. It was a beautiful moment for me to watch the intense gaze on his face. Then we turned and walked to the plane.

I asked Bryan to circle the mountain so that Norman could see it one more time. The day was clear and sunny, and we had no obstructions. Bryan circled twice, and our eyes followed our route all the way to the summit. I think each of us relived in our own minds those eight days, especially those hours on the summit. In our individual ways, each of us said good-bye to Mount Vaughan. For me, it was one of the most memorable moments of the entire trip.

We flew back to Patriot Hills, where everyone greeted us with great fanfare. We loved it, of course, but we had already had our best celebration at the summit.

We had summited December 16, 1994, three days before Norman's birthday. On December 19, we returned to Patriot Hills. The people there prepared a birthday cake made out of a circle of cream puffs, with candles on each one.

"We did it," Norman said several times to the people gathered there. "We did it."

His words summed it up well. Norman had fulfilled a dream born sixty-five years earlier.

"What's next?" someone asked.

Norman only smiled.

A full-length account of Norman Vaughan's experiences on the Byrd Antarctic Expedition is contained in *With Byrd at the Bottom of the World* by Norman Vaughan and Cecil Murphey, available at your local bookstore or from Stackpole Books. Call (800) 732-3669 to order.